ed Land,
ck Land

Joan Bingham

Barbara Mertz, one of the world's leading authorities on ancient Egypt, wrote the widely acclaimed *Temples, Tombs and Hieroglyphs: A Popular History of Ancient Egypt*. She received her Ph.D. from the famed Oriental Institute of the University of Chicago. Ms. Mertz has two grown children and lives just outside Washington, D.C.

# Red Land, Black Land

## DAILY LIFE IN ANCIENT EGYPT

REVISED EDITION

## Barbara Mertz

*Illustrated with map,
photographs, and drawings*

**DODD, MEAD & COMPANY**
NEW YORK

1   2   3   4   5   6   7   8   9   10


Library of Congress Cataloging in Publication Data

Mertz, Barbara.
Red land, black land.

Bibliography: p.
Includes index.
1. Egypt—Civilization—To 332 B.C.   I. Title.
DT61.M53   1978      932'.01      78-9552
ISBN 0-396-07575-4

*For My Mother and Father*

# CONTENTS

**PART TWO**
# The World of the Dead

# FOREWORD

THIS is not a book about ancient Egyptian culture; it is a book about ancient Egyptians. It might even be subtitled "How To Be an Ancient Egyptian," for, if properly studied, it will teach the reader how to make papyrus, how to build a pyramid, and how to dress, dine, and furnish a house in the Egyptian manner, among other matters of equal interest. The objects of our study are, for the most part, anonymous; but they are, or were, people —human beings—Egyptians. I have tried, therefore, to talk about them *as* people, not as featureless statistics or as the vague blur of humanity underlying such academic topics as Egyptian Literature or Egyptian Architecture. The reader will not find a chapter on Egyptian Literature in this book, although a good many literary works are discussed. He will not find a chapter on Architecture, either, but houses, temples, and tombs will be described. We do have a longish chapter on Egyptian Religion; however, the chapter on Costume is almost as long, although it concerns itself with a subject which is decidedly frivolous compared to theology. Yet I suspect that a well-to-do Egyptian lady, like her descendants in other countries and other ages, sometimes spent as much time thinking about her clothing as about her gods.

I apologized, in another book, for what might strike a sensitive reader as a frivolous approach to ancient Egypt; but I do not really believe that an apology is necessary. The popular view of Egyptian civilization as dignified and austere is incorrect. It comes from the massive temples, the grisly mummies, the crumbled and ruined tombs. Yet the temples were once bright with paint and aglitter with gold; the mummies were men, women and children who enjoyed life so much that they went to unusual extremes in the hope of perpetuating it; the tombs were Houses of Eternity, equipped with "every good and pure thing" for the enjoyment of life everlasting. We are not insulting the Egyptians, or falsifying their view of the world, if we catch a glimpse of them telling bawdy stories about the gods, getting drunk, writing sentimental poems to their sweethearts, or lecturing their bored children. If we laugh at them just a little, it will not diminish them; and if we fail to see that we are also laughing at ourselves, we are missing the best part of the joke.

Let me begin my acknowledgments to the many people who have helped me with this book by thanking two—appropriately— anonymous groups: the Egyptian artists who created the originals of most of the illustrations, and the many archaeologists, philologists and historians who have contributed to my understanding of ancient Egypt. A work of this kind is, inevitably, a composite, drawing on the knowledge amassed by the dedicated efforts of hundreds of scholars. I have mentioned many names in the text and in the Bibliography, but it was impossible to mention all of them; and my debt to these men and women—English, Italian, French, German, and American—is enormous.

Specifically, I would like to acknowledge the graciousness of Professors Sol Tax and Carleton Coon, who answered questions on specific anthropological problems; of Professor Walter B. Emery, who brought me up to date on Imhotep; and of Professor Otto Neugebauer, who replied to my anxious query on a point of Egyptian mathematics. I need not say that these gentlemen are in no way responsible for the interpretations of their respective subjects which appear in these pages. They did their best to enlighten me, and if they failed the fault is my own.

I am indebted also to the Directors of the American Academy in Rome and of the German Archaeological Institute, Rome, for permission to use the libraries of those institutions. Various museums have been good enough to let me use photographs from their collections. Specific acknowledgments are made elsewhere, but I would like to direct a particularly warm "thank you" to Mr. A. F. Shore of the British Museum's Egyptian section for spending so much time finding suitable photographs for me.

BARBARA MERTZ

DECEMBER 1965
ROME

PART ONE
# The World
# of the Living

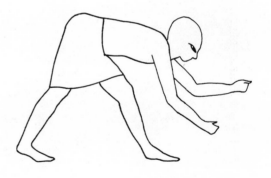

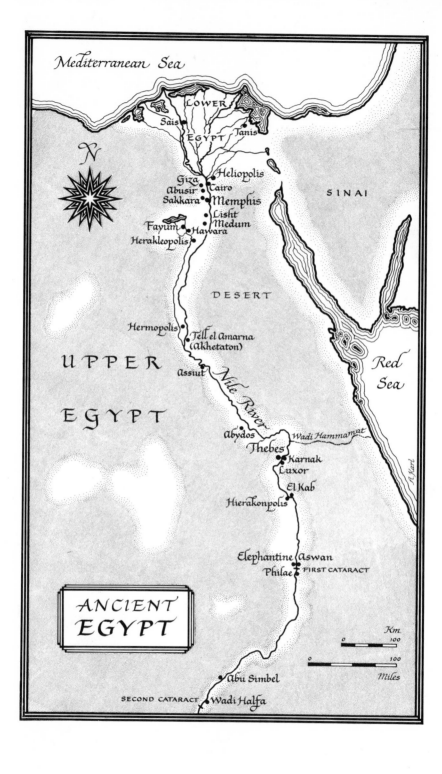

Mediterranean Sea

LOWER

Sais

EGYPT    Tanis

SINAI

Heliopolis

Giza    Cairo

Abusir

Sakkara    Memphis

Lisht

Medum

Fayum    Hawara

Herakleopolis

DESERT

Hermopolis    Tell el Amarna
(Akhetaton)

Assiut    Nile River

UPPER

EGYPT

Abydos    Wadi Hammamat

Thebes    Karnak

Luxor

El Kab

Hierakonpolis

Red
Sea

A. Karl

Elephantine Aswan

Philae    FIRST CATARACT

ANCIENT
EGYPT

Km.
0    100

0    100

Miles

Abu Simbel

SECOND CATARACT    Wadi Halfa

# I

# People of the Two Lands

May she flow away—she who comes in the darkness,
Who enters in furtively
With her nose behind her, her face turned backward—
Failing in that for which she came!

Hast thou come to kiss this child?
  I will not let thee kiss him!

Hast thou come to injure him?
  I will not let thee injure him!

Hast thou come to take him away?
  I will not let thee take him away from me!

KNEELING on the bare earthen floor, the woman chants softly, lest she wake the child asleep in her arms. The little one-room hut is dark, except for the dim red glow from the brazier, where the cooking fire still smolders. A last expiring flame leaps up, and shows the crouching form more clearly: a slender brown girl with long black hair and dark eyes—eyes that dart glances half-defiant, half-apprehensive toward the door. It is closed and barred, but she can feel the dark pressing in—the dark from which "she with her face turned backward" may enter furtively, to steal the breath of the sleeping child.

I see this picture whenever I read the lines quoted above. They are singularly effective lines, even in translation; the original text was written several thousand years ago, in the ancient Egyptian language. Surely the night-demon is one of the most dreadful specters in the folklore of any people, with her head twisted about on her neck, and with the suggestion of melting shapelessness in the words "flow away." Like the old Scottish prayer against "ghost-ies and ghoulies and *things that go bump in the night*," this Egyptian spell carries a hint of diabolic danger which is all the more terrifying for never being made explicit.

There is another point of similarity between the Scottish poem and the Egyptian one. We quote the first as a joke nowadays, laughing and pretending to look nervously over our shoulders; but, like its Egyptian counterpart, it was not a joke nor an exercise in literature for its own sake. It was a charm—a prayer, if you will—against the powers of evil. In both examples we have first a description of the threatening forces. Then the counterspell is re-cited. In the Egyptian example, defensive measures take the form of powerful denials, made more potent by mounting repetition— "I will not let thee kiss him! I will not let thee injure him!"—and also by a recipe of magic herbs, which I have not quoted. In the Scottish prayer the invocation of defensive powers is simple— "Good Lord, deliver us."

Well, we mustn't press the comparison too far; it has no signifi-cance, except to show that many people, in many times and places, have been afraid of the dark and of that which may come out of the dark. What touches me most about this Egyptian prayer is that it is designed for the protection of children. There is no sphere of life in which man feels his vulnerability to the caprice of Fate more poignantly than in that which threatens his children; and at no time in his life is he more helpless than when he comes forth, naked and squalling. This volume concerns itself with the daily life of the ancient Egyptians, so it is fitting that we should begin when the Egyptian began—at birth. Having pronounced the proper protective incantation, we may proceed to bring our ficti-tious baby into the world.

## *Childbirth*

Once upon a time there was an Egyptian lady who attracted the interest of no less a personage than the great sun-god, Re. Perhaps the god's attentions were motivated not so much by the lady's charms as by his desire to produce three offspring who would eventually rule the land of Egypt. Yet, the lady was only the wife of a humble priest of Re; his name was Rauser and hers was Reddjetet; and

"One of these days it happened that Reddjetet felt the pains of labor; and her labor was hard. So the majesty of Re said to Isis, Nephthys, Meskhenet, Heket, and Khnum, 'Go on and deliver Reddjetet of the three children who are in her womb, and who will exercise the kingship in the entire land.' "

The informed reader will recognize in Isis and Nephthys two of the great goddesses of the Egyptian pantheon; they were the wife and sister of Osiris. Meskhenet was another goddess—the patroness of childbirth, appropriately enough. Khnum, the only male in the party, also had a role in creation. He was the potter who fashioned the bodies of newborn children, in clay, on his divine wheel. Heket assisted at the birth of the sun-god each morning, so she was a logical person to supervise the birth of his children.

The goddesses disguised themselves as dancing girls, with the lordly Khnum as their porter, and all five of them set out for the priest's house. They found the supposed father-to-be in a pitiable state, which is described with concise eloquence by the Egyptian author; he was "sitting motionless, his clothing in disarray." To me, the priest is a most sympathetic character. Although he was desperately worried about his wife, he took the trouble to speak courteously to the itinerant entertainers: "You see, ladies, the mistress of the house is in labor; and her labor is hard."

The dancing girls took up their cue. "Let us see her. We know how to facilitate a birth."

The father could not refuse the offer; Re, looking down from his golden boat, would see to that. Still, we have a feeling that it was a natural suggestion. The function of midwife was not a medical specialty. As in most primitive societies, including that of medieval Europe, a woman in labor was probably attended by the other women in the house or the village, with a local "wise woman" on call in case the situation became complicated. Even a dancing girl might claim special skill in obstetrics, and the distracted husband's response is perfectly understandable. At that point he would be willing to try anything and anybody. He gave the five divinities his permission, and they locked themselves up with the lady.

"Then Isis put herself before her, Nephthys behind her, and Heket assisted the birth." One wonders how she assisted—by massage or magic? A little of both, perhaps; or perhaps the decisive factor was the speech of Isis to the child struggling to be born: "Do not be too *strong* in her womb, in this thy name of User-kaf." The word "strong" in Egyptian is "user," so the speech involves a sort of pun on the child's name. Puns may be the lowest form of humor, but they are potent magic when the spoken word is regarded as powerful in itself. This speech is a command as well as a play on words, and it would probably have been efficacious even if it had not been spoken by a goddess.

"This baby then glided out upon her hands." It was an impressive baby; its body was encrusted with gold and its hair was real lapis-lazuli. Portents and wonders are common at the birth of a king, but it is possible that this wild description may be figurative. The newborn Egyptian baby had black hair, and lapis is a dark blue stone. To a mother's fond eye, the little brown body might seem to glow like gold. "Teeth of pearls, ruby lips"—the technique is not unknown in our own literature.

The goddesses washed the child, cut the umbilical cord, and put the baby on a "box of brick." Then Meskhenet, who had been strangely passive, considering that she was the real expert, blessed the child, and Khnum "gave health to its body," whatever that may mean. The same procedure was followed for the second child and the third, including the important pun-command.

Their task finished, the goddesses, still in disguise, came out of the birth chamber and found Rauser, the husband, still waiting before the door. "Let your heart be glad, Rauser," they reassured him, "three children are born to you." He answered: "Ladies—

what can I do for you? I beg you, give this sack of grain to your porter, and take it for yourselves, as payment, in order to make beer."

This story, part of a long, complicated fairy tale, is the most detailed account we have of an actual ancient Egyptian birth. Other sources are maddeningly vague. We know how the Egyptian mother delivered her baby. She sat or crouched on a seat made out of bricks. No obstetrical divans or chairs have survived, so the construction must have been a temporary affair, dismantled when it was not needed. But certain inscriptions refer to the expectant mother as being "on the bricks," and the position is familiar to us from, of all things, hieroglyphic writing. The normal sign used to designate woman and her affairs shows a seated female with knees drawn up. The hieroglyph for "give birth" is a drawing of a woman kneeling; she is distinctly pregnant in outline, and below her body the arms and head of the child are visible. We also have a few crude (in the aesthetic sense) little statuettes depicting the process, which take almost the same form as the hieroglyphic sign. As the expectant mother knelt, she was supported fore and aft by two women of the household, and the midwife, in front of her, prepared to receive the child on her hands.

And that's about all we know. One potential source of information has proved a disappointment: the medical papyri, though they include one of a specifically gynecological nature, give no information on labor or the techniques of the obstetrician.

It may seem surprising that the Egyptians, who preserved for us so many details of the activities of life and death, left so little material about the essentials preliminary to both these phenomena. Yet the seeming wealth of documentation is illusory; it is only rich by comparison with that left by other pre-Greek cultures. Just to give an idea: An Egyptologist can read, during his professional lifetime, every single document written by the ancient Egyptians—all the original source materials—and still have time to read most of the secondary sources, and produce a book or two himself. A scholar in the field of modern history would find it impossible to do this for a period of thirty years, let alone three thousand. He probably couldn't even cover the source materials—the novelists and essayists, major and minor, the wills, court reports and legal documents, the personal and business letters, the treaties and laws, the scientific treatises. . . .

I make this point, not to gloat over the thoroughness of the student of Egyptology, but to mourn for his limited sources. Books on ancient Egypt often give the reader a misleading impression, presenting hypotheses as if they were facts and possibilities as if they were certainties. Some of this is inevitable; one cannot explain in painful detail the evidential background for every statement. But the most reliable books are loaded with boring words like "probably" and "perhaps" and "possibly"; scholars avoid "maybe" for stylistic reasons, but it should be prefixed to fifty percent of the statements made in any book on Egypt—including this one.

We cannot conclude, when we know nothing about a particular facet of Egyptian culture, that it was either nonexistent or produced by some "lost science" or occult power. We are ignorant only because that particular body of information has not survived four thousand years of time, or because the Egyptians did not bother to tell us about it. Egyptian culture was literate, but it was not self-analytical, nor was writing a universal skill. The Egyptians were busy people; they had fields to sow and harvest and irrigate, pyramids to build, battles to fight, and tombs to equip; they preserved in writing only the things they needed to know, not all the matters which might be of interest to alien peoples in some unimaginable future. It is no wonder we know so little about childbirth; in fact, it is surprising that we know as much as we do.

## The People in Art

Having gotten our Egyptian into the world, we can now pause to ask what sort of person he was. His habits, and beliefs, and mannerisms will emerge, let us hope, in future pages. We will restrict ourselves here to his physical characteristics.

But before describing the Egyptians as they look to us, it might be interesting to see them first through their own eyes. How did they want to look? What was the ideal physical type?

Paintings and sculptures give a good idea of the desired norm. In fact, the similarity of the types depicted, the lack of deviation, is astounding when you consider the number of centuries involved— from somewhere in the neighborhood of 3000 B.C. (give or take a few hundred years) down to the first century of our own era. The ladies are slim, so slender that their bodies look almost flat in profile from waist to knee. Rounded hips were evidently not admired; shapely breasts were. The ladies in the paintings have small but firm bosoms, and some of the mummies of older women, whose natural equipment had sagged under the relentless pressure of the years, were stuffed with wax or sawdust in the pectoral region to give the necessary curves. One late mummy, described by Elliot Smith in his classic book on mummification, had an entirely new body surface molded over the withered flesh in a kind of papier mâché, made of bandages and resinous paste. The breasts were beautifully modeled, and tipped with copper buttons. This mummy is uniquely well-made; Smith says, enthusiastically, that it resembles an exquisite statue of Venus.

The male physique, which became the model for sculptors of kings and commoners, was one which we would approve—very broad shoulders tapering down to a flat abdomen and lean flanks. When customers came to a sculptor to order statues of themselves, or hired an artist to paint their forms on the walls of their tombs, it was in bodies like these that they expected to appear.

There are a few exceptions to the general rule. Most of them are famous, known to every working Egyptologist, just because they are exceptions: the old blind harper, with his bent shoulders and wrinkled face; the emaciated herdsman, whose ribs stand out under his skin; the dwarf, squatting proudly beside his normal-sized wife. The art of the Amarna period is exceptional, too. We'll talk about that later. Some of the exceptions are truly exceptional, superb pieces of the sculptor's art.

My particular favorite is the figure we call the "Sheikh el-Beled." This means "Mayor of the Village," and the way in which the statue came by its name makes a nice little story.

The statue was found by Auguste Mariette, one of the great French Egyptologists of the last century. For me, the names of Mariette and Maspero, like ham and eggs, always go together:

Maspero, the founder of the Egyptian Antiquities Service, who established the regulations which preserved most of the ancient treasures of Egypt for the modern Egyptians; and Mariette, his equally dedicated successor. Though Mariette had to supervise all the archaeological work carried on in Egypt, to make sure the rules were being followed, he liked to do some digging of his own. One morning his workers were shoveling away when the head and shoulders of a statue came into sight. The statue was carefully freed from its covering; and as it was drawn out of the earth, a simultaneous gasp of recognition came from a dozen Arab throats. "The Sheikh el-Beled!" they cried with one accord.

One can easily believe, looking at the statue—which is now in the Cairo Museum, in the collection begun and cherished by Maspero and Mariette—that it reminded the men of their mayor. It looks like someone I used to know, too. The figure is life-sized, carved of wood and cunningly fitted together at the joints. The form is that of a man of middle age, rather portly, with a round face which combines joviality and firmness. He stands in the conventional Egyptian attitude, stepping forward, one foot before the other. One arm hangs at his side. The other hand holds a long walking stick which is obviously, despite his corpulence, designed for prestige rather than support. He is a man of dignity and of authority. The eyes of the figure are incredibly lifelike; they seem to stare back at the beholder, not with the expressionless blankness of wood but with calm curiosity. Indeed, the eyes are masterpieces of craftsmanship. The eye sockets are lined with copper, and the eyeballs are composites of inlaid pieces—opaque quartz for the white of the eye, rock crystal for the cornea, and a little round cylinder, filled with dark resin and sunken behind the crystal cornea, for the pupil. The statue is probably four thousand years old. That it survived at all is due to the miracle of the dry Egyptian climate.

The Sheikh—whose real name was Ka-aper—is broader around the middle than at the shoulders; he certainly doesn't exemplify manly beauty, like the majority of the other male statues. But he is, as I said, an exception; and even he is a handsome figure in his way. He is portly, not fat. Indeed, he is a joy to behold. And although there are a few exceptions like Ka-aper, none of these are hideously malformed. I know of no hunchbacks, or cripples, or hideously fat old women. (The famous Queen of Punt, who is certainly shaped like a nightmare, is not an Egyptian; barbarians were not entitled to the same courtesies as were inhabitants of the great land of Egypt.) Nobody ever seemed to have a wart on his nose, or scoliosis, or buck teeth.

*The Queen of Punt*
From Hatshepsut's mortuary temple
at Deir el Bahri

Scholars who are specialists in Egyptian art have explained the reason for the persistence of the artistic norm. This involves profound speculations on Egyptian mass psychology, attitudes toward the universe, and the function of art—which served a magical rather than an aesthetic function. We'll go into this later. But it amuses me to wonder if there might not be another, more simpleminded reason in operation when an Egyptian merchant stalked into a sculptor's studio to order his mortuary statue. Who would chose to have his double chin and protruding belly immortalized when he can go down to posterity looking like Apollo?

Obviously we can't take the Egyptians' pictures of themselves too literally. There never was a population of any size without the maimed and the deformed, and the just plain homely. And yet some Egyptologists, nice, trusting fellows that they are, do take the pictures literally.

## The Problem of Queen Ti

History is not a series of facts; it is a series of opinions and theories, some solidly based, some sheer nonsense, most more or less probable. Unless a historian who is writing a book confines himself to a particular problem within a limited era of history, he cannot possibly explain all the evidence, pro and con, or give all the variant theories for every debatable problem. There are usually too many debatable problems! Yet it is important to remember how flimsy some of our historical reconstructions actually are, and it is interesting to see how some of them have developed.

We have been talking about a fairly basic point—the physical appearance of the ancient Egyptians. It is not an important point, in terms of cultural history, nor does it seem like a difficult one. Either you know what people looked like, or you don't know. Either you have mummies and skeletons, or you lack them. Either these people painted pictures of themselves, or they didn't.

Physical remains and pictorial representations—these are the basic sources for the description of a man. But the relative reliability of these sources may be quite different. A skeleton is finite and objective. It can tell us height, build, sex, and age. With a mummy we get more data—hair color and texture, skin color, body weight. Even this evidence is subject to variation because it must be interpreted by human beings. Read the learned discussions on the skeleton which was believed to be Akhenaton's if you doubt that two qualified physicians can disagree on anything as solid as bones.

But the evidence derived from pictures and statues is almost hopelessly subjective. We have seen that the Egyptians didn't show themselves as they actually looked. Yet archaeologists—good ones —often fall into the error of talking about the Egyptians, not in terms of how they really were, but how they wanted to be. I am fascinated by two popular books on Egyptology which describe Queen Ti, the commoner who rose to be King's Great Wife and mother of the heretic Akhenaton. In one book she is described as blue-eyed and fair; the other calls her a Negro.

It doesn't really matter whether Queen Ti was blond or black or spotted with purple polka dots, and yet descriptions like the ones I mentioned are vexing. They are not wild flights of fancy on the part of writers who are not specialists in the field; they are based on interpretations of professional Egyptologists. How, then, can they be so disparate?

The answer is obvious: Because the learned authorities are talking about pictures, not people. Let's take the fair queens of

Egypt to begin with. I discussed them in another book, but this point seems to require repetition. As far as I know, there never was a blond queen of Egypt. The famous Fourth Dynasty lady, who was believed to be blond or red-headed, has been shown to be wearing a yellow headcloth. There never were any other candidates for the description.

I hope that disposes of the blond queens—but it is a feeble hope. These theories have a habit of perpetuating themselves. The view that Queen Ti was a Nubian is more popular in Egyptological circles than the blue-eyed version. I think I know how this particular fallacy started, and it pleases me because of its very simplicity.

There is, in the Berlin Museum, a famous head which is usually identified as that of Queen Ti. It is a wonderful piece of work, evoking, as the best "portrait" sculpture does, a personality as well as a set of features. The personality suggested by Ti's head is not the kind you would want to live with permanently, nor make an enemy of. This impression may be unfair to the long-dead queen; but the impact of the head cannot be denied. Because it is so expert, so evocative, it makes a lasting impression. It is carved of black wood.

I am sure that it would be doing the Egyptologists who make Ti a Nubian an injustice to claim that they think of her as black just because this great, forceful face is black. However, I have a strong suspicion that such is the case. Naturally, none of the scholars involved would ever admit that this was a factor in their decision, nor would such a decision be made on a conscious level. Experts talk, expertly, about Negroid features in Ti's portraits, and the prominence of Nubians in the court hierarchy of the period, and the popularity of Nubian hair styles. These last are meaningless points, even if they are correct, and the description of the Berlin head as Negroid is highly subjective. The features do not show the characteristics defined as Negroid by physical anthropologists. And, to complete the joke, the real evidence about Ti's ancestry is available—objective and indisputable. We don't have her mummy, which would be the best thing. But we do have the mummies of both her parents, Yuya and Tuya, which were discovered by Theodore Davis in 1905.

Theodore Davis was an American millionaire, a tourist, and an enthusiastic amateur in Egyptology. Like Carnarvon twenty years later, he spent his winters in the genial climate of Egypt and amused himself by excavating. He had come to an agreement with the Egyptian government; Davis had a concession for the Valley of the Kings. Without his permission, no one else could dig there. He paid for all the work he conducted, and all the objects found went to the Egyptian government.

This arrangement might strike a nonenthusiast as somewhat one-sided. Davis, who had not the reputation of an "easy man," accepted it, and anyone who has ever felt the thrill of archaeology would agree with him. In fact, he managed to acquire quite a fine collection of objects, but the fun of digging, and of discovery, would have been worth the money by itself.

Davis, whom even his friends described as "brusque and eccentric," was also amazingly lucky. Of course he was working at a time before the Valley had been thoroughly excavated, but even so, he made some exciting discoveries. Among the royal tombs he found were those of Thutmose IV, Hatshepsut, Siptah of the Twentieth Dynasty, and the cache containing the disputed mummy which has been successively described as that of Queen Ti, Akhenaton, and Smenkhkare. One gets the impression that Davis was not an easy man to deal with, but his services to Egyptology were great. He supplied money and enthusiasm, and at his death, he left his collection to the Metropolitan Museum, where it can be enjoyed by the public.

In February of 1905 Davis' crew was working in a space between the tombs of Ramses III and XI, not far from the spot which, twenty years later, was to yield up the fabulous treasures of Tutankhamon to another millionnaire amateur and his assistant, Howard Carter. Davis had little hope of finding a royal tomb in this area; there wasn't room enough. But in the Valley of the Kings one never knows.

On February 5, Davis' men uncovered the top step of a tomb. Davis sent for Weigall, who was then Inspector of Antiquities for Upper Egypt, and about a week later the stairs were dug out and the top of the tomb doorway appeared. The excavators' excitement was dimmed by the discovery that the original seals on the door had been broken. Someone—thieves, undoubtedly—had been there before them.

They were in for a pleasant surprise. The funerary chamber itself lay just beyond the door, without intervening corridors or antechambers, and the first sight that met their eyes was a wooden sarcophagus, broken and dismantled. Within it were three coffins, nested like Chinese boxes. The lids of all three were off; they had been flung against the side of the sarcophagus, as if in guilty haste. The mummy lay, exposed, its face wrappings torn away, within the innermost coffin.

It was the mummy of an "an old man of striking appearance and dignity. His splendid head and fine features bore a marked resemblance to Lincoln."

So wrote a contemporary observer, who was with Davis at the first moment of entry. Another wooden sarcophagus lay to the left. Its lid had also been flung aside, and the mummy exposed. It was that of a woman, in a gilded coffin. "The face was serene and interesting, a low brow and eyes wide apart, and a curiously expressive, sensitive mouth."

The chamber was packed with wonders—boxes and furniture, a chariot, perfectly intact, the gleam of gold on the inner two coffins of the mummies, the blue faience ornaments. Thieves had tunneled into the tomb, but evidently they had been interrupted before doing much damage. Best of all, the inscriptions on the coffins and other articles had not been mutilated. The identity of the mummies was easily discovered. They were Yuya and Tuya, the parents of Queen Ti.

As wonderful as the contents of the tomb were, the most important aspect of the discovery, for our present purposes, was the mummies. I've seen pictures of them, and the descriptions quoted above are fair enough if one allows for the sensitive imagination of the beholder. I lack this type of imagination. I can't look at the wrinkled face of a mummy—leathery brown skin, shrunken lips and protruding teeth, sunken cheeks—and tell myself that the lady may, in life, have been the toast of ancient Thebes. The bones, the basic structure of beauty, still remain; one can describe a brow as oval and high, a set of teeth as even and white, a face as charmingly oval. But the mental picture disintegrates under the impact of the grisly face.

However, the mummy of Yuya, Ti's father, isn't bad. Yuya, who was an officer of charioteers (hence, perhaps, the chariot in

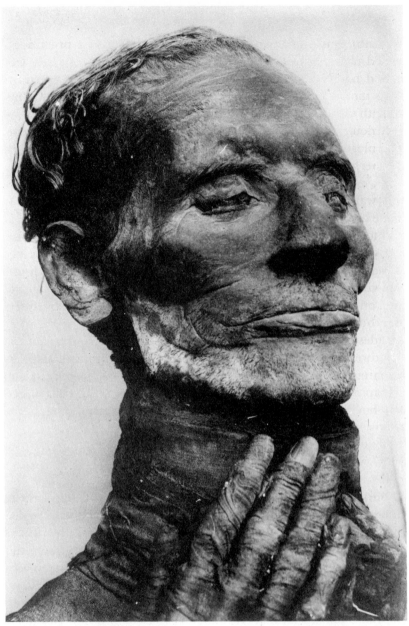

Mummy of Yuya, father of Queen Ti. Eighteenth Dynasty. *The Metropolitan Museum of Art.*

his tomb), was a tall man with strong features and a prominent hooked nose. Elliot Smith, the mummy expert of the period, examined both bodies and described the skull of Yuya as unusual. Smith thought he might have been a Semite. Tuya, the lady, was, in Smith's words, a typical Egyptian of her time and place.

I don't know whether Yuya was a Semite or not. Some Egyptologists like to make him one, usually to prove some theory or other. There is no indication that he was an immigrant to Egypt, except for the fact that his name is not always spelled the same way. That is sometimes a sign that the Egyptians couldn't decide on the proper rendering of a foreign-sounding name. I find this inconclusive evidence, one way or the other. If Yuya did move to Egypt from some other country, he must have arrived when he was fairly young; his career, and titles, seem to be perfectly consistent with those of any other Egyptian bureaucrat. Nor would I insist on Smith's expertise. He was an excellent scholar in many ways, but he too had his favorite theories, and there is nothing more destructive of objective scholarship than a pet theory.

However, whether Yuya was a Semite or an Egyptian, there is one thing he pretty surely was not—a Nubian. And if he wasn't a Nubian and his wife wasn't one either, it is very difficult to explain how their daughter could have been one.

### The People in Actuality

Turning from the Egyptians as they weren't, to the Egyptians as they were, we find that we can describe them as general types without resorting to works of art. On the average they were shorter than we are; the women were about five feet tall, the men perhaps five feet five inches. Again, as always, we must note variations; Amenhotep II was a towering six feet in height. Their skin color was brownish; we could assume that even without mummies, from our own experience with the baking Egyptian sun. Unless it has turned white with age, the hair of mummies is usually dark, either black or brown; it may be straight or it may wave. In general they were a small people. Smith often describes the women as having small delicate hands and feet. The features are regular, with narrow noses, although some mummies exhibit what I like to call the Thutmosid nose. It was like George Washington's.

Anthropologists distinguish two main physical strains in Egypt. Predynastic Egyptians, we are told, were not the same people as the "Giza" men of the Third and Fourth Dynasties. The earliest Egyptians were dainty little people with small delicate faces; the men must have been slender, since the skeletons of males and females are indistinguishable, with none of the heavier bone formation which male skeletons usually exhibit. The only exceptions, among predynastic skeletons, are the people of Tasa, one of the very early predynastic cultures. They had square heads, coarser bones, more robust skeletons. (That word is not a particularly happy one to use in describing a skeleton, but it's the one the excavator used, and it does give one an idea.)

The later people of Giza resemble the Tasian type. Doctor Derry, one of the leading medical authorities on ancient Egypt, claimed that they also represented the ruling class of the Twenty-Second Dynasty, which came from Libya.

I don't want to go into the problem of two separate races in ancient Egypt. It gets confused with other arguments, particularly the vexed question of which "race" brought classical Egyptian culture into Egypt. Even allowing for disagreements about the physical types involved, there is probably too much emphasis placed on the notion that culture had to be brought in by somebody. No one has ever proved that the traits we use to define civilization—such as writing, monumental architecture, complex social organization, to name only a few—are connected with one of these two groups, to the exclusion of the other. The oldest physical type—the small fine-boned predynastic Egyptians—may be related to the brown Mediterranean type, and to the Abyssinians and Somalis. We can call them "Hamites" if we like, although this word is more usefully employed to describe language, not racial classes. (Anthropological terminology could stand revision; there are too many such confusions.) And maybe the later Egyptians, the dynastic people, are Semites. Except, of course, that "Semite" is a linguistic description, too. Let's just say that there were two different strains who probably looked the same to a casual observer—brown skin, dark hair, dark eyes, on the short side. No race remains "pure" for long unless it is completely isolated; and if it gets too "pure" it may just commit racial suicide through inbreeding. Like the rest of us, the Egyptians were probably mongrels. In the north there would be an Arab, or Semite element; in the south, the Nubian strain would be stronger.

With such a heritage, racial discrimination, as such, was one error the ancient Egyptians never fell into. They discriminated, naturally, but not on the basis of skin color. Like the Greeks, and others, the Egyptians called themselves "the people." Other men were not people; they were only barbarians. When the texts refer to Cush, the land of Nubia, it is always as "wretched Cush." "Don't worry about the Asiatics," a Thirteenth Dynasty prince advised his son, "they are *only* Asiatics." Later, the fine contempt for outlanders was shaken by bitter experiences. Some of the *mere* Asiatics came down and conquered Egypt; later still, wretched Cush had her turn. Then came the Greeks, the Persians, and the Romans. It is unlikely, however, that the hard cold facts of conquest and annexation ever altered the Egyptian's view of his own superiority. In this he was no better and no worse than the rest of us; we have a long way to go before we will be able to face the fact that greatness is not a national but an individual phenomenon, and that all men are brothers in their weaknesses, if in nothing else.

# II

# The Red
# and Black Lands

*The Two Lands*

THE world into which the Egyptian baby emerged was a narrow one, especially in the physical sense; the Valley of the Nile is some six hundred miles long, and only about ten miles wide. Pharaonic Egypt consisted of the elongated valley and the triangular delta, where the river breaks up into several mouths before it reaches the Mediterranean Sea. The two parts of Egypt are very different in physical geography, and the Egyptians as always thought of them as distinct areas. Before the First Dynasty, when Egypt emerges into historic times as a united nation, under a single king, the Delta and the Valley were probably separate kingdoms. Since we have no written records from this period, the existence of the prehistoric kingdoms must be inferred from indirect evidence; but this is about as solid as circumstantial proof can be.

The king of Egypt always wore two hats—literally. His Double Crown was made up of the crowns of Upper Egypt and Lower Egypt. The duality of the monarchy is indicated by many other signs: the two goddesses, Nekhbet of the south and Buto of the north, protected the king; and his titles include "King of Upper and Lower Egypt" and "Lord of the Two Lands." We could go on, but this is enough to indicate why we feel we are safe in assuming that, at some point, there was political separation as well as topographical difference between Upper and Lower Egypt.

To the Egyptians, their country was "the Two Lands." These were the areas we call Upper Egypt and Lower Egypt, corresponding, roughly, to the Valley and the Delta. (The Nile flows from south to north, so Upper Egypt is "under" Lower Egypt on a normal map.) You may encounter a reference to Middle Egypt, meaning the area between Cairo and Assiut, but the threefold division was not natural to the Egyptians. They apparently enjoyed parallels, for in addition to the contrast between Upper and Lower Egypt, they emphasized the difference between the Red Land and the Black.

The Black Land was Egypt, and anyone who has ever visited the Nile Valley can understand why the Egyptians chose this name for their own land, in comparison with the Red Land of the desert. On either side of the Nile there is a strip of rich, dark soil which is fertilized annually by the inundation of the river. The Black Land ends so abruptly that it is as if a divine finger had drawn a line down the length of the land, decreeing: on this side life, the green of growing crops; on that side, death and sterility in the lifeless sand. The sterility which begins within the Valley itself extends on, up and out, over the cliffs and into the two deserts of Libya and Arabia which border Egypt on east and west.

For the Egyptians, the desert was a place of abhorrence. There dwelt the wretched Bedouin, the wanderers who did not know the gods; there the traveler found heat and thirst and misery. Yet without the Red Land, Egypt, as we know it, would never have existed. From the barren plateaus the Egyptians drew the gold

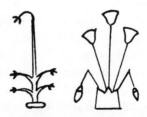

*Symbols of Upper and Lower Egypt*

which made them an object of envy among the other ancient powers of the Near East and gave them the power that comes from wealth. In the red lands of the desert they found copper, the source of the tools that cut the Pyramids and the weapons that won Nubia and the East. And on the sands which bordered the Black Land below the cliffs, they built the temples and tombs which have survived to tell us of the grandeur that was Egypt. The rich black soil which the Egyptians prized so highly gives life to the ephemeral things that live for one season; the sterile desert sand has preserved not only stone, but such frail objects as textiles and papyrus and human flesh. Ancient Egypt was the product of both Black Land and Red Land, though its people called it Kemit, the Black.

The Delta region was all black land—flat, green, and often swampy. Thus we know less about it than we do about the narrow ribbon of valley. The great majority of the artifacts which fill our museums today come from Upper Egypt; indeed, the Delta represents a big gap in our knowledge of Egyptian culture, and it is a gap which badly needs to be filled.

A number of the Delta sites were important and already ancient cities in pharaonic times. In the western Delta was the primitive northern capital of Buto, "the place of the throne." It lay deep within the marshes, and its goddess, the cobra, later became one of the two protective powers that guarded the king. South of Buto was Sais, with its sacred lake, the home of the goddess Neith. Farther east, almost in the center of the Delta, was Busiris, where Osiris lived before he moved south to Abydos, in Upper Egypt. Bubastis, southeast of Busiris, should be an object of interest to all cat fanciers, since it was here that the feline-headed goddess Bastet had her chief shrine. North and east of Bubastis lay Mendes, home of the ram-god Khnum, and directly east of that city was Tanis, on the salty plain south of Lake Menzalah. It was not so old a city as Sais or Buto, but it has an intriguing history. Scholars are still arguing about the identification of Tanis with two important ancient cities—Avaris, the stronghold of the invading Hyksos, and Pi-Ramses, where the Israelites toiled to raise a treasure city for their oppressors. Tanis was the capital of Egypt in the late period, and important royal tombs were found there by a French expedition under Pierre Montet. In its neighborhood the Ramesside kings built palaces and pleasure-domes. One source of pleasure, surely, was the fine wine of the Tanis area, and that of Inet, south of Tanis.

The northeast Delta was famous for wine in ancient times, and it also provided pasturage for the great herds of the king and the gods. Great stretches of the region, however, must have been pure swamp, filled with the pretty feathery papyrus and with reeds which grew higher than a man's head. The reeds sheltered geese and duck and other fowl, including ibis and heron. Perhaps there were even hippopotami there at one time, although these animals have now vanished. The Delta cities and villages were often raised, on hillocks or man-made eminences. The area is wet today, and it may have been wetter in ancient times. Now there are two main exits for the river, the Damietta and Rosetta mouths. In the time of Herodotus there were no less than seven mouths, and between the main branches there were streams and canals and lakes.

It is a pity we don't know more about the Delta, with its handsome palaces and temples, its prized vintages, its herds and wildfowl and fields. We have had to be content with a hasty, bird's-eye survey of the area. Now let us compensate by viewing Upper Egypt in more detail. Naturally, we will go by boat. It is still the pleasantest way of seeing Egypt, and in ancient times it was the only way.

We cast off from the docks at Memphis before dawn on a pleasant summer morning in the fifty-second year of the Lord of the Two Lands Userma'atre Setepenre Ramses Meriamon—whom later generations will know, more conveniently, as Ramses II. We have the king's permission to hitch a ride, and such permission is necessary because the ship and its cargo belong to him, as does almost everything in Egypt that doesn't belong to the gods—grain, temples, animals and men. The voyage is not a commercial enterprise for profit. The boat carries wine of the king's vineyards of Inet to be delivered to the god Khnum of Elephantine, and to the god's priests, who will probably enjoy it more than he does. Along the way we will stop to drop off a few jars at certain cities especially favored by the king.

The skies are a pale brightening blue as we lean against the rail, yawning, and look back to see the stately triangles of the Giza pyramids outlined on the horizon. Above our heads the great sails swell and grow taut; boats coming downstream to Memphis go with the current, but we must depend on the north wind for power. Luckily it is almost always blowing from that direction. We pick up speed, leaving Memphis behind—the White Wall, the first capital of united Egypt, which has stood at the junction of the Two Lands since the time of Menes the Unifier. From afar we can see the pylon gate of the temple of Ptah rising high above the massed greenery of palms and tamarisks that beautifies its courts.

The light grows stronger; then the glowing disk of the sun, Re-Harakhte, soars on falcon wings up over the rim of the world. His beams illumine the mighty bulk of the Step Pyramid, marking the old cemetery of Sakkara. Across the river, on our left, the black holes of the limestone quarries at Ma'sarah are conspicuous against the pale gold of the cliffs. From these quarries came the stones which smoothed the slopes of the pyramids of Giza, and still the pharaohs delve into the heart of the hills to extract blocks for their tombs and temples.

The sun is high when we pass the Dahshur pyramids; their slopes shine golden in the light. Next comes Lisht, as it will be called, with more pyramids—smaller, already crumbling. At Medum we see the last of the big pyramid tombs of the Old Kingdom. It is a landmark for miles around. Still pyramid-shaped, it will not remain so much longer. Soon the pillaging of stone from its sides will begin, and in the twentieth century it will look like a tall, squat tower.

Near Medum we will have to stop and tie up for the night. Nothing short of a dying mother or a threat to the crown could make a captain sail his craft in the darkness. There are too many sandbars, for one thing; and the spiritual dangers are equally grave. The dead wander at night—the ones with their faces turned backwards. And perhaps other things wander as well.

The captain has invited us to dine with him up on the poop. It is a pleasant spot, with the cool night breeze touching our faces and the glitter of stars overhead. The captain apologizes for the meal—just rough sailor's food—but we find it more than ample. A roast duck, onions and radishes, fresh baked bread from the village where we lie at anchor, and fruit to finish up with—dates and apricots and figs. And—can it be?—wine of Inet!

The captain is surprised and a bit hurt when we mention the wine, although we do so tactfully. Certainly it's wine of Inet. Would you expect him to travel 600 miles with that nectar in the hold and not have so much as a taste? He shrugs, throwing out his hands in a gesture which must have been born with the human race. A little wine here and there will never be missed; everyone expects that sort of thing, it's the custom. He is an honest man; he won't sell a quarter of the cargo on the side, with a share of the profits to the scribe who checks the king's accounts at the end of the trip. None of that sort of thing for him! Indeed, it is not too safe at this point in history, for Userma'atre (may he live, prosper, and be healthy!) is not patient with trifling of that nature. In past times, the captain has heard, such things were done with impunity. The good old days . . . But who is going to make a fuss over a jar or two? It *is* excellent wine, isn't it? We agree, and empty another cup, safe in the knowledge that if anyone is going to suffer for the missing wine it won't be us.

Next day we pass the entrance to the Fayum. If we could see that far—which we can't—we would behold a wide lake surrounded by green fields, and temples, towns and palaces. The wonder of the Fayum area is the Labyrinth, as it will be called by a Greek named Strabo, a thousand years from now. The captain knows it as the temple of Amenemhat, an ancient king; it contains 2,000 rooms built of monolithic slabs of stone. The Fayum is like a big oasis, attached to the Nile by a tributary which will be called the Bahr Yusuf—Joseph's Canal—to commemorate a man and an event of which Egyptian records hold not the slightest trace. Is this because Joseph never existed, except in the poetic imaginations of the Hebrews, or is it because we Egyptians prefer not to notice aliens, barbarians, in our midst? If the latter is the true explanation, Joseph's descendants may be, even now, laboring in the marshes of the Delta, trying to scrounge straw for their bricks. Perhaps Moses is on his way, and the magicians of the royal court of Tanis are reading strange omens in the sacrifices. But—all this is fantasy. If we were on that boat, in the fifty-second year of Ramses, we might find out what really did happen. If an evil spirit appeared and offered an Egyptologist the chance to take a trip like that in exchange for his immortal soul, many of them, I imagine, would be sorely tempted.

One hundred and eighty miles south of Memphis, we pull into the docks at Beni Hassan, our first real stop, to drop off a few jars of wine. The local prince is partial to Delta wine, and he is a close friend of the king's. They shared many a jar on the Kadesh campaign. The town is on the east bank, and up in the cliffs behind it there are tombs, already ancient, which archaeologists of future generations will cherish tenderly. The prince is not at home just now; he's off in the desert hunting, so we are not invited to drop in for a drink. The captain is anxious to get on, so as soon as the prince's porters have carried off the jars we set sail again.

Next day we pass a spot where the eastern cliffs fall back, leaving a fertile cup of land along the river. We crowd to the side and stare; the sailors whisper among themselves and finger the amulets hung around their necks on bits of string. There is not much to see now—only some ruined walls and heaps of stone. But once this was a city, the capital of the arch-heretic who tried to defy the king of the gods himself. He met the fate he deserved, that criminal of Akhetaton. Even his name is forbidden now.

Just below Akhetaton, which we know better as Tell el Amarna, we are conscious of a tightening of tension on board. The captain comes out from under his shelter and stands alert in the prow, eyes sweeping the river. The oars are manned. Then we see that the cliffs which bound the river on the east have moved in. They form a sheer wall down into the water, and from countless holes in the rock an army of birds emerges, fluttering and screaming. This is one of the worst spots on the river, where gusts of wind, dropping down the cliffs, seize the boat and whirl it into hidden sandbars. Just then the oars dig in, at a shouted command, and we swing away from the cliffs, missing a sandbar by inches. There are twenty miles of this sort of thing, and when we emerge from the narrows of the Gebel Abu Feda (a name, of course, which our captain has never heard of), we are ready to stop for the night. The captain took a chance coming through so late; twilight falls as we drop anchor and prepare the evening meal.

Eighty miles from Beni Hassan, over two hundred and fifty from Memphis, and we are approaching Assiut. We have been on the way for over ten days now, and we are less than halfway to Elephantine. Assiut is a great city, whose rulers once came close to being kings of Egypt, and the prince of Assiut is still an important nobleman. Perhaps if we reach the city at nightfall we will have time for a visit to the tombs of his ancestors, up in the cliffs.

Date palms and sycamores, pomegranate and persea, fields of flax and wheat—it is through a green, fertile district that we pass on from Assiut, reaching the holy city of Abydos two weeks after leaving Memphis. Osiris himself lies buried here and the waters are crowded with boats. Some are barges, bringing stone for the great temple Ramses is building here, but most are carrying pilgrims to the shrine of Osiris—live pilgrims and dead ones. A funeral boat, with a gilded mummy case on deck under an awning, cuts under our prow, and the captain, forgetting respect for the dead, hurls a string of curses at the sweating rowers. Then he steps to the side and makes an obeisance, and says a prayer or two, in the general direction of the Great Temple. He will make this journey again one day, in the same shape as the Osiris on the boat he nearly ran down—if he can save enough to pay for the pilgrimage.

When we reach Hu (which the Greeks will call Diospolis Parva) the perpetual low undercurrent of grumbling which marks the Egyptian sailor rises to an audible growl. We have had stretches before where the men had to man the oars, not only in the narrows but in spots where the river turned east or west for a short distance. Here begins the great bend, going almost due east for thirty miles and then turning back on itself for another thirty miles westward. There will be blisters, even on the sailors' callused hands, three days from now.

The last of the cities on the eastward section of the bend is Denderah, the site of the Hathor temple. In the twentieth century A.D., men will travel a long way to visit the Temple of Denderah, but they will see only a graceless, late version of the wonder we now behold—a shrine built by the great conqueror of the Eighteenth Dynasty after a plan handed down from the time of Khufu.

Past the cities of Coptos and Kus and Nagadah, still laboriously rowing; and then we are in the long westward stretch, and ahead of us, red in the sunset, rise the obelisks and pylons of Thebes. The capital of Egypt's present kings lies far to the north, in Tanis, but they still come here for burial, where the capital of the king of the gods will always remain—Thebes of the Hundred Gates, with its massive temples of Karnak and Luxor. A little farther, and we can see both temples; the gold-tipped flagstaffs before the painted pylons bear scarlet banners that flutter bravely in the evening breeze. As we move in toward the docks on the east bank the panorama of west Thebes, City of the Dead, glides into view: first the giant seated statues flanking the handsome mortuary temple of Amenhotep III, then the temple of our own Ramses, looking raw and new against the weathered cliffs. It makes a brave show, however, even in comparison with the other rich temples that run in a colorful line along the western cliffs. In a sheltered bay there is one structure that holds the eye, among all the other marvels—a temple of sweeping colonnades and soaring ramps, its terraces green with myrrh trees. This temple is dedicated to Amon and Hathor and to the Thutmosid kings, says the captain, and he ought to know; he is a widely traveled man, and has visited many of the temples himself. We nod politely; but we, travelers from a world distant in time as well as in space, for once know better than the native of the era of Ramses Userma'atre. This was the temple of Hatshepsut, the woman who dared to be king. Her name is not mentioned in the king lists. Her cartouches and her form have been cut out and covered over on the walls of her own temple. It will remain for archaeologists of a future day to bring her back to life.

It is still a few hours before dark, but the captain decides to lie over at Thebes till morning. He is an indulgent captain, for he lets the men go ashore. We seize the opportunity too, and go up to pay our respects to Amon—a sheep, perhaps, to be offered at the sunset service. After our religious obligations are fulfilled we can visit the town. We owe it to ourselves to see the night life of this great city of the past. There is not time to visit the tombs on the west bank, even if we were allowed to do so. The Valley of the Kings is guarded, and there is nothing visible there save the frowning cliff walls.

Unfortunately, the sailors found the night life of Thebes equally fascinating, though they lack our antiquarian bent. In the morning they are sleepy and disagreeable, and two of them never show up at all. The captain comments on their ancestors and personal habits, hires two of the hangers-on around the dock, and we set sail, only an hour behind schedule.

The men have another ten or fifteen miles of rowing ahead of them, but we leisured tourists can lean over the boat's side and watch the obelisks of Karnak fade into the distance. Before long we are passing Hermonthis, also on the Theban plain. Montu lives here, Montu the war god. Then at last we round the far bend and head south under a stiff breeze. The pace seems like flying after the hard days of rowing; two days after leaving Thebes we pass the twin cities, El Kab with the remains of its ancient wall and Hieraconpolis on the opposite side of the river. A little farther on is Edfu, one of the sanctuaries of Horus. As at Denderah, we now see something finer than the Ptolemaic temple which will one day attract hordes of tourists; this is the original, designed by the great Imhotep himself, who erected the Step Pyramid. His plan has been cherished and preserved by all succeeding kings.

Two more days, and we approach Silsileh, sacred to Sobek the crocodile god. There is a good reason for being polite to crocodiles here. The plateaus of the northern part of Egypt are limestone rock, which changes to sandstone near Silsileh, where the river cliffs come together like the pylons of a giant gateway. Whirlpools, rocks and sandbars make this into a treacherous stretch; often in the past, boats have struck and capsized. Then the proper prayers to Sobek might have paid dividends. Gape as we may we see no crocodiles; they have become scarce in past generations. But, as the captain pessimistically remarks, you usually don't see them until it's too late.

There is another small bend, and a group of islands, at Kom Ombo, which will be a favorite tourist spot in a few thousand years; from there we have a straight stretch twenty-five miles long into Elephantine. The scenery makes a wonderful close to this part of our trip. Straight ahead is the end of the island of Elephantine, with a cluster of houses around the temple, which is on the high point at the south end of the island. The sandstone cliffs begin to show outbreaks of granite, and granite boulders protrude above the brown water of the river.

The house of the prince is on the island—his earthly house. His House of Eternity is being built for him in the north, so he can lie near his royal master. But there are tombs high in the western cliffs across from the island; we can see them, if the sun is right, as rectangular black holes against the cliff face. If we feel like it, we can climb the cliff and walk right in; these Houses of Eternity are empty now. Perhaps the prince of Elephantine, who is also vizier of Cush, is wise to locate his own tomb in the capital where the cemeteries are guarded against thieves. His predecessors, the owners of the empty tombs, however, were not men who leaned on someone else for protection. Explorers and adventurers, they set out for the next world just as they had ventured into the wild jungles of inner Africa—alone, leading instead of following. We can read about their exploits if we like; they are carved on the walls of their tombs and in perfectly good Egyptian, too. Some of the words are a little odd, old-fashioned, but any literate person can read them. There is a lot to see at Elephantine: the granite quarries; the two holes out of which the Nile flows; on the island of Sehel, to the south, the Nilometer which measures the height of the inundation, so important to the prosperity of the nation.

## Nubia and the Deserts

Elephantine is the border between Egypt proper and the land of Nubia; the boundary is marked by a particularly nasty cataract region filled with granite rocks. To get to Nubia we go overland for a few miles and join our boat, which has been towed over the rocks, below the cataract. We get on board opposite a big island which will one day be called Philae.

The next part of the trip is not as interesting; the land is poor and not so green with growing crops. As far as the monuments go, however, we might still be in Egypt. We pass temples built in the traditional style at half a dozen places, and at least half of *them* were built by Ramses, a not immodest pharaoh. His most impressive enterprise is at Abu Simbel, which we reach on the eighth day after leaving Assuan. Two of the huge statues of Ramses, sixty-six feet high, have been finished, on one side of the doorway of the temple, and there is an antlike swarm of little black figures on the scaffolding that masks the other two figures. The inside of the temple is cut out of the cliff.

One of the passengers on our boat is a scribe, on his way to Abu Simbel to supervise the cutting of the inscriptions in the temple. He carries a bag of scrolls with the texts which are to be copied, and he tells us that the king wants to commemorate—once more—his great victories over the Hittites, that presumptuous group of people far away in the north. The scribe is a middle-aged man, run to fat a trifle around the waistline, as scribes usually are; his face has the blank amiability of the trained bureaucrat of any age. But we think we see a twitch at the corner of his mouth as he refers, respectfully, to the king's famous victory. We, too, know a few things about the battle of Kadesh, but we are just as tactful as the scribe.

The statues at Abu Simbel seem too big, and rather stumpy. In fact, the façade of the temple looks overloaded with the four colossi, a complicated sculptured group over the doorway, and a row of carved apes on top of the whole thing. Beautiful or not, it is certainly solid. As the captain says, it will surely endure as long as the pyramids of Giza.

A further two days' travel brings us to the second cataract, where the river descends in a series of rapids and a chaos of glistening black boulders, wet with foam. Beyond the gorge is our destination, and it is quite a sight: on either side of the river the cliffs are crowned by a massive fort, with battlements and ramparts. Our messages are for the commander of Semna, on the west bank, where we are welcomed by a crowd which consists of most of the inhabitants of the fort. It is a dull life, and they are always glad to see someone from home.

Semna is a good place to stop on this trip, for it marks the end of the area which has been under Egyptian control for so long that it is Egyptian in manners and customs. More cataracts, rocks, and barren cliffs line the river all the way down into the Sudan, but there are Egyptian temples and forts for a long distance south. We decide not to go on; we are five hundred years too early for the

pyramids of Napata and Meroe, which will be built by the descendants of the wretched Nubians whom the commander of Semna
has just mentioned with such sneering condescension. He seems
like a pleasant fellow; we need not tell him that within a few
centuries the wretched Nubians will be on their way north to take
over the throne of Egypt.

We have seen most of the Black Land now, and without so
much as leaving the deck of the ship. Boat travel is pleasant; but as
we turn from the Black Land to a quick survey of the Red, we can
be thankful that our journey is only an imaginary one. We are
going into the desert, and that requires fortitude.

The deserts—the Libyan on the west and the Arabian on the
east—are high above the valley. In prehistoric times the river cut
its way through a plateau which is composed of limestone in the
north and sandstone in the south, so that by the pharaonic period,
as today, the valley lay at the bottom of a trench whose cliffs are
several hundred feet high.

If we were going into the eastern desert with the ancient Egyptians, we would probably backtrack down the Nile to Coptos,
which lies on the eastward bend where the river comes closest to
the Red Sea. Here we would fit out a caravan of donkeys—the
camel will not be known for a long time yet—and start out along
the Wadi Hammamat, heading due east.

The eastern plateau is full of these wadis, which are something
like small canyons or arroyos, and we follow them when we can.
There are wells along this particular wadi, which has been a traveled route for centuries. Even so, it is a dreadful trip. The landscape is as barren and dead as a scene on the moon; high
mountains parallel the coast, and at one point in our route we
have to climb over a pass that rises to 2,500 feet above sea level.
The sun is baking hot, and the short-lived spring flowers, products
of the winter rains, have long since died. Remembering the cool
gardens around the prince's palace in Coptos, we wipe our streaming brows and wonder why anyone but a madman would venture
into these purgatorial rocks. The clue lies, in part, in the ancient
name of Coptos. It was called "Nebet," and Nebet means "the
Golden Place."

Some of the gold that made Egypt great among the nations came from Nubia, but a goodly share of it was found in the desert east of Egypt proper. Some of the gold is still there. Corporations to rework the ancient mines were formed in the present century, but the effort had to be abandoned after a few years because the ores were not worth the expense of extraction. This problem would not have worried the Egyptians; if they wanted something they were willing to put forth a degree of energy which we would consider prohibitive—as witness the Pyramids. Perhaps, too, they got all the richer ores and left the rest.

In the Museum at Turin there is a particularly fascinating papyrus, perhaps the oldest treasure map in the world. It may have been drawn at about the time of this imaginary journey to ancient Egypt, and it shows the location of some of the gold mines of the eastern desert. Archaeologists are not sure which mines were meant, but they may have been the very mines that lie along the Hammamat route. These mines, those of Fuakhir, are almost on Egypt's front doorstep compared with some of the others. At some

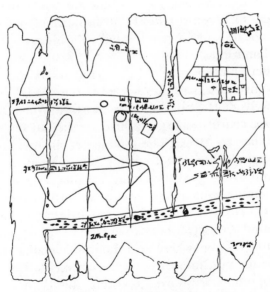

*Ancient map of gold mining area*

of the desolate, isolated sites there are ruins of ancient camps—stalls for cattle and for the miserable human cattle who worked the mines, barracks for the troops who kept them at a job none of them would have endured unless they had been forced to do it. Perhaps only criminals and prisoners of war were sent to these godforsaken spots; it would have been punishment to suit any crime.

There are jewels in this desert as well as gold—garnets, agate, chalcedony, jasper, rock crystal, carnelian—all prized by the Egyptians for jewelry. Apparently the ancients never discovered the beryls and emeralds which were found later.

Hard stone was quarried in this barren landscape. True, all stones are hard but some, I am told, are a lot harder than others. The limestone and sandstone of the valley cliffs, from which most temples were constructed, are soft stones. The Egyptians wanted finer material for special objects, such as the sarcophagus that held a king's body and the statue that depicted his divine form. At Assuan they quarried granite, from a quarry northeast of Cairo they obtained quartzite, and from the Wadi Hammamat they got the "beautiful bekhen stone," a gray-blue graywacke prized for the mirrorlike polish it could take. Flint also came from the desert; the ancient mines have been located. Marble, porphyry, slate, basalt—the list is long.

Under its forbidding surface, the desert was a treasure house. But the Egyptians had still another motive for venturing into it. Through the Wadi Hammamat, ancient caravans made their way to the Red Sea, and from ports on the coast they set sail on trading expeditions south to Africa. The products of the mysterious country the Egyptians called "God's Land" are as poetic as the name itself—apes and ivory, gold and ebony, panther skins, ostrich feathers, frankincense and myrrh. The strange little dancing dwarfs, who made such popular royal "pets," also came from God's Land. We don't know precisely where this exotic country was located, but we think it was somewhere near modern Somaliland.

Having made one jump from Elephantine to Coptos, let us make another one northward, to where the Delta spreads out green arms to east and west. The desert east of the Delta merges into the peninsula of Sinai, also a source of wealth and a high road to distant lands.

Sinai has copper. The Egyptians had copper. It would be reasonable to suppose that the Egyptians got their copper from Sinai. We suppose they did, but oddly enough, we can't prove it. The Egyptian mines in Sinai, at Magharah and Serabit el-Khadim are unmistakably Egyptian because of the numerous inscriptions scratched on the rocks nearby, but they were turquoise mines, not copper. There are ancient copper mines in Sinai, but nothing to prove that these miners were Egyptians. Some of the copper which was so essential to Egypt must have come from the eastern desert, although we have a hard time finding inscriptional evidence to prove it. And it is certainly probable, if not provable, that other copper came from Sinai.

The rocky, sandy roads of Sinai led into Asia. The Egyptians got tin and silver, amber, lapiz lazuli and jade from the east, not to mention the famous cedar of Lebanon. Under the empire, when they conquered—and were conquered—they also acquired slaves, mercenary soldiers, cattle, and miscellaneous booty. Unfortunately, roads go two ways—if the Egyptians could get out, the Asiatics could get in. They could not get in so easily, since the Egyptians guarded the paths; by garrisoning the few wells they could pretty well control the goings and comings of the "wretched Asiatics." Still, the Asiatics came, and at certain periods they came in a flood instead of a trickle. The hated Hyksos were Asiatics who brought to Egypt a national humiliation which was not wiped out until the warrior kings of the Eighteenth Dynasty drove the invaders back out into the deserts from which they had come. Even from the invaders the Egyptians got new and useful ideas, and at all periods contacts with the other civilized powers of the Near East—Sumner, Babylon, Assyria, Mitanni, Hatti—led to important developments in Egyptian history and culture. The other great civilized powers with whom Egypt had trade relations were 'way off in the middle of the "Great Green"—Crete, Cyprus, and, later, the Mycenean culture.

The desert on the west of Egypt, the one we call the Libyan, was not so exciting as the eastern desert. It had some valuable minerals, notably diorite and amethyst, but its most distinguishing characteristic was the string of oases that ran in a line roughly paralleling the Nile. There are six oases, five of which were controlled by the ancient Egyptians. Khargah, the "southern oasis," was one of the most important; it was famous for wine, as was Bahriyah, the "northern oasis." Perhaps the most useful was the Wadi Natrun, the source of natron, the salt used by the Egyptians in embalming. Far to the northwest of the Wadi Natrun lay Siwa, the only one of the group which was probably not under Egyptian control until late. This was where Alexander the Great went to be recognized as king of Egypt by Amon.

The water which makes the oases possible comes up in pools or springs, some of them thermal in nature. There is so much water that, ironically, the oases used to be quite unhealthy because of malarial fevers. Perhaps the ancient Egyptians were more skillful at handling their water supply than were the Arabs of the nineteenth century A.D., but it is interesting to note that the oases were dumping grounds for undesirables in pharaonic times—political enemies and criminals were exiled to them. The isolation of the oases did make them good prisons without bars; once you were there, there you stayed unless you could bribe the soldiers of the desert patrol to look the other way while you loaded a donkey caravan with food and water. But if the places were as unhealthy in ancient times as they were a century ago, they might also have been a slow sentence of death for anyone the king wanted to get rid of.

The Egyptian word for oasis was "wahe"; it is one of the few ancient Egyptian loan words in English. (Another one is adobe, from Egyptian djebat, mud brick.) The original inhabitants of the oases may have been the wandering tribes the Egyptians called the Tjemehu and Tjehenu. These people had to live somewhere, and there is no place else to live in that area; a few days away from the oases the great sand sea of the Sahara begins. Other nomads lived up north, near the western side of the Delta. They were relatively primitive peoples compared with the Egyptians, who were constantly having to go out and "chastise" them. Living where and as they did, we can hardly blame the Libyan tribes for occasionally raiding one of the oases or a western Delta village; but they never seem to have been a serious problem until they were backed up, in the twelfth century B.C., by other wandering tribes.

In our armchair sail up the Nile, we have seen more of Egypt than most ancient Egyptians did. Even if they were adventurous travelers who had gone all the way from Coptos to Memphis, or Amarna to Elephantine, they still saw the same eternally unchanging landscape—the river and the valley, the high cliffs, the desert and the sown. In the heyday of the empire a commoner might indeed see exotic foreign lands, but usually as a soldier. And even if he did not leave his bones in the unconsecrated soil of Asia or Cush, the Egyptian hated every minute away from home. For him the world was small and serene, and blessedly predictable; and that was just the way he wanted it to be.

# III
# "Beloved of
# His Father
# and Mother"

### *Children*

WHEN an Egyptian nobleman went hunting, he took the whole family along. The gentleman in our illustration is Nebamon, an official of the Eighteenth Dynasty; his little girl squats at his feet and his wife, beautifully and inappropriately dressed, stands behind him, in a pose which would, in reality, probably tip over the light papyrus skiff. Nebamon has draped some of the lotus flowers his child is picking over one shoulder; one can almost hear the high, childish voice insisting, 'They look *pretty* there, Daddy!' In one hand he holds the live ducks which act as decoys, and in the other he wields a throw stick shaped like a serpent. Even the family cat is there, grabbing a duck as it takes wing in a futile attempt to escape. Under the boat the fish swim placidly along in a line, and to the left we see the tall reeds and flowers of the swamp.

This is a very popular scene in tombs. Another nobleman named Menna had three children, two girls and a boy, and the entire family—wife, boy, and girls—accompanied their father on an expedition which was probably designed for fun as much as for food production.

Egyptian fathers may have preferred sons for practical reasons; only a boy could play the part of Horus, the dutiful son, when the

Fowling in the marshes. Painted relief from the tomb of Nebamon, Eighteenth Dynasty. *The Trustees, British Museum.*

sad hour of making offerings to his deceased father came around. But there is no reason to suppose that men were not equally fond of their daughters. To take little girls along on a duck-hunting trip is a sign of affection which few modern fathers would be willing to emulate.

One of the most affectionate fathers in ancient Egypt was Akhenaton, the husband of beautiful Nefertiti, and the great Egyptian heretic. Akhenaton had no sons by Nefertiti, and this is assumed by some to have distressed him immeasurably. If it did, he showed no signs of it. His six daughters were the pride of his heart, and he must have spoiled them badly. Wherever he went, they went too—to the temple to worship Aton, to state banquets, to ceremonies honoring virtuous officials. When Akhenaton and Nefertiti went for a drive in their chariot, the girls came along in their own chariots, or in that of their parents. In one such scene, we observe that Akhenaton has turned to give his pretty wife an affectionate kiss, and one of the girls, riding with them in their chariot, takes advantage of her parents' distraction to stir up the horses with a stick. Akhenaton lost one of his daughters when she was still quite young. On the walls of the royal tomb where the child was buried, he had himself depicted in attitudes of frenzied mourning which no other king ever ventured to employ.

Akhenaton was unique in the candor with which he allowed his love for his children to be shown, but he was surely not the only Egyptian parent who felt that way. The formal attitudes to which Egyptian art was usually restricted do not allow intimate family scenes. We know, however, from exceptions such as the hunting parties, and from other hints, that family life was close and warm. Among the most honorable epithets a man could claim, when he inscribed his dignities on his tomb stela, was the one we have chosen as the title of this chapter: *Beloved of his father and mother.*

Children led a fairly carefree existence when they were small. What did they play with? Sticks and stones, and mud, and bits of broken pottery, probably, as modern children do when their parents do not harass them with educational toys. Some ancient toys have survived—tops, miniature weapons, and several elaborate mechanical toys. One of these has a row of little dancing dwarfs on a platform; they are made to jog up and down by means of a string. An expensive toy, this one, for some nobleman's son—who probably left it lying in the dust after five minutes, and went back to his mud pies. Another mechanical toy was the cat shown in our illustration. A string made the jaws move.

You can find Egyptian dolls in many museum collections, but they may not have been children's toys. Some obviously are not; they are little naked female figures with certain characteristics which make their magical utility to the owner of the tomb where they were found uncompromisingly clear. Other dolls are very crude, just paddle-shaped chunks of wood with roughly painted features and a mop of clay curls. Since these have also been found in tombs, they may have had magical significance. But one suspects that female children of almost any era would demand a "baby" to play with, and Egyptian girls may have played with these unprepossessing specimens whatever their original purpose.

A mechanical toy in the shape of a cat. *The Trustees, British Museum.*

Dolls. Sometimes called "paddle dolls," they are of painted wood with hair of clay pellets strung on cord, in imitation of the heavy wigs of Egyptian ladies. *The Trustees, British Museum.*

Swimming must have been a popular sport for children. The houses of wealthy nobles boasted garden pools, and the villagers had the Nile or a handy canal. The youngsters played ball; the object they used was similar to a modern baseball, made of hide stitched together and stuffed. Races and wrestling matches were popular with the boys, dancing and playing house with the girls. Some games are shown in the tomb reliefs; one is played by four children, two mounted on the backs of two others, with a ball flying back and forth between the two riders. The point of this game is not hard to discover; it looks like fun, too, for the young and agile. In another game, one boy stands in the center with four or five others hanging onto his arms and forming a circle. This one is called "Going Around Four Times," but we do not know how it was played.

### Household Pets

Domestic pets were much enjoyed by children and adults. Egypt was probably the original home of *Felis catus*, the domesticated cat. The wild variety from which our alley cats (excuse me, "domestic short hairs") probably derive is a small animal, grayish in color, with dark stripes or spots. The Egyptians discovered the usefulness of this delightful creature at an early stage, perhaps in connection with their cultivation of grain. Wherever there are granaries there will be rodents, and no man-made mousetrap is as effective as a cooperative cat. With the subtle presumption of the

*A cat under its owner's chair*

*A hunting cat*

breed, Egyptian cats soon made their way out of the granary and into the house, ending up in a favorite feline position under their owner's chair.

One popular Egyptian goddess was cat-headed, which is in itself no sign of distinction, since many animal species were connected with one divinity or another. Not all cats were sacred animals, but there may have been sacred cats at Bubastis, where the cat goddess had her principal shrine. Mummified cats have been found; some may have been sacred beasts, some beloved pets. The beauty of the cat's graceful body must have appealed to Egyptian sculptors because there are a lot of cat figurines, ranging in size from little ones which could be worn as amulets up to nearly full-sized statues. In the latter the graceful curves of the back and flanks, and the proud pointed face, are beautifully modeled. In all the representations we have, the cat in question looks sleek and well tended. That they actually were tended with loving care we may see by a formula for removing poison from a cat who has been stung by a scorpion. It comes from a very late text, but the formula is similar to medical prescriptions of all periods and, like most Egyptian medical prescriptions, it relies heavily on what we would call magic. "Oh, Re, come to your daughter," it begins, "whom a scorpion has stung on a lonely road. Her cries reach heaven; harken on your way! She has used her mouth against it [sucked the wound] but lo, the poison is in her limbs." Re says he will come to the cat's aid, and then, to make sure, each part of the animal is placed under the protection of a particular god. "Oh cat, your head is the head of Re; oh cat, your nose is the nose of Thoth . . ." and so on. After this, there is the more practical recommendation that a tourniquet be applied.

Yes, the Egyptians must have been fond of cats. They even gave their daughters pet names which mean "little cat"—the equivalent of our own "kitten." We must mention that the Egyptian word for cat was spelled "miw." How it was vocalized we may safely leave to the imagination of any cat-owning reader.

Dogs seem to have been domesticated early, in many parts of the world. By the time they make their appearance in Egyptian reliefs, there were already several breeds differentiated. One is a lanky, long-legged greyhound type, probably related to the saluki hounds of Africa, which are still used for hunting. Another looks something like a short-haired terrier, except for the peculiar blob on the end of its tail, which is not found in any known species and which may have been some Egyptian dog-lover's idea of a pretty decoration. The most charming of the Egyptian dogs of my acquaintance is a little female with the bandy legs, sausage body, and long muzzle of a dachshund. The ears are different, however.

While dogs appear in numerous paintings and reliefs, as house pets and hunting companions, they were not a popular subject for sculpture. There may, or may not, be some relation to the fact that dogs were not deified—unless the peculiar creature known as the "Set-animal" was a dog. It does look something like a greyhound, but there are confusing details.

Modern dog-lovers claim that canines are more "lovable" than cats. Maybe the Egyptians felt the same way; at least they gave their dogs names, like other members of the family. A list of dogs' names has been compiled by Professor J.M.A. Janssen, and it is extensive enough to suggest that a good many dogs did have names —quite a distinction in ancient Egyptian terms, since a name had magical importance. Perhaps the most famous ancient dogs belonged to a budding pharaoh of pre-Middle Kingdom Thebes. His name was Wahankh, and on his tomb stela he had five dogs shown with him. Possibly he hoped, in this way, to assure their affectionate companionship in the next world. All the dogs had names written next to them; three have been translated as "the Gazelle," "the

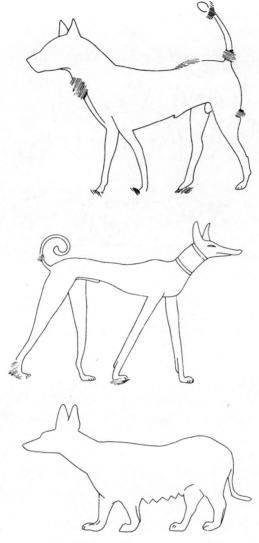

*Three breeds of Egyptian dogs*
a. Terrier type; b. Saluki hound type; c. Dachshund type

Black One," and "the Cook-pot" (?). The last one is questionable, but it is not hard to think of an explanation for it. Cooking pots are full of food, and this dog may have had a hearty appetite.

Baboons and monkeys were also household pets. There are a few pictures of them squatting morosely under the master's chair, in the position usually occupied by the family cat. A more cheerful

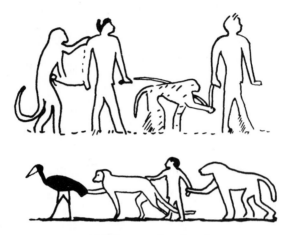

*Children and animals*

picture shows several monkeys hand in hand with children. One of my favorite pet scenes has a cat, a goose, and a monkey. The monkey is swinging gaily from the rung of a chair; cat and goose are in a loving embrace, with the cat's paw wrapped around the neck of the goose. The fowl seems to have doubts as to its friend's intentions; its eye has a terrified glare and its feet are off the ground, as if it were trying to fly. I wish I could reproduce this scene, but some ancient vandal removed the cat's head and spoiled the picture. Only the tips of the ears and the ends of the whiskers remain—enough, however, to clear the cat of the suspicion we might otherwise entertain, from the goose's agitation, that puss's jaws are buried in her companion's neck.

Many other animals were domesticated, but we cannot always say which ones were regarded as pets. Horses might be included in this select category; they were always relatively rare beasts. Senmut, the parvenu friend of Queen Hatshepsut, had a little mare mummified and buried near his tomb. He may have been an animal-lover, since his pet ape was also buried with him. The Nubian kings of the Twenty-Fifth Dynasty were great horse fanciers. One unfortunate Egyptian prince, whose city was besieged and conquered by Piankhi, the first of the Nubian dynasty, almost lost his head when the conqueror discovered that the horses in the princely stable had suffered from the long siege. Piankhi expressed himself as more distressed by the discomfort of the horses than by anything else—including, one presumes, the near-starvation of the citizens of the town and the death and mutilation of soldiers of both sides. I am an animal-lover myself, but I find this attitude somewhat exaggerated. It is not unique to ancient Egypt, however.

Perhaps these were the only animals that could actually be called pets; but I am sure that the children of ancient Egypt enjoyed playing with the other animals, especially the young ones. The Egyptians did not employ the camel; their beast of burden was the donkey. For food they raised goats and pigs and cattle of all kinds, including some wild varieties. Gazelles and ibexes were domesticated, and the young of these species must have appealed to the young humans. Baby ducks and geese would have had their admirers too. But there were no baby chicks; the domestic fowl was unknown in Egypt.

## Growing Up

When they were very little, children didn't have to bother with clothing. Considering the Egyptian climate and the habits of children, this was an admirable idea. Older children wore clothing like that of their parents, a kilt for boys, a simple linen dress for girls. The girls let their hair hang loose or braided it into pigtails,

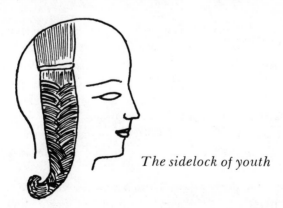

*The sidelock of youth*

but boys had an unusual coiffure—the head was shaved except for one long lock on the side, which was braided.

The distinctive sidelock is known from the reliefs, and it was actually found on a mummy, that of a boy about eleven years old. He had not been circumcised, although we know that this was standard Egyptian practice. There may have been a ceremony marking a boy's coming of age, when the sidelock was ceremonially cut off and the act of circumcision performed. One text mentions a mass circumcision of 120 men and adds that none of them hit out or was hit, none scratched or was scratched! Such mass puberty rites are known in many cultures, and manly fortitude in the presence of pain is expected of the initiates. There is no proof that the cutting of the sidelock was part of the coming of age ritual, but it was certainly one of the things that separated the men from the boys. The "sidelock of youth" is often mentioned in the texts, and men refer to the carefree days of boyhood as the time "before I had cut off the sidelock."

After the ceremony the boy was no longer a boy, nor was he that modern abomination, a teen-ager. He was a man, and ready for adult responsibilities. Boys and girls in the Near East today seem to mature physically at an earlier age than their western counterparts, so probably Egyptian children entered into adulthood at an age which would seem scandalously young to us. The tomb autobiographies are infuriatingly vague about the age at which the protagonist began his career, but they suggest that he had entered his chosen profession, and married, when he was still in his early teens.

Setting up a household was a proper adult activity. A man needed to beget sons to carry out his funeral ceremonies and see that his spirit was provided with food and drink. This is the formal reasoning, but it would be absurd to suppose that it was the only reason why the ancient Egyptians got married. We don't know how often marriages were arranged by parents, but there was none of the modern Near Eastern seclusion of the female, and in some cases at least a boy and girl married because they had fallen in love.

Egyptian love poetry dates from a relatively late period, but we need not conclude that the state of mind it describes so eloquently only occurred after, let us say, 1500 B.C. It is a state of mind which we find quite familiar, expressed in figures of speech which sound ridiculous only to those who have never experienced the emotion in question themselves.

It is up to the boy to make his feelings known first; the girl remains modest and shy until he does so:

> "I met Mehi driving on the road,
>   With his companions.
>   I don't know how to get out of his way;
>   Shall I pass casually by him?
>   See, the river is the same as the road [to me].
>   I don't know where to put my feet!"

Seeing the unaware object of her adoration, the girl dares not betray her love; in her efforts to appear calm and unconcerned she can hardly see where she is walking. But once she knows she is beloved, she voices her longing passionately:

> "Oh, that you would come to me
>   Like a stallion of the king,
>   Chosen from among all the horses,
>   The finest of the stable!"

The boy suffers from the same pains and exultations that vex a modern hero of romantic fiction. When his beloved returns his love, he indulges in boastful fantasies:

"The love of the beloved is on yonder bank;
The river lies between, and a crocodile lurks on the sandbank.
But I go into the water, and I wade through the waves,
And my heart is strong in the flood.

The water is like land to my feet, the love of her protects me.
It makes a water-magic for me!"

When she leaves him, he sinks into a decline:

"Seven days from yesterday I have not seen the beloved.
And sickness has overcome me.

My body has become heavy; I am forgetful of myself.
If the chief physicians come to me,
My heart is not satisfied 'with their medicines.
The priests—no solution is in them.
My malady will not be diagnosed.

When I see her, *then* will I be well;
When she opens her eye, my body is rejuvenated.
When she speaks, I am strong,
When I embrace her, she banishes evil from me.

But—she has been gone, for seven days."

These poems are not erotica; they express romantic love, although some experts seem to think that emotion is not found in
other cultures than our own. No doubt physical union is the cul-
mination both lovers desire, but it is not the only aspect of love
that interests them. Both the *chagrin* and the *plaisir d'amour* are
admirably expressed. The mere presence of the beloved is enough
to transport boy or girl, and a kiss makes them think they are in an
earthly paradise of perfume and incense. One young man remarks
ecstatically,

"When I kiss her, and her lips are open,
Then I am happy even without beer!"

Intoxicated with love, in other words. There is a general impression that the Egyptians did not kiss, but rubbed noses. The
last-quoted verse is clear testimony, it seems to me, that they had
gone beyond nose-rubbing. The verb translated as "kiss" is determined by the drawing of the upper half of the face, whose most
prominent feature is admittedly the nose, and in some reliefs two
people are shown familiarly "nose to nose." I suppose we would use
the mouth sign for kissing if we wrote with pictures, so either the
Egyptians looked at the problem differently—noses do get involved
in osculation—or they started out by rubbing noses and, at least
occasionally, proceeded to something more dangerous. As for the
reliefs, it would have been impossible for an Egyptian artist to
show two faces in such close contact as kissing demands; nose to

*Akhenaton and Nefertiti*

nose was as close as he could get his lovers without overlapping the nasal members, which would have been against all the rules. I feel quite sure that Akhenaton kissed his wife; he was an iconoclast in any case, and Nefertiti was certainly beautiful enough to inspire a husband. Certain of the Amarna reliefs show the royal couple in romantic poses. In one case Nefertiti's head is tipped back, and it is obvious that lips, not noses, are about to meet. In another relief she has her mouth set in the proper shape for a kiss. With the new freedom of pose which Amarna art permitted, it may be that the artist was attempting to show a custom which had existed, but which the artistic canons were unable to depict.

The Egyptians even admitted the possibility of that despised notion, love at first sight. Ramses II fell in love with his bride, the princess of Mitanni, the moment he set eyes on her, "because she was more beautiful than anything." And in one of the nicest of all Egyptian stories, the princess . . . But let's take it in its proper order.

"Once upon a time there was a king who had no son. So His Majesty asked the gods to give him a son, and they ordered that one be born to him. He lay that night with his wife, and she became pregnant. And when she had fulfilled the months of bearing, behold, a son was born. Then came the Seven Hathors [a cross between the Fates and the good fairies] to settle his destiny. They said: 'He will die by the crocodile, or by the snake, or else by the dog.'

"The people who were near the child heard, and they reported to His Majesty. So His Majesty's heart became very sad. And His Majesty caused to be built, on a desert plateau, a house of stone

equipped with servants and every good thing from the palace—
because the boy was not supposed to go outside the house.

"When the boy grew up, being, one day, out on the terrace, he
saw a dog following a man who was walking along the road. So he
said to his servant, who was with him, 'What is that thing walking
behind the man who is going on the road?' He (the servant)
answered: 'It is a dog.' And the boy said, 'Let someone bring me
one.' Then the servant reported these words to His Majesty, and
His Majesty said, 'Let one bring just a little dog, so that he won't
be sad.' And so they brought him the dog."

Arriving at manhood, the boy chafes at his imprisonment, and
finally persuades his father to let him go, arguing that the will of
the gods will be fulfilled whatever he does. Equipped in style, he
sets out on his travels and ends up in Naharin, where he finds an
interesting situation. "The king of Naharin had no child, except
one daughter, for whom he had built a house whose window was
seventy feet above the ground. He called all the sons of the princes
of Syria and said to them: 'The one who reaches my daughter's
window, to him will I give her as wife.' "

The prince, newly arrived, is welcomed by the Syrian boys
because of his beauty and because of the sad tale he tells; conceal-
ing his birth he says that a new stepmother made life at home
miserable for him. He asks them what they are doing, jumping up
at the high tower all day long, and they explain the situation.
"And he said to them, 'Oh, if my feet didn't bother me, I would
jump with you.' So they went to jump, as was their daily custom,
while the young prince remained aloof, to watch. And the princess
of Naharin saw him.

"Now after several days had passed, the young prince went to
jump with the sons of the princes. He jumped—and he reached the
window of the princess of Naharin! She kissed him, and embraced
him in all his limbs. They (the onlookers) went to tell her father
. . . who asked, 'Is it the son of one of the princes?' They answered,
'It is the son of an officer who has come from Egypt, running away
from his stepmother.'

"So the prince of Naharin flew into a great rage, and said,
'Shall I give my daughter to a fugitive from Egypt? Let him go
back!' And they went to tell him: 'You must return to the place

from which you have come!' But the young girl seized him, saying: 'By Re-Harachte, if they take him away from me I will stop eating, I will stop drinking, I will die at once!' So the messenger went back and told her father all that she had said. And her father sent men to kill him where he was. But the young girl said: 'By Re, if you kill him, when the sun sets I will be dead! I will not survive him a single hour!' "

Naturally the prince of Naharin has to give in to his infatuated and headstrong daughter; he is impressed by the boy's beauty and royal manner, too. So the prince, and the girl who fell in love with him at first sight, are married. When the prince tells his bride of the destiny foretold by the Seven Hathors, she urges him to get rid of his dog; but he replies that he has raised the animal from a puppy, and can't part with him. By her watchful devotion the wife saves the prince from his first fate, the serpent; but later he is frightened by his dog, and in fleeing from the pet he runs straight into the jaws of the crocodile. The beast presents him with an "out." If the prince will fight a water-spirit with whom the crocodile has been vainly struggling for months, he can go free.

Just at this desperate moment the manuscript breaks off; it is one of the most exasperating breaks in Egyptological literature, because while we can almost guess at the ending we cannot be sure whether the prince escapes the snake and the crocodile only to fall victim to his own cherished pet, or whether the dog is allowed to be his salvation rather than his doom. I incline toward the latter ending, not only because I am an optimist, but because the Egyptians were optimists too; most tales of this type have happy endings. The astute reader will recognize a number of familiar elements in this story, which is less famous than I think it deserves to be. Not only do we have the immediate passion of the princess for the prince—standard emotional fare in western fairy tales—but the disguised prince, the princess in the inaccessible tower, whose hand is to be the reward of prowess, the threatened doom and the father's attempt to avert it by secluding the boy—all these are elements in a dozen well-known European stories. It makes us wonder where the origins of our own folklore are to be found. And yet, from the early centuries of the Christian era up to the middle of the nineteenth century, there was not a single man on earth who could read "The Doomed Prince," as our story is called. How then did bits of it get into "Rapunzel," "The Princess on the Glass Hill," and all the others? Or are we, perhaps, dealing with basic human psychological traits?

Basic or not, the Egyptian view of love was similar to our own in many ways. Their attitudes toward marriage—which is, of course, quite another thing—we will consider in another chapter.

# IV
## Lady of
## the House

### The Egyptian Woman

SOMEONE—I think it was Dr. Margaret Murray—once said that a country's state of civilization could be judged by the position of its women. The higher the culture, the more honored were the female members of it.

Much as I would like to support this admirable idea, I must point out that it falls apart at the first critical prod. To take a single example: The outburst of creative genius that took place in Periclean Athens puts that culture high up on any man's list of great civilizations, and in no ancient culture, perhaps, have women been held so cheap as they were in the age of Sophocles, Socrates, and Phidias. The rule was not even "Kinder, Küchen und Kirche," for women were not encouraged to hang around the temples. Conversely, some of the societies in which the female has a high position are the more primitive ones.

We cannot claim, then, that Egypt's greatness was the result of the way she treated her women. Although they were well off by most standards, they never had the "equal rights" that modern women demand. The professions were not open to them, nor were any of the crafts except those which were traditionally feminine.

*Egyptian lady*

They were not carpenters or sculptors or scribes—although some, at least, of the royal women did know how to read and write. They were not priests, either, although each temple had its corps of women attendants. The commonest title of the temple women was "singer"; they formed a choir of singers and dancers, who performed for the god's amusement and accompanied themselves on the rattlelike sistra. Sometimes they were regarded as the god's concubines, although there is no evidence of the sacred prostitution found in some cultures.

Women might be singers, dancers, or musicians and in these capacities they are depicted entertaining guests at private banquets. But the girls—most of whom were young and pretty—may not have been professionals who worked for pay; they may have been household servants or slaves. In one story, however, a group of itinerant female musicians is mentioned in such a way as to suggest that they were familiar figures. But, for the most part, woman's place was in the home.

> If you are a man of standing, you should establish your household and love your wife at home, as is proper. Fill her belly and clothe her back; ointment is the prescription for her body. Make her heart glad as long as you live—she is a profitable field for her lord. You should not judge her, or let her gain control. . . . Let her

heart be soothed through what may accrue to you; it means keeping her long in your house.

That's the way to treat a wife, according to Ptahhotep, the Old Kingdom sage who left a book of advice for the benefit of posterity. We can hardly picture him offering to wade across a river filled with crocodiles for his lady's sake, or sinking into a decline when she went back to spend a week with her parents. Ptahhotep wrote during the Old Kingdom, and the love songs come from a period almost a thousand years later, but I suspect that the difference in tone is not the result of cultural change but of the change from romantic love to practical marriage. The words of a later sage, more nearly contemporary with the love songs, are more sentimental, but no more romantic:

> When you are a young man and take yourself a wife and are settled in your house, remember how your mother gave birth to you, and all her raising of you besides. Do not let her blame you, so that she lifts her hands to god and he hears her lamentations. . . . Do not supervise your wife in her house if you know that she is capable; don't say to her, "Where is it? Get it for us!" when she has [already] put it in the [most] useful place. Watch and be silent, so that you may recognize her talents.

The last sentences imply a high degree of sensitivity on the wise old gentleman's part; few men realize how annoying it is to be "heckled" about details of household management!

There is a difference in attitude between these two quotations so widely separated in time; and it may be that the women of the later period had more rights than they did at the beginning of Egyptian history. They had property rights, certainly; there are dozens of legal documents relating to the sale or rental of property in which women dispose of houses or land as they wish, without reference to the permission of husband or father. This is an "advanced" state of things, according to Miss Murray's definition, and it puts ancient Egypt several steps higher on her scale than Victorian England, for instance.

If there is no romance in Ptahhotep, there is another element which is very pleasant. Although the husband should be the mas-

ter, his supremacy should be established by fairness and consideration, not by brute force. One has the feeling that the sage would
have considered wife-beating too crude even to mention, although
it may well have occurred. There is a suavity and subtlety about
many aspects of Egyptian culture, including the relations between
man and wife—not the tortuous subtlety which Westerners consider typical of the Near East—but sophistication, even refinement.

We know very little about the ceremony of marriage, but most
authorities agree that it was unimpressive, if indeed it existed.
Perhaps a man simply built a house and invited a woman to share
it; when she moved in, the couple was married. Some sort of legal
settlement may have been drawn up, but there are no traces of
religious rites.

While polygamy was permitted, it was not necessarily common.
The difference in status between a wife and a concubine was considerable. The first or chief wife was called the "lady of the
house." (I am always delighted to have salesmen inquire after me
in those terms; some day I intend to greet one of them in Egyptian.) Marriage was not for eternity—divorce was practiced—but
usually a man and wife expected to live together in the West just as
they lived together in life, and some of the tomb statues which show
husband and wife seated side by side, facing eternity with smiling
faces and arms embracing one another's bodies, are attractive tes-
timonials to the fact that affection did not end with death or marriage.

A woman gained additional prestige when she became a
mother. Sons were supposed to honor and care for their mothers,
and the tomb inscriptions of the late Old Kingdom and First Intermediate Period, which listed the writer's claims to virtue, commonly mentioned that he was loved by his mother. Strangely
enough, none of these inscriptions mentions the wife. A man is
praised and loved by his parents, children, and brothers and sisters, but never, so far as I know, by his wife. It is an unexpected
omission, and one whose implications, if any, are difficult to explain.

We have seen what the rights of women were. What were their
obligations? "To be a fertile field for their lords" for one thing—to
present them with children, preferably sons. Although other du-

ties are seldom specifically named, naturally a wife was expected to tend to her husband's comfort, prepare his food, keep his house and clothing in order, and be a good mother to his children. If her husband was a farmer she helped in the fields; wives of officials and "businessmen" often managed their husbands' affairs when the men had to leave home temporarily. In the humbler households women were kept busy grinding grain, baking bread and brewing beer, weaving and making clothing. However, nobody expected them to fix electrical appliances, unstop a drain, discuss politics, drive a car, mix a good dry martini, or be an expert on dietetics, child psychology, interior decoration, bridge, or educational theory. Although they may not have known it, they were well off.

In comparison to the women of many other cultures, the Egyptian wife had little to complain of. She had prestige as the mistress of a household, and her husband was expected to treat her well. Her children owed her respect as well as affection. Her property rights were assured and, at one period at least, she was entitled, in case of separation, to a third of what the couple had acquired after marriage. Although children were desired, I know of no cases of divorce because of the wife's seeming barrenness—a common injustice in many nations, even modern ones. (In polygamous societies, admittedly, the problem is more easily solved.)

There was one serious crime against marriage—infidelity. Since we have no Egyptian civil law codes, we have to infer from other sources just what constituted a crime, but several stories make it clear that adultery—for the wife, at least—was a dangerous game. There is one such story about a great magician and his faithless wife. The lady must have been sorely tempted to take chances with a man of her husband's profession; of course, the seer found out. Her lover was given to a crocodile that, presumably, did something unpleasant to him. By the king's command, the wife was burned alive. In another story the erring wife—who was not guilty of actual adultery, but only of aspiring to it—was killed by her husband and thrown to the dogs.

The literature unfortunately gives us no examples of what happened to unfaithful husbands, but it is evident that promiscuity, before and after marriage, was frowned upon. We have already noted the punishment of the lover of the magician's wife. The wisdom literature does not neglect the subject. Says Ptahhotep: "If you want to make friendship last, in a house to which you have access as son, brother, or friend . . . beware of approaching the women. . . . Do not do it . . . it really is an abomination." A later sage, Ani, warns: "Be on guard against a woman from abroad, one who is not known in her town. Do not stare at her when she passes by; do not 'know' her—a deep water, whose windings one does not know, a woman who is far away from her husband. . . . It is a great crime, [deserving] of death. . . ."

One of the truisms about ancient Egypt that everybody seems to believe is that brother-sister marriages were practiced. I am generally suspicious of truisms, and it was with great pleasure that I found that this one is indeed suspect. Some years ago the assumption was reexamined by Professor Jaroslav Černý; his name deserves mention not only because he was willing to challenge a long-held generalization, but because he had a tedious and frustrating job disproving it. The job was tedious because it involved searching through hundreds of inscriptions for examples. It was frustrating because of the Egyptian vagueness about relationships. The most misleading of their habits, which may have led to the formation of the brother-sister theory in the first place, was that they did not always use "sister" in its literal meaning. By the Eighteenth Dynasty, if not before, it had come to mean "wife" as well, and in the love poems it is a synonym for "beloved." The only way we can be sure that man and wife are also brother and sister is when the parents of both are named, and when the parents are the same. This ideal case does not occur very often. Still, Professor Černý found enough examples to make a good sampling, and the results were startling. His Middle Kingdom examples produced several possible cases of brother-sister marriage; but one of these depends on the assumption that "sister" was not used to mean "wife" before the Eighteenth Dynasty. The other cases are those of a man and wife who had mothers with the same name—a name which was very common during the period. Professor Černý found no cases of brother-sister marriage in the Eighteenth Dynasty. We cannot conclude from this that they did not occur, since we do not have enough data to check every known Egyptian marriage. But if marriages between siblings were legal, they were very uncommon —which is in direct opposition to the popular theory.

Commoners, then, usually didn't marry their sisters. Kings certainly did—not always, but often. Why?

## The Queen

At this point it is necessary to discuss the prevailing theory in regard to the queen's role in the inheritance of the throne—and I find myself in an embarrassing position. I strive, always, to give my readers the most widely held interpretation of data on which Egyptologists disagree—which includes most of the data. In this case, however, my disagreement with the traditional interpretation is so profound that it would be inhuman to expect me to pass it over without comment.

The traditional theory argues that the queen could not reign, but it was only through her that the right to reign could be obtained. The "heiress-ship" passed from mother to daughter, and only by marriage with the heiress could a man, king's son or not, legally hold the throne.

You will find this explanation repeated, I expect, in most books written about Egypt. So wide is its acceptance that it is almost impossible to find out how it ever began. Certainly by the 1890's, when Sir James Frazer was compiling *The Golden Bough,* he wrote that "Mr. William Petrie assured me that all Egyptologists accepted the doctrine of royal descent through the female."

Sir James was interested because he, and other anthropologists, had just discovered the primitive matriarchy. The idea was that most, if not all, societies were originally ruled by women. The mother goddess, symbol of fertility, was the top deity, and the mother was the head of the family—possibly even of the tribe. All this happened in the dawn of history, before written records; by the time the great civilizations arose men had rebelled and taken over. But traces of the old order of things survived in religious practices, inheritance, kinship terms, and so on.

At first glance this theory seems reasonable. The physical relationship between mother and child is obvious, but the father's role may be obscure. In the early part of the present century there were tribes in Australia who did not know anything about the male role in conception. Babies were brought by spirits. Europeans found this naïve doctrine highly amusing, and Frazer tells one pathetic story about an Australian whose wife had just borne a child after he had been away from home for a year. He couldn't understand why the Europeans for whom he was working kept snickering.

In all fairness, we must admit that the paternal role in conception is not the sort of conclusion that leaps to mind on the basis of the evidence. Some married women never conceive, and some girls who deny all contact with men do. The time between conception and parturition is great; it is five months before the embryo shows signs of life, and "quickening" might be the first indication a neolithic female had of her pregnancy. There would be no reason to connect conception with intercourse any more than with eating, sleeping, or planting taro; and, in fact, it is a wonder that so many people did eventually figure out the connection, without any knowledge of the complex physiological processes involved. We need not strain our credulity too much to admit that possibly primitive man did not know who his father was.

But it is a long jump from such an admission—which is not based on any concrete *evidence* from prehistoric cultures—to a conclusion that such cultures were matriarchies. Even if a man only knew his mother, he would not necessarily want to make her chief. Physical and political power do not need to be related to genealogy.

The brutal truth is that men have always been stronger than women. In primitive times, before agriculture, they were the hunters, who produced the food on which the very existence of the family or tribe depended. Childbearing, in such cultures, was not an asset to a female, but a positive handicap. For several months each year she was slow on her feet, sluggish, and clumsy. The baby picked its own time to be born—as it still does—and this might be a very inconvenient time: on the march, during a war, or right in the middle of the harvest. Admitting that primitive women may have been tougher than their spoiled modern descendants and took little time out to bear the child, they had to take some time;

we can fancy the skin-clad husband stamping up and down as the tribe gets farther ahead, looking impatiently at the sun moving up the sky and yelling to his mate to hurry up! Childbirth is also a perilous time. The mortality rate may not have been as high in Neanderthal times as it was in eighteenth-century Europe, when the honest physicians brought the germs of puerperal fever into the wards from the dissecting room, but some primitive women did die bearing children. I may be prejudiced, but it seems to me that a pregnant chief would not be an asset to any tribe, particularly a tribe of wandering hunters.

It might be postulated that women only came into their own with the advent of agriculture. The first farmers might have been female, and some bright Neolithic husband might have seen the connection between the fertility of the earth and that of his wife. This could conceivably lead to a deification, if not of women, of the female principle. But the oldest statues which have been thought to be those of a mother goddess come from paleolithic, not neolithic, levels; so we get back to the caveman, leaning over his wife, his eyes misted and his mouth trembling, as she smiles up at him and presents him with his son. . . .

No, it won't do. Let us leave this fooling and say simply that anthropologists no longer accept the blanket theory of primitive matriarchies. So we can't quote the general thesis to support what looks like a survival of matriarchal conditions in Egypt.

In fact, when we examine the evidence from Egypt we find that the theory of inheritance through the female—a hangover from the time of the now dubious primitive matriarchy—can only be supported by a series of exceptions, and unreasonable explanations of exceptions. There are too many exceptions. I will not weary the reader by detailing them, but if he knows anything about Egyptian history he can probably think of a few exceptions himself. (Ti and Nefertiti, the mother and wife of Akhenaton, are conspicuous examples.) One or two exceptions may prove the rule, but too many exceptions mean that we need a new rule. I prefer to explain the inheritance of the throne in ancient Egypt by the simplest notion of royal succession—that the king was succeeded by the oldest son of his chief wife. If the chief wife bore only daughters, the oldest of them, and the husband selected for her—preferably the king's son by a secondary wife or concubine—inherited the throne. Since women could not rule, an heiress princess needed a husband, but a properly legitimate crown prince could reign in his own right.

Let me reiterate that this interpretation of royal inheritance is not very popular among Egyptologists. The old truism of the heiress princess has never been seriously challenged; neither was the truism about brother-sister marriage until Professor Černý took a cold hard look at it. Just because one hoary tradition turned out to be unsound does not mean that the other one will too; but it does provide a hopeful precedent.

Since we have wandered, by logical progression, onto the subject of royal women, we will have to consider them at greater length, for while they were subject to some of the generalizations we have made about women, they naturally held a unique position. At all periods the queens of Egypt were the First Ladies of the land. Even in the First Dynasty there were tombs, as big and elaborate as those of the kings of that distant period, which were designed for the royal wives. The pyramid builders made little pyramids for their queens—and the relative sizes of the monuments suggest that, however important the queen might be with regard to other women, she was distinctly smaller than the king. The queen's titles of this period are suggestive of high rank; one of them is almost impossible to translate literally, but a reasonable compromise between sense and grammar might go like this: "She for whom anything she says is done." Impressive, if true! According to legend, the Old Kingdom ended with a queen on the throne, actually ruling Egypt. That was the end of the Old Kingdom; whether the reigning lady was a cause of the decline, or a symptom, we cannot say.

Although the queen was respected in earlier times, her prestige increased formidably in the Eighteenth Dynasty. The royal women of the Theban house that united Egypt after the Hyksos invasion must have been remarkable individuals; they were cherished by their husbands and sons, and even grandsons, and they sometimes exercised real power. It is possible that earlier queens acted as regents for absent husbands or infant sons, but none of them got as much publicity as the Eighteenth Dynasty ladies. The rise of the royal women culminated in Hatshepsut, the female king, who stole the throne out from under her young nephew and wielded the scepters for over twenty years. Hatshepsut may have come to a bad end, but her unconventional behavior did not deter future queens. A century later, Amenhotep III married a humble commoner, and his attitude toward Ti was definitely uxorious. Letters from foreign potentates during this period make it clear that Ti had a hand, potent if unofficial, in affairs of state, and she ruled supreme in the harem, taking precedence over kings' daughters and noblewomen. Her son, Akhenaton, not only continued to pay her homage, but raised his own wife to a high position. Nefertiti was so beautiful, if we can believe the evidence of the statues which have come down to us, that Akhenaton's infatuation is understandable; but by the same evidence Ti was no beauty. She must have had "it," or "sex appeal," or the Egyptian equivalent.

Hatshepsut was not the only woman to sit on the throne. There seem to have been at least three others. Two of them are such dim figures that we have a hard time proving they existed at all, and nothing useful about the queen's role can be deduced from them. Another queen, Tausert, sometimes has the title of king. She finished up the Nineteenth Dynasty, as the first two queen-kings finished the Sixth and Twelfth. But we know very little about Tausert; the only point of interest is that she probably was not a king's daughter. Some Egyptologists proceed, blandly, to remark that Tausert must have been the heiress, because she took the throne. They fail to see that this is one of those nasty circular arguments, and that Tausert's case is one of several that casts serious doubts on the commonly accepted theory of the heiress queen. If Tausert was not of royal birth, her assumption of the throne is quite remarkable since she had no hereditary claim to partially balance the handicap of her sex. But don't ask me how she did it, because I don't know.

Hatshepsut is, of course, the great female usurper. Her violation of tradition lay not only in the fact that she ruled, but that she ruled as a king. Obviously the reigning monarch of Egypt had to be male; the titles, laudatory inscriptions, and ceremonies were all designed for men, and they were so deeply rooted in tradition and dogma that it was easier for woman to change her sex— ritually speaking—than change the titles.

During the post-Empire period, certain royal women acquired

a new position which probably implied genuine political power. This position, held by the virgin daughters of the kings, was signified by the title of "God's Wife," which was originally a religious title belonging to queens of the New Kingdom. Presumably it referred to the intimate relations of the queen with the God Amon, who was, according to one story, the father of her royal son. The later princesses who held the same title may also have been brides of Amon-Re, but their marriages were not blessed with issue. They remained celibate, taking no earthly husband, and they lived in Thebes, where they assumed some of the powers of the High Priests of Amon. Since the capital of Egypt during this period was in the Delta, the king thus secured a valuable viceroy in the south—all the more valuable because she could rule in his name, but never in her own. Since the God's Wife could have no children, she adopted the daughter of the king who succeeded her father, and this girl became God's Wife when her adopted mother died.

The God's Wife may have gained her title because of her relationship to Amon, but the title of "God's Mother," which the queen occasionally bore, probably refers to the divine king. The king was a god in several senses; he was not only Horus himself, he was also the son of Re and, later, the son of Amon. The Egyptians were not worried by such apparent contradictions. Re and Amon might be regarded as manifestations of the same supernatural force, and Amon was certainly the king's divine father; two separate sets of reliefs make his paternity very clear. Although the god came to visit the queen in the form of her mortal husband, he was careful to announce his true identity, which naturally pleased her very much.

Queen or commoner, the Egyptian woman had a relatively pleasant life, and we do not need to resort to questionable generalizations like that of the primitive matriarchy in order to explain her prestige. The Egyptians were a "civilized" people in the looser meaning of that much abused word—urbane, amiable, fairminded. We need not explain why they were nice to their wives; indeed—if I may be permitted some slight feminine bias—we ought to explain why other people were not nice to theirs. The notion of the primitive matriarchy seems to have blossomed in the depths of the nineteenth century, when women were described as sexless angels and treated like feeble-minded children; perhaps this theory was the only way in which the bearded scholars of Victorian England could account for the peculiar customs they observed in other, inferior cultures.

# V
# "Clothe Her Back"

### *Clothing*

WOMEN seem to be inherently and incurably fashion conscious. (Men are too, but they don't like to admit it.) In all ages and all climes they have taxed the resources of their men and their nations to secure that with which they might make themselves beautiful. It need not be pointed out that fashion is arbitrary; some of the styles of even the recent past look hilariously funny to us, and the *haute couture* of alien cultures may seem actually grotesque.

By our standards, Egyptian female costume and makeup look just alien enough to be exotic. Essentially the only material used for clothing was linen; wool was ceremonially unclean, and cotton and silk were not known until a very late period. A lot of variety was possible with linen, however. Egyptian weavers were skillful, and the cloth they produced ranged from a coarse canvas texture to the most delicate, semitransparent gauze.

The Egyptian lady's version of our "good basic black dress," suitable for all occasions, was a form-fitting garment which went from below the breasts down to the ankles. Wide straps ran over the shoulders, covering the bosom but leaving a deep décolletage.

This dress is often worn by women in statues and painted reliefs, but the casual observer might not recognize it at once, owing to the conventions of Egyptian drawing, which have trouble with female anatomy. Usually one breast is shown in profile and the other is indicated only by a neat round nipple in some arbitrarily selected spot. The straps of the dress, however, are shown in front view, so that they look like the topless bathing suit straps of a few years ago. We know they weren't actually worn that way by the statues which show the same garment. In both statues and paintings it is sometimes hard to make out the dress at all, except as a pair of straps and an incised line for the hem. The dress must have been designed to fit the figure as tightly as possible, and it may have been stylish to make it of thin material. A becoming style for the slim and graceful, but I wonder how plump ladies felt about it? They could at least cover themselves with a mantle, which would have been comfortable on cool evenings. It could be draped to suit the fancy of the owner—over one shoulder and under the other arm, or wrapped around the shoulders like a shawl or a stole.

Basic woman's dress
of Old Kingdom

Elaborate woman's gown
of New Kingdom

In later periods, coincident with the growing sophistication of society in general, another style came into fashion among the well-to-do. This was a robe made of the sheerest linen obtainable and covered with delicate accordion pleats. Over the shoulders went a capelike affair whose ends were crossed and tied on the breast; it gave the effect of wide elbow-length sleeves, also narrowly pleated. Alas, there was still no relief for the obese female. Not only were these robes transparently thin, but they were open in front from breast to ankle, and they hung free unless confined at the waist by a bright embroidered or gold-ornamented sash. The ends of the sash hung down almost to the floor. Under the robe a modest lady might wear a shift like the older style dress, but some of them seem to have worn nothing at all.

There has probably never been any period in which male attire was so drab as it is today, when changes in fashion are limited to the number of buttons on a coat or the width of a lapel. The modern masculine contempt for fashion, as something which should concern only women, is uncommon; I suspect that in Egypt men commented approvingly on Setnakhte's new collar, and asked Amenhotep where he got his kilt pleated. The kilt or short skirt was the basic costume for men; trousers were still centuries off in the future. But the kilt was capable of fascinating variations. Basically it was just a rectangle of linen, knee length, which was wrapped around the waist and anchored in front by knots or sashes or by a simple overlap and tuck-in. Then some Egyptian Beau Brummell decided to have his kilt pleated; a rival lengthened the material and arranged the long overlapping end in a series of folds, fastened in front so that it fell like a pleated apron over the front of the thighs. One variant shortened the ends and brought them up in a sharp curve to meet at the waist; the resultant gap in front was filled in by a stiffened piece of material like a phallic sheath.

The man's elaborate robe, corresponding to the later woman's dress, was like that of his wife: sheer, accordion pleated, and long. He might also wear a two-piece outfit, consisting of a pleated skirt and a plain shirt with wide pleated sleeves. The shirt was collarless, and tied at the neck.

There are many variations in the standard costume, many of them depending on the occupation of the wearer. Field workers,

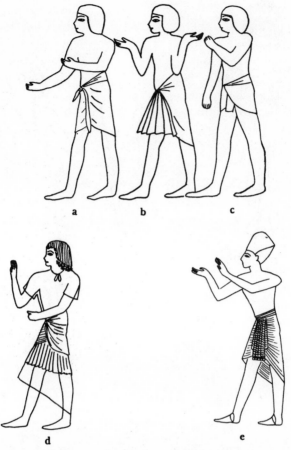

*The man's kilt—various types*

a., b., c, commoners; d. noble, with shirt and transparent
overskirt; e. king, with elaborate sash and Blue Crown

men and women alike, wore only a loincloth or short kilt. The
graceful acrobats and the dainty little serving girls who waited on
guests at parties were adorned only with narrow girdles and strings
of beads. Men's working costumes varied even more; some could
almost be called uniforms. The vizier affected a straight unpleated
robe which fell from below the armpits to the ankles; it was held
up by narrow tapes around the neck. Sailors seem to have preferred an odd nether garment made of coarse netting, with a
leather patch on the seat to compensate for the wear and tear of

Nobleman's costume
of the New Kingdom

A vizier

Costume of a Sem priest

the rowers' bench. Priests wore various ornaments to indicate
rank; the most picturesque uniform was that of the *sem*-priest, a
leopard skin arranged so that the snarling head lay on his breast.

Although most people went barefoot, they did wear sandals
when they got dressed up. Even the poorer classes could afford
papyrus sandals, but of course they didn't last long; leather was

more practical. The gold and silver shoes, of which a few examples have been found, were probably only for funerary use. They certainly would have been hideously uncomfortable in the hot climate of Egypt—but then, people are notoriously willing to suffer in order to be beautiful.

Our knowledge of Egyptian costume comes, for the most part, from painting and sculpture. The marvelous climate of Egypt preserves fragile materials remarkably well, but, as it happens, mummies were usually buried with no covering except the mummy wrappings. We do have a few garments which were actually worn, and these shed some interesting sidelights on the fashion story told by the monuments.

Perhaps we never realized how extensive and elaborate a royal Egyptian wardrobe could be until Tutankhamon's tomb was discovered by Lord Carnarvon and Howard Carter. The gold coffins and mask, the shrines, the jewelry, have obscured some of the less conspicuous but equally important objects. Among these were garments once worn by Tutankhamon, and packed carefully into chests and boxes so that he would be just as fashionable in the world of the dead. We have the jewelry which belonged to certain queens and princesses, but no clothing; probably we never will have it until an intact queen's tomb is found—if ever.

One of the first objects to catch the eyes of the excited discoverers of Tutankhamon was a gorgeous painted chest, with scenes of the king hunting and fighting in battle. It is so beautiful that one forgets it was not an object in itself. It was, of course, a container, and it contained many things: four pairs of sandals, a head rest, robes, a glove, an archer's gauntlet, caps, loincloths, and other pieces of material. Carter's description of the way this chest was handled, after being tenderly removed from the tomb, is an example of the varieties of expertise necessary to archaeologists, and also an explanation of why it took him five years to clear four small rooms.

When he first opened the chest, Carter found a pair of sandals on top and, to the left of them, a crumpled bundle which his expert eye immediately recognized as a royal robe. Its surface was entirely covered with a network of faience beads, arranged in squares with a gold sequin filling in each alternate square. The robe was bordered with bands of tiny colored glass beads, arranged in patterns. The patterns could still be seen, but all the threads which had held the beads in place had rotted away, and the smallest movement was sufficient to jar the loosened beads into a meaningless jumble.

How on earth, Carter wondered, could he get this unique object out of the chest without losing the design of the beads? Tutankhamon's tomb was not, strictly speaking, untouched; it had been entered by robbers in antiquity, and although they left a lot of things they pulled everything out of the chests and boxes in their search for portable loot. This robe had been tossed onto the floor, and when the priestly restorers came to straighten up the tomb they did not fold the garment neatly, but wadded it up and jammed it into the box.

The cloth, which looked so solid, fell apart under Carter's careful fingers when he tried to touch it. He might have stiffened the cloth and fixed the beads in place by means of wax or some other substance, but then he might not have been able to unstiffen it in order to see what the underneath portions of the robe were like. Something had to go, either cloth or pattern, and Carter decided, sensibly, to sacrifice the cloth. He picked it out, fragment by rotting fragment, and removed the decoration in its original pattern.

Once this tedious task was finished, Carter was not even halfway through with the chest. Luckily the sandals were in good condition, and could easily be removed. Under them, and the robe, was a second layer—three pairs of sandals made of leather elaborately decorated with gold. Two pairs were of the type that children wear, in a plastic version, during the summer, with one strap coming up between the toes to join a band encircling the instep. In one pair of Tutankhamon's sandals the thong was made in the shape of a lotus. The stem was inlaid with tiny bits of gem material, and the flower was attached to the wide side straps, which were gracefully curved and beautifully inlaid. The third set of footwear was a pair of slippers; heelless, they had leather toes and sides covered with little golden sequins.

Under the sandals Carter found a sadly decayed mass which was beyond hope of preservation. He thought there were at least seven different garments tangled up in the bundle, all covered with spangles and sequins and rosettes of precious metal.

*Sandal of Tutankhamon*

Two other robes, bundled hastily into another box in the Annex of the tomb, had resisted time and decay somewhat better. Carter believed them to be ceremonial garments. Both were shaped like long, loose vestments, with rich tapestry-woven decoration and fringe. One had needlework of palmettes, desert flower and animals in a broad pattern at the hem and at the neck opening. Another was covered with colored rosettes, flowers and cartouches woven into the fabric, and its neck opening had the shape of a falcon with outspread wings.

So far as I know, there is no relief which shows a king wearing a garment like these robes, or heelless slippers like Tutankhamon's. Some statues depict men and women wearing embroidered or woven robes, but these are rare. We wonder, therefore, whether the representations tell the whole story. The conventions of Egyptian art limited poses and attitudes, so perhaps they limited clothing styles as well. We can't even be sure that the paintings are literally accurate; the case of the ladies' shoulder straps is a case in point. With this in mind, some authorities have suggested that women's dresses were not so tight nor so sheer as the paintings suggest. We can't be sure, of course, but I see no reason why they should not have been both tight and sheer. The Egyptians had no complexes about nakedness. They may not have been the first nudists—as, I believe, some nudist magazine has suggested—because nudism, in the modern sense, implies self-conscious violation of the society's customs. Normally, the sexual organs of adults, male and female, were covered, but the rest of the body was exposed whenever weather or convenience made this comfortable.

## Coiffures

I suspect that the art forms are equally limited in regard to hair styles, but it must be admitted that they show quite a variety. Men were just as fashion-conscious about their coiffures as women were. Ladies usually wore their black hair long, although some female heads from the earlier dynasties display a "mannish" short haircut. A popular and becoming style was to let the long hair hang loose, thick and waving, from under a fillet or wreath of flowers; but women were not always content with such simplicity. Sometimes they braided their hair into many tiny plaits, or separated it into ringlets bound with gold. Some of the styles are enormously puffed, like the bouffant hairdos of today. But the Egyptian lady's coiffure was all hair, not air. When her own locks were inadequate they were padded out with hairpieces, and when she tired of black or brown hair she could dye it red with henna.

In the "classical" time of the Old Kingdom, men often wore a simple short cut like the one prevalent today. Other popular styles were the long, shoulder-length bob and the short cap of tight curls set in formal rows. The characteristic Middle Kingdom style was the "shawl-shape," with bangs across the forehead and the long side hair cut to a point in front. In the New Kingdom a new coiffure swept the country, at least among noblemen. It was cut in two layers. The top consisted of long thin sausage curls, and the underlayer was made up of rows of shorter curls or marcelled waves hanging to the shoulders.

During the Eighteenth Dynasty this marcelled men's wig came in two varieties, long and short. The short type, sometimes called (for reasons which are none too logical) the "Nubian style," was also worn by the ladies of Akhenaton's court. For this reason some of the sculptured heads of the period are very hard to identify. It has been suggested that the adoption of male styles by women was another of the "degenerate" customs which some scholars like to

*Hair styles of Old and Middle Kingdoms*

a., b., c., styles of men—Old Kingdom; d., e., styles of women —Old Kingdom; f. typical men's hair style of Middle Kingdom; g. women's hair style of Middle Kingdom, front and back views

*Hair styles of New Kingdom*
a. styles of men; b. styles of women

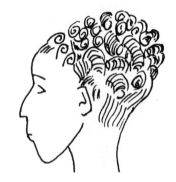

*Upswept hairdo on*
*mummy of a woman*

find in the heretic Akhenaton and his family. We are somewhat degenerate ourselves, so the hair styles popular with some of our young people may tend to prove this thesis. However, the ladies of the Fourth Dynasty—a period of classic dignity, with no discernibly nasty habits—also favored a mannish haircut upon occasion. Also, while fashions in clothing and hair styles may be bound up with cultural progress and cultural decline, I have yet to see anyone prove it.

I have said that I suspect the reliefs do not tell all there is to be told about hair styles. This suspicion is based on the mummy of a middle-aged woman who was found among the royal mummies of Deir el Bahri. She has the most extraordinary hairdo for an Egyptian woman. One cannot expect a mummy's hair to remain perfectly set, but judging from its present condition the lady wore an upswept hair style with sausage curls on top and waves over the ears. It is very "un-Egyptian," and I know of nothing like it in the pictorial representations.

Many of the elaborate coiffures, male and female, were wigs. These were made of human hair. Actual wigs have been found, and in some of the statues and paintings you can see the owner's real hair under the wig if you look closely.

As a rule, facial hair was not cultivated by the Egyptian male— nor, I hardly need say, by the female. Sometimes neat little mustaches were worn, or a short beard, like a chopped-off goatee. But the Egyptian gentleman, and peasant, was usually clean-shaven. The long stiff beards worn by kings, for ceremonial reasons, were artificial.

## Jewelry and Cosmetics

Although some robes and dresses were woven in colors, the Egyptians usually preferred to wear white clothing and depend on their ornaments for color. Egyptian jewelry is marvelous; the craftsmen of the earliest periods had attained real excellence. Inlay, embossing, filigree, gilding and plating—they could do most of the things modern jewelers could do. One of their supreme efforts was granulated gold work, in which tiny spherical grains of gold are fused onto the golden background. They also did a kind of work

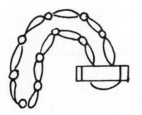

*Necklace*

which looks like cloisonné; instead of enamel, bits of precious stones or faience were set into cells outlined by thin gold strips.

The gems used in jewelry were the semiprecious stones; except for an isolated case of pearls, none of the precious stones were known to the Egyptians, although emeralds do occur in the eastern desert. Carnelian, turquoise, garnets, feldspar, rock crystal, and lapis lazuli were favored. The most useful and ubiquitous material used for jewelry was faience, which is an artificial product made of ground quartz mixed with an adhesive and molded into the desired shape. Faience could be glazed in a number of colors, to imitate gem stones; a turquoise color was perhaps the most popular.

The main metals used in jewelry were copper and gold—copper for the commoner, gold for the nobly born. The gold was used as found, without refining, so it varies in purity; it is for this reason that much ancient gold is colored. The shades range from gray to reddish-brown, and owe their coloring to mixtures of silver or copper or iron. The best known of these natural alloys is electrum, a blend of silver and gold, which comes out a pale yellow. Being harder than gold, it was often used for jewelry, and the Egyptians probably got it in its natural state from veins in the desert. There is one variety of colored gold which appears to be deliberate—a handsome rose-pink. This red-gold has been described as the product of one of those "lost Egyptian sciences" which people are fond of discovering; but actually it has been reproduced by modern scientists. The color is due to iron.

Luckily we do not have to depend on pictorial representations for our knowledge of ornaments; it would be very limited if we did. It is extraordinary how much jewelry has survived from ancient Egypt. Of course there was a lot of it, and it was made of imperishable materials. On the other hand, it was the most sought-after loot of the tomb robbers. Yet in addition to Tutankhamon's famous collection, there are at least half a dozen sets of jewelry in various museums.

The most common ornament was the wide flexible collar, made of concentric rows of beads, some of which might be shaped like animals or flowers or leaves. It covered the front of the wearer's body from the base of the neck to the middle of the breast,

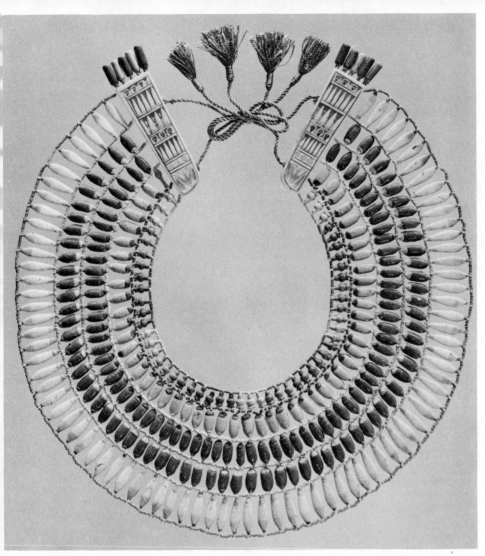

Faience collar, late Eighteenth Dynasty. A relatively inexpensive example of the most popular Egyptian piece of jewelry. The elements of the collar are not semiprecious stones, but are formed of the vitreous paste called faience. *The Metropolitan Museum of Art, Rogers Fund, 1940.*

and since it was made of bright, gay colors, it formed an important part of the overall costume. Instead of a collar, necklaces or pendants might be worn. The simple bead necklaces, strung on cord, have been found in such numbers that you can sometimes buy them at the sales counters of museums which have Egyptian

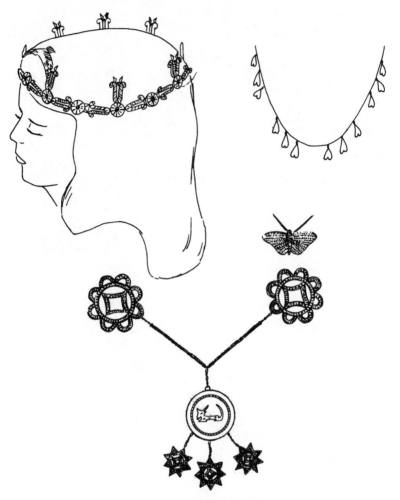

*Jewelry of Princess Khnumit*

collections; but the ones on sale are not very attractive. The best, naturally, are in the museum cases. Pendants, hung on cord or gold, depending on the wearer's income, ranged from faience amulets in the shape of gods or magical hieroglyphs to elaborate cloisonné pieces which have a whole miniature scene done in relief. Then there were bracelets, some flexible rows of beads, some rigid, of copper or gold. Earrings were worn by women and boys, possibly by men; diadems and fillets held back the hair, gold

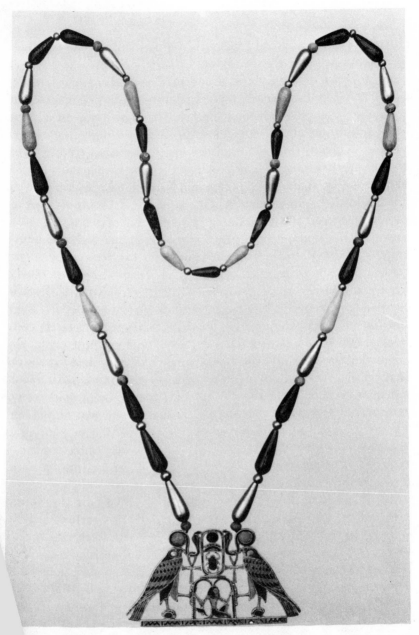

klace of gold, carnelian, lapis lazuli and green feldspar, belonging
rincess Sithathoryunet, Twelfth Dynasty. The cartouche in the
ral contains one of the names of the princess's father, King Senu-
. *The Metropolitan Museum of Art, Contribution from Henry*
s *and the Rogers Fund, 1916.*

ribbons or rings confined long curls. Girdles, anklets, finger rings of all types—the variety is endless.

The prettiest jewelry ever found in Egypt belonged to a princess of the Twelfth Dynasty named Khnumit. I have been unable to find good photographs of these lovely things, but even a good black-and-white photo does not do them justice. My rough sketches probably do them even less justice, but they enable us to appreciate the designs. The crown shown here is made of gold with insets of lapis blue, orange-red carnelian, red jasper, and green feldspar. Another crown was one of the daintiest ever worn by any princess of any country: it consisted of very fine gold threads, set at random with tiny flowers of red and blue. At intervals the golden strands were caught together by a cruciform shape made up of four papyrus flowers. The designs are exquisitely simple; the princess's necklaces were plain gold chains with various pendants. Some of the latter, such as the large pendant stars and the butterfly, are covered with the delicate granulated gold work at which Egyptian jewelers excelled. One piece is unusual— the medallion hanging from the openworked, granulated rosettes. On a pale blue background a miniature white bull with black spots has been painted; the picture was then set in a gold frame and covered with a thin piece of rock crystal.

Crown of Princess Khnumit. *The Met*

Khnumit's jewelry has been described as "un-Egyptian," perhaps because of its very simplicity. But the workmanship is typically Egyptian, exemplifying the high degree of skill which craftsmen had attained by the Twelfth Dynasty, and which was never surpassed later. The miniature painting is uncommon; a Cretan origin has been suggested for the little bull, but he reminds me unmistakably of a certain Egyptian hieroglyph. I wonder, though, what was in the princess's mind when she ordered this piece? Could it have had a personal meaning for her?

There are several other elegant parures of Middle Kingdom princesses in various museums, and later periods are also well represented. The most extensive and most famous personal collection is certainly that of Tutankhamon.

When we view this collection, filling case after case in the Cairo Museum, we ought to remember that according to the excavator, it is only a part of what was originally buried with the king. Being small and extremely valuable for its size, jewelry would have been the first things the thieves who broke into the tomb looked for, and Carter was sure that they had made off with quite a bit of it. Neat dockets written on the storage chests listed the objects which were supposed to be in them, and Carter estimated that some of the jewel boxes had lost at least 60 percent of their contents. He actually found one group of heavy gold rings tied loosely in a cloth and lying on the floor of the Antechamber— mute evidence not only of the robbery, but of its interruption, perhaps by necropolis police.

The earrings and pendants and pectorals worn by the young king strike us as extremely ornate compared with earlier designs. The pendant illustrated is typical; indeed, it is a more satisfactory design, despite its overcrowded look, than many other pieces. Of course I am not playing fair by Tutankhamon's court jeweler to show this piece in a dull line drawing; it omits the brilliance, the glorious blend of colors, and the general gorgeousness of the ornament. But it does allow us to study the design, undistracted by other considerations, and I think most of us would agree that the design is a bit overdone. However, similarly crowded designs are found in the Twelfth Dynasty; some of the pectorals owned by the princesses have everything in them but the kitchen sink. And Tutankhamon possessed some pieces of jewelry which compare

*Pectoral of Tutankhamon*

favorably with the elegant simplicity of earlier designs. The hilts
of his daggers, which have to be considered examples of the jeweler's craft, are beautiful by any standards, and so are some of his
rings and one of his diadems. The pectorals and pendants do
compensate for their heavy designs by the skill of the workmanship and the lavishness of color and material. The colors may
sound garish when we describe them—dark blue lapis, orange-red
carnelian, turquoise, amethyst, green feldspar—but they were
made up into remarkably harmonious combinations, especially
when separated by the thin gold line of the cloisons, or cells, into
which the stones were set. Comparisons are odious, and we can't
really generalize about differences between Twelfth- and Eigh-
teenth-Dynasty jewelry. All I can say is that while I admire

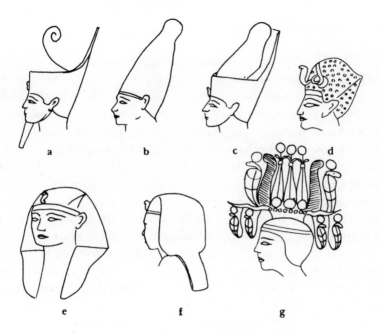

*Crowns of the King*

a. Red Crown; b. White Crown; c. Double Crown; d. Blue (battle) Crown; e. *nemset* headdress; f. *afnet* headdress; g. *atef* crown

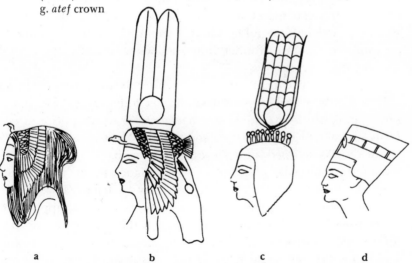

*Crowns of the Queen*

a. early form of vulture crown; b. later form of same crown with plumes; c. moon disc and horns crown; d. tall blue crown of Nefertiti

Tutankhamon's jewels, I would wear Princess Khnumit's, if I could get my hands on them.

Although Tutankhamon and the princesses have handed down to us several diadems or simple crowns, none of the formal crowns known from the paintings have survived. The king wore the tall White Crown or the basket-shaped Red Crown, which rose to a point in the back, or else he wore the two combined. The Blue Battle Crown may have been a war helmet originally. The Atef crown is a complex, heavy-looking affair, almost too cumbersome to be worn on the head. For ordinary occasions the king had linen headdresses on the order of a "babushka" whose ends are tied at the nape of the neck instead of under the chin. The queens' crowns were just as fancy, although once again we know them only from reliefs and statues. Nefertiti's tall blue crown is well known from her bust; she preferred this type, which covered all of her hair (I wonder if she had trouble with her hair?) but it was not a common type for queens. The most popular was the vulture crown, made of gold and inlaid with bits of colored stone in the wonderful Egyptian technique which looks like cloisonné. On top of this the queen might wear the tall plumes and moon disk of Hathor, modeled in gold. There were other crowns, some so complicated that we wonder how the poor woman's neck could support their weight.

To complete the picture of ravishing beauty, the Egyptian lady had only to make up her face. At her toilet table—which was not a table, but a low chest—she had metal mirrors, pots and jars for cosmetics, tweezers, razors, and combs. Most of her time and attention was lavished on her eyes. Black eye paint, called kohl, is still used in the Near East, but it is now made of soot; the ancient equivalent was green (malachite) or gray (galena). These minerals were ground and made into a paste, which was applied in heavy lines over the eyebrows and around the eyes by means of a little wooden or bone rod, or by that handy implement, the finger. Rouge, in the form of red ochre, was used, and there is one picture of a lady applying it to her lips—with a brush.

Most of the nice little pots and jars on the lady's dressing table probably held ointments. The Egyptians were fond of oiling

Toilet articles of an Egyptian lady. Background, the inlaid box; foreground, left to right: cosmetic spoon, comb, cosmetic jar, polished metal mirror. *The Trustees, British Museum.*

themselves—understandably so, in a climate so hot and dry as theirs—and their perfumes were not true perfume, which has an alcohol base, but scented oils. Myrrh and sweet-smelling resin were used to make the lady smell nice, but she also used flower scents, such as "perfume of lily."

# VI

# "Spend the
Day Merrily"

***Towns and Houses***

IF we could arrange to visit the Luxor area as it was a hundred and
fifty years ago, we would probably expect to find it looking just
about the same as it does now. Many of the monuments on that site
had already suffered three thousand years of wear and tear; an
additional century and a half would not, one might suppose, do
that much more damage. But this assumption would not be correct. Some of the saddest stories of archaeology deal with the
wreckage of ancient monuments, caused not by time or carelessness or the search for treasure but by people who thought they
were serving knowledge. "The passion for antiquity . . . destroyed
what the centuries had spread."

I am quoting Bernard Bruyère, the excavator of Deir el
Medineh, a site located on the west bank of Thebes. Bruyère,
heading an expedition of the Institut Français d'Archéologie
Orientale, worked at this one site for over twenty years, and he
mentions that, at the beginning of the last century, a visitor to Deir
el Medineh might have seen houses with their walls still intact,
and tombs still capped by the little pyramids which were characteristic of the period. By the time he arrived it was all gone,

wrecked by amateur archaeologists and by some professionals who did not know their trade well enough.

Deir el Medineh is not well known except to Egyptologists, yet it is an extremely important place—one of the few town sites found in Egypt. Unlike tombs, houses were built of perishable materials, and many of the most important ancient cities are hidden under modern villages. Therefore, the town sites we have found are vital, rounding out a picture of Egyptian culture still heavily biased by mortuary material. Thanks to the devoted efforts of the French mission, Deir el Medineh has yielded more useful information about town life than any other such site, with the possible exception of Tell el Amarna. Although Amarna was a bigger city, with considerably more variety in house types, it was atypical in the sense that it was an artificial creation, inhabited *in extenso* for less than twenty years. When the inhabitants left it,

Model of an Amarna villa. Reconstruction of the estate of a nobleman of the court of Akhenaton. Within the walled enclosure are the villa, outbuildings, a pool, jars for the storage of grain, and a small shrine. *The Oriental Institute, University of Chicago.*

they stripped the houses down to the very columns and doorposts. Deir el Medineh yielded masses of ostraca and papyri, most of them fragmentary. Some are still being studied, and they give unique insights into the activities and interests of a group of average men of the Nineteenth and Twentieth Dynasties.

The isolation of Deir el Medineh explains in part why it was spared for so long. It lies in a hidden valley behind a spur of the desert cliffs, away from the regular tourist routes. The area is desolate and inhospitable; there is not even a water supply at the village. We might wonder why a town was ever located there. The answer lies in another valley, not far distant from Deir el Medineh. The inhabitants of the village were necropolis workers —the stonemasons, scribes, and other craftsmen who built, among others, the tombs in the Valley of the Kings.

The town was probably founded in the early Eighteenth Dynasty when the first royal tomb was constructed in the Valley, and it was inhabited for about 450 years. A wall surrounded the site, and a single gate led into the main street, which was straight and only four or five feet wide. The houses, built of mud brick, faced directly on the street. Most of them were small, having on the average only four rooms. The room facing the street had no windows, except for small gratings high up near the roof. Behind was an all-purpose room in which the family slept, dined, worked, and entertained; columns supported the ceiling, which was higher than that of the neighboring rooms and which thus allowed light to penetrate through clerestory-style windows. There was usually a raised platform in this room, to serve as a couch and/or bed platform. Behind the main room were two smaller chambers. One was the kitchen and one a storeroom or extra bedroom. Most of the houses had basements, for storage, reached by stairs from the main room. Other stairs led up to the roof, which was flat and served as extra living space.

Not very glamorous, is it? Undoubtedly we would prefer a nobleman's villa—as the Egyptians did, if they could afford one. Our model comes from Tell el Amarna, which was no workman's village, but the one-time, if short-lived, capital of Egypt. Most of the excavators of Amarna have pointed out that the name is incorrect; it is a misunderstanding of the names of two of the modern villages at the site. However, it has been used for so long that it has acquired a meaning, whether it had one originally or not, and I would rather use it than the ancient name, Akhetaton, which is confusingly like the name of its founder, Akhenaton.

Amarna was not a walled city, being bounded by the river on one side and the valley cliffs on the other. The main street of the ancient city, called the "Royal Road" by archaeologists, is still being used. Along this street the city mushroomed in three major subdivisions. The central section, with the royal palace, Great Temple, and fine private houses, was the first to be built. Later a southern residential section was added, with another palace. Just before the city was abandoned, work had begun on the northern suburb, including a northern palace.

Since the site had never been inhabited before Akhenaton's time, his chief courtiers could lay out elegant houses with ample grounds around them. The gardens—in which the Egyptians delighted—were filled with choice flowers and trees, carefully tended by gardeners. When the water supply permitted there was also a pool, meant for beauty rather than for swimming, and some gardens had a little kiosk or shrine. The house itself was sprawling and one-storied. Set on a low platform, it was approached by steps or ramps. The main entrance led into a reception hall with painted wooden columns. Behind it was a central hall, a sort of family room, with columns, a brazier for heat on cool evenings, and a built-in divan along one wall. The private quarters of the family were little suites separated from the public part of the house. Some had small private sitting rooms. Then there was a bedroom, identified by the raised platforms on which the beds were placed, and a bathroom with stone or plaster walls. The bather stood on a stone slab with a low coping and the water drained off through a hole into the floor. Since there were, naturally, no closets, storage space was provided by a separate room with rows of shelves. The amenities of the villa were topped off by a small, walled-off space with a seat supported by bricks and a removable vessel underneath.

Still not satisfied? Then we will offer a royal palace. Not many of them have survived, since they were built of the same brick and wood that constituted private dwellings. The plans of the Amarna palaces are known, but an even more interesting one was the palace of Amenhotep III, Akhenaton's father, on the west bank at Thebes. The site is called Malkata.

Amenhotep's palace was almost a city in itself; it consisted of four separate royal residences, a temple, a workers' village, and a series of houses for officials. Possibly one palace was the king's, and the others belonged to the 'queens and crown prince. Amenhotep III had two important wives and a son who turned out to be Akhenaton, so the theory is neatly tempting, but of course we don't know whether it is true or not. Let's take a look at the building which has been called the King's Palace.

At the northern end were three audience halls, two big and one small. Each had a dais for the throne, and the largest was reached by a wide corridor, the main entrance to the palace. The king's private apartments consisted of a long columned hall with a throne room behind it. Behind *that* were the king's bedroom, bath and robing room. On either side of the long hall there were four suites of rooms—for ladies of the harem?—each consisting of a storeroom with shelves, a robing room with more shelves, a bedroom, a parlor, and a bath.

The glory of the palace was not its spaciousness but its decoration. Floors, ceilings, and walls were painted in brilliant colors, and with a naturalistic skill which reached its height at this period. A favorite motif for floors was a pool, surrounded by plants and water birds, and filled with fishes, lilies, and swimming ducks. Ceilings had grape trellises, or flying birds; walls might be adorned with animals or graceful court ladies. In the bedrooms there were prancing figures of the odd little dwarf god Bes, who was a popular household deity. Even the brick supports for the shelves were painted with papyrus plants and animals. The decoration of the throne rooms was more formal—figures of the king, and of kneeling captives. The wooden columns which supported the ceilings of some rooms were made in the graceful shapes of plants, papyrus or lotus, and they also were brightly painted. No greater contrast to the general view of Egyptian architecture— grim, gray and monolithic—could possibly be imagined than these palaces, aglow with color and alive with the fluttering of birds' wings.

We have had a small sampling of Egyptian houses, from the humble dwellings of workers to the abode of the king himself. Although they may be considered "typical" in a wide sense, other examples do show different features. The Malkata palace, which was similar to those of Amarna, particularly in decoration, may have been exceptional; this was an exceptional period, particularly in art. Plant columns were always popular, even in private homes, but the walls, floors and ceilings of earlier palaces were probably painted with more formal designs, or covered with woven matting. Egyptian animal and bird figures are always quite charming, but animal forms of the Amarna period have a liveliness which is lacking in earlier times. We have no evidence that such motifs, appropriate and lovely as they are, were used in earlier palaces.

One important difference between the Amarna villas and those of other periods must be noted: There were no separate women's quarters at Amarna. Other well-to-do houses give the mistress her own suite, separate from that of the master. At Amarna, husband and wife apparently occupied the same suite. What does this mean? We could make some pretty generalizations about the changed position of women under the iconoclastic, uxorious Akhenaton, but they would only be guesses.

Villas and palaces are unusual in one important aspect—their spaciousness. The king naturally took all the room he wanted, and the villas were country houses. A townhouse, even one belonging to a nobleman, was more cramped because Egyptian cities were limited in space; they had to encroach as little as possible on the precious black soil used for crops. We think that houses in a city such as Thebes were several stories in height. Except in rare cases there would be no land available for gardens or "front yards," so the family had to take their airings on the roof, which was often surrounded by screens of matting.

I imagine most of us could endure living at a place like the Malkata palace; we wouldn't even mind the absence of plumbing if we had slaves to run back and forth carrying water jars. The cramped quarters of the workman's village might not appeal so much. Even the humbler houses, however, were well adapted to the Egyptian climate and customs. The main features of the climate are its rainlessness and its brilliant sunshine, with resultant heat. The sun-dried brick of which most houses were built was perfectly adequate in a rainless area; sloping roofs were unnecessary. Thus a cheap, easy source of building material was readily available, and the flat roofs could be used as terraces, which would be an agreeable addition to city houses. To keep the houses cool, sunlight was excluded as much as possible; windows were few, high, and small. Walls were thick—twenty inches in the Deir el Medineh houses—and there were ventilators on the roofs to catch the prevalent north wind. The city houses were limited in space, so cooking had to be done in the house itself, but whenever possible the kitchens were outside, in separate buildings. Other outbuildings, on a villa estate, included servants' quarters and pens for animals. The country estate of a nobleman might comprehend buildings for brewing, baking, and weaving, and a butchers' shop.

The Egyptians did not clutter up their houses with furniture, but some of the pieces which have survived are elegant enough to stand comparison with fine modern work. In fact, they are better-looking than a lot of my furniture. Like their friends the jewelers, Egyptian carpenters had reason to be proud of their skill, all the more so because of the materials they had to work with. Egypt is poor in large trees, and early in pharaonic times she began importing cedar from the Lebanon for fine wood-working. Such imports were expensive, of course, so Egyptian carpenters had to learn to work, for the most part, with their scrubby native trees—sycamore fig, acacia, tamarisk, sidder, and willow. Mortise and tenon joints, dovetailing, and wooden pegs joined together the small planks which were obtained from these local trees. The tools were of copper; they included chisels, adzes, axes and drills. Saws were of the "pull" type, with the teeth set toward the handle. I do very little sawing myself, but I understand that our saws are "push" saws, with the teeth set *away* from the handle. We usually lay the wood to be cut with a saw on a table or sawhorse, but the Egyptians tied theirs to a post and cut down from the top, this being the best position for using their "pull" saws. When the wood was cut and jointed it was "planed" by a lump of stone.

### Furniture and Household Equipment

Softened as we are by our posture-pedic inner-spring or foam rubber mattresses, most of us would find Egyptian beds uncomfortable. They had wooden frames and springs of woven cord or leather strips. Most were higher at the head than at the foot, so they have a footboard—but no headboard—to keep the sleeper from sliding gently down onto the floor. Over the springs were placed pads of folded linen, with sheets of the same material as the covering. I imagine these beds were as comfortable as our camp beds, but the item that would finish most of us was the pillow, which was not a pillow at all but a headrest of shoulder height, with a support curved to fit the neck. I have always wondered whether the Egyptians didn't use cushions with these devices of torture, but I know of no examples, and apparently the headrest is not as painful as it looks once you get accustomed to it. Other peoples use them, and a modern archaeologist, H. E. Winlock, remarked that they were surprisingly comfortable after some little practice "if you didn't pinch your ear." Obviously Mr. Winlock tried a headrest himself. Certainly a headrest is more sensible than a pillow in a hot climate.

There was very little in the bedroom besides the bed—only a few boxes and baskets for clothing. Most of these containers, though, were kept on the shelves of the storeroom next to the bedroom, if the house boasted such an arrangement. Women kept their toilet articles in a chest or a basket, and perhaps these were placed on low tables when the lady made up her face. Some storage chests could be provided with legs, forming a sort of stand. There was one such object in Tutankhamon's tomb, and it is an extremely handsome piece of furniture; some day I intend to have it copied. Unlike many of Tutankhamon's possessions, it is of simple design, but the proportions, and the row of ornamental hieroglyphs, are quite elegant. Tutankhamon had some chests which are real *objets d'art*, especially the one painted with scenes of hunting and warfare, but of course they are not representative

Tutankhamon's chest on legs. The chest can be "locked" by means of a cord wound between the two knobs (one on top) and sealed with a clay stamp. *The Griffith Institute, Ashmolean Museum, Oxford.*

of those ordinarily used. Plainer wooden boxes and woven baskets
were more common. Some had lids which could be tied on and—if
the owner was of a suspicious nature—sealed, over the knot. The
boxes were often ingeniously designed, with separate compartments for different articles. One had a shallow space under the lid
for a mirror, with supporting pieces set in to hold the handle and
keep the mirror from banging around when the box was moved.
The hollow interior of the box held pots for unguents and perfumes.

Living room furniture consisted of chairs, stools, and tables.
The common people squatted on the floor or on the built-in
divan; wealthier folk naturally had more furniture. Chairs exhibit
a wide variety of forms, having long legs and short legs, arms or no
arms, but most of them seem broad by our standards, especially
for the slender Egyptians of the reliefs. The most gorgeous chair
we have is one belonging to Tutankhamon; it was probably a

Egyptian chairs. Both illustrate the type of furniture owned by non-
royal but well-to-do Egyptians. *The Trustees, British Museum.*

throne rather than a household item, and it is inlaid with hundreds of little pieces of ebony, ivory and colored wood. Stools usually had short legs and seats of woven rushes. There were no dining tables seating twenty-four, not even in the king's palace. At banquets each guest or pair of guests had his own little table.

The furniture demonstrates the taste as well as the skill of the ancient craftsmen. Imagination and a sense of the beautiful transform even prosaic items of daily use. Tutankhamon's headrests, for instance, are all decorated. Even the simplest are prettily colored and, except for the gold band around the "neck," they would not be beyond the means of a moderately well-to-do tradesman. One headrest was ivory, with carved heads of the grotesque god of the bedchamber, Bes, on either end, and with the legs ending in graceful stylized duck's heads.

The imaginative talents of the artisan show up most clearly in the objects we might lump together under the heading of toilet articles. Mirrors were circles of polished metal with handles cunningly carved into the shape of an animal or a lotus flower or a slim naked girl. The little ointment spoons may be seen in many museum collections. The covered, spoon-shaped space which held the ointment might be made in the form of a duck, with a swimming girl for a handle. Even the humble baskets of the poor were

*Headrest of Tutankhamon*

Mirror with handle in the shape of
a girl holding a bird. *The Trustees,
British Museum.*

finely made, with strips of colored grass woven in to form patterns. The Egyptians were very much aware of natural beauty, and their ornamental designs reflect this awareness, making frequent use of plant and animal forms and graceful poses of the human body.

Although the furniture was scanty, the interior of an Egyptian house was cheerful and colorful. Woven mats were used as floor coverings, wall hangings, or even ceiling covers. As we have seen, some surfaces were painted.

Kitchen furniture was limited to utensils and the indispensable oven. Strange as it may seem, the Egyptian housewife cooked without any "counter space" at all. She squatted on the ground when she ground grain, and apparently she stayed there while she mixed and kneaded her bread. Her oven was a pottery shell about thirty inches high, with two doors, one at floor level for fire-building and another, fitted with a lid, on top. The fire was allowed to die down into a bed of coals before the bread was put in, via the top hole, onto a shelf about a third of the way up. The housewife could cook on top of the stove or on a brazier. I wish I could tell you how she washed the dishes; I would like to know myself. But no painting or model has preserved this homely detail.

Some kitchens had niches built into the wall for storage, but otherwise pots and jars just stood in rows along the walls. The Egyptians made good pottery of a variety of shapes—bowls and jars, spouted jugs, pots with handles. The material was the useful Nile mud, which produced a reddish-brown pottery. From the area near Qena in Upper Egypt came a special type of light-colored clay which made especially handsome pots.

And that is all I intend to say about pottery. A detailed description of types would only interest a specialist and, to be candid, Egyptian pottery of the historic period is not exciting. It was well made and nicely shaped, but there were no types as attractive as the painted wares of other Near Eastern countries. It was utilitarian, meant for the prosaic functions of the household. Luxury ware was not made of clay. In the earliest dynasties the best tableware, the vessels designed for the service of the gods and the royal dead, was laboriously shaped out of stone—alabaster, marble, porphyry, limestone, rock crystal, even basalt. I don't know which is more impressive, the sheer number of these stone vessels or the wonderful skill with which they were made. Professor Walter Emery found over 1,500 stone vessels in a single First Dynasty tomb at Sakkara. The finest of the stoneware comes from the first three Dynasties, and it is cut with such skill and accuracy that the walls are sometimes as thin as those of a modern dinner plate.

Metal vessels appear as early as the First Dynasty, and eventually royalty dined off gold and silver. A hoard of such vessels was found by Pierre Montet in the royal tombs of the Twenty-First Dynasty at Tanis; even as far back as the Fourth Dynasty Queen Hetepheres owned a gold drinking cup and several small bowls of the same metal.

The Egyptians also used glass. It seems to have appeared rather suddenly, around the time of the Eighteenth Dynasty. Unlike modern glass, it was not transparent; the opacity is due to the incomplete fusion of the materials. Apparently glass vases were made on a clay core which was dipped into the molten glass and then twirled rapidly to distribute the glass evenly. The hot material could be colored and rolled out into thin rods. When these were wound around a vase, and dragged up and down, they produced the wavy effect which is so common in Egyptian glassware.

Glass vessels. *The Metropolitan Museum of Art, The Theodore M. Davis Collection. Bequest of Theodore M. Davis, 1915.*

Glass vessels are not often found, possibly because of the fragility of the material, and possibly because much of the glass made in the factories of Thebes and Tell el Amarna was used for jewelry, in the form of beads or inlay.

## Food and Entertainment

What did the Egyptians eat out of all those pots? Quite a variety of things, if they could afford them. Bread was the staple food. Some loaves have survived to the present day; they are like rock, the stalest bread you can imagine. The yeast used was a wild variety, relatively impure, although one specimen from an Eighteenth Dynasty tomb turned out, upon analysis, to be as pure as modern yeast. We know about the yeast from beer, not from bread itself. There are no actual pots of that beverage still around, but it was possible to analyze it from the dried residue left in the bottoms of jars.

"A thousand [loaves] of bread, a thousand [jars] of beer"— so the Egyptian mortuary formulas began, when they listed the food items desired in the next world. The two staples of the Egyptian diet are connected in another way, for both went through the same initial process. When the dough had been mixed and shaped into loaves, they were left to rise. If the housewife wanted bread she popped the pans (pots) into the oven. If she wanted beer, she crumbled the loaves and mixed them with water to form a mash. This "sat" for a few days till it fermented; it was then strained and poured off into jars. A similar beverage, called "bouza," is still being made today. It has an alcoholic content of about 7 percent.

With bread and beer and a few vegetables, the poorer Egyptians could get by. They ate onions and leeks, beans and lentils. Meat was probably scarce in poor households except on festival days, but the villagers may have eaten fish. They were regarded as unclean in some contexts, and certain mortuary inscriptions have the fish-hieroglyphs carefully mutilated, to keep them from harming the dead. But it is unlikely that people would have neglected such an accessible source of protein, especially in view of the rarity of meat.

The diet of a wealthy nobleman was extensive. Beef and mutton, goose, duck, and other birds were prepared in various ways. Honey was the main sweetener, sugar being unknown, and fruit such as dates, figs and grapes was popular. The sophisticated Egyptian of the New Kingdom had developed quite a taste for fine wines. Jars were labeled, not only with the year of the vintage, but with the vineyard of origin, and certain wines were prized above others.

The Egyptians ate not only for nourishment but for conviviality. Some of the tomb reliefs which show people eating together may have been designed to assure the dead a perpetual banquet in the afterlife, but they probably also reflect the pleasant custom of dinner parties. People ate with their fingers, and when the meal was over a servant, or a daughter of the household, came around with water which was poured over the hands. Judging from some reliefs, such as the ones from Amarna which show the royal family dining on rolled roasts and whole roast ducks, à la Henry VIII, some substitute for napkins was certainly necessary.

But the important part of the banquet, one imagines, was not so much the eating as the drinking. Quiet family parties did not end in orgies, of course, but big celebrations, given, no doubt, like modern cocktail parties, to get rid of one's social obligations or impress one's friends, often ended in unhappy spectacles of undue merriment. One banquet scene shows a lady guest in the last extremity of misery, and other diners look as if they need help to stand erect. We need not conclude that everybody got roaring drunk at these parties, but the euphoric effects of wine and beer were certainly enjoyed.

At banquets like these there was a floor show. Singing and musical instruments accompanied the feasting. A basic orchestral instrument was the harp; several different types are shown in the reliefs, from small portable instruments to big floor models, taller than the harpist. Percussion instruments, small drums, and tambourines beat out the rhythm, and were augmented by the hand clapping and finger snapping of the dancers. Other instruments appear later, after the beginning of the Eighteenth Dynasty; they may be Asiatic in origin—the lyre, the oboe and the lute.

Unfortunately we cannot give the music to any ancient Egyptian tunes. But we do know some lyrics. This is one of the Harper's Songs:

> Spend the day merrily; put unguent and fine oil to thy nostrils, and lotus flowers on the body of thy beloved. Set singing and music before thy face. Cast all evil behind thee and think thee of joy— until that day comes when harbor is reached in the land that loves silence. Spend the day merrily, and weary not therein; lo, none can take his goods with him; lo, none that has departed can come again.

Not a very cheerful song—but perhaps it all depends on the point of view. However, songs like this one—and there are a number of different versions of the same theme—are known to us from the tombs, where the singer is performing for his dead master. Maybe they were not sung at real parties. However, there is no reason to suppose that they would have seemed morbid to the Egyptians. The advice is practical, really—"eat, drink and be merry" because "you can't take it with you."

A stock figure in the orchestra was a bent, elderly male harper, often blind. The rest of the musicians were girls, and if they were as young and pretty as the paintings suggest, their appearance provided additional pleasure for the feasters. Their costumes, like those of the dancers who appeared with them, were quite flimsy; sometimes they wore only a string of beads and a girdle.

Dancing seems to have been a spectator sport or a religious exercise; I know of no representations of boys and girls dancing together for fun. The slim little girl dancers were professionals, and some were trained to do acrobatic tricks. Music also seems to have been reserved for professionals. However, one relief shows a vizier's lady playing a harp, so it is possible that people of leisure enjoyed performing music as well as listening to it.

Thus the wealthy entertained their friends. The middle classes probably tried to imitate their betters, on a smaller scale; and for people who enjoyed drinking for its own sake there was always the corner tavern. Egyptian towns had such establishments, and they may also have had their town drunkards. Although mild inebriation was permissible, even commended, public drunkenness was regarded as disgusting. One of the sages warns his audience of the dangers of the corner pub:

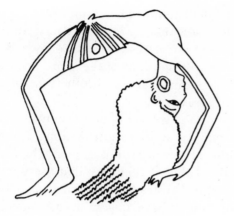

*Acrobatic dancer*

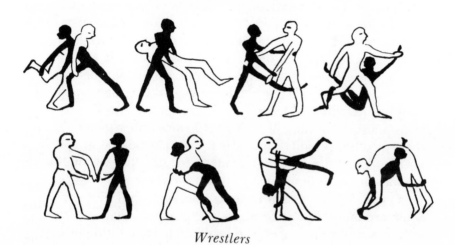

*Wrestlers*

"Don't take to drinking," says Ani, "because if you speak, something else [other than what you meant] will come out of your mouth; you won't know what you are saying. You will fall down and break your limbs. Nobody will take you by the hand; your drinking companions will stand apart and say: Look at that sot! If someone comes to look for you, to ask your advice, he will find you lying on the floor, like a little baby."

Another popular spectator sport was wrestling. Our illustration shows only a few of the dozens of wrestling holds illustrated in a Middle Kingdom tomb. They look quite expert, and I am told by those who know that some are like modern holds. Incidentally, the match was not necessarily waged by a Nubian and an Egyptian. The contrasting colors of the men's bodies is a device of the artist, to make clear what would otherwise be an impossible tangle of arms and legs.

While we are on the subject of amusements, we must mention storytelling. It may seem like quite a jump from wrestling to literature; but the latter word is misleading. The reader will note, if he examines the Table of Contents, that there is no chapter on "Egyptian Literature." Instead, I have tried to look at the subject as the Egyptians might have looked at it, under a number of different categories—love songs under love and marriage, hymns and prayers under religion, the maxims of the sages under the subjects to which they pertain. A student of comparative literature is justified in lumping all these compositions together into a single category, but the unity is artificial because it is a modern, not an ancient, viewpoint. By the time we are through we will have examined the major subdivisions of "Egyptian literature," with one exception—the epic, which did not exist. The compositions praising the valor of a king are hymns rather than epics, and the only other possible contender for the position of an epic hero is Osiris who must be counted out, if for no other reason, on the grounds that he is dead during most of the story.

Egyptian prose fiction includes tales of several different types. Some are more sophisticated, more "literary," than others; they were meant for audiences who could appreciate puns, an elegant flow of rhetoric, and refined style. Other stories rely on plot rather than style for their interest, and a few are as melodramatic, as bloodthirsty, and as implausible as any bad modern thriller.

The question of humor in Egyptian stories is not so easy; it is always hard to tell what strikes someone else as funny. The Egyptians' sense of humor shows up in other media, particularly in painting and relief. There are several late drawings, on papyri and ostraca, which are obviously meant to be satirical; they show animals busily engaged in a number of human activities. A mouse lady, seated at a dressing table, is being attended by a number of cat servants, while a cat nurse carries a mouse baby; a mouse king,

Scene from a "satirical papyrus." A lion and a gazelle playing *senet*, or some other board game. *The Trustees, British Museum.*

mounted in a chariot, attacks a fortress manned by cats; a lion plays a board game with a gazelle. One devastating little model from Tell el Amarna shows a group of monkeys driving in a chariot; the charioteer monkey has, upon close examination, a terrible resemblance to the king, Akhenaton, who is often seen in his own chariot. Other humorous touches are less satirical, and broader—a very fat woman and her very small donkey. We can be reasonably sure that these satirical pictures appealed to the Egyptians' sense of humor. As for the stories, there is only one which was almost certainly regarded as a comic tale—the "Contendings of Horus and Set," which we will consider in detail in another chapter. It is a broad, bawdy story which pays scant respect to the immortal gods, and much of its humor is of a visual nature. The divine assembly of the gods brawls and bickers like a group of spoiled children, Isis bustles about playing tricks on her enemies, Astarte gets the supreme god Re out of a fit of the sulks by exposing herself to him—these touches are not especially subtle, and they are certainly meant to be funny. Some of the other tales are not so easy to diagnose. Take the story of Wenamon, for instance.

Wenamon was an Egyptian official who was sent to Byblos to get cedar at a time when Egyptian prestige abroad was pretty low. He had a perfectly terrible time, being robbed, insulted, threatened, and sneered at. After he got to Byblos he sat around for a month without being allowed even to see the prince, and, as he remarks, "[The prince] sent to me every day, saying, 'Get out of my harbor.'"

I think this is funny; in fact, all of Wenamon's tribulations amuse me tremendously. Did they amuse the Egyptian readers of the story? Probably not. I don't know.

Since most Egyptians were illiterate, and since they lacked those blessings of the illiterate, movies and TV, they probably relied on professional storytellers. These itinerant figures are known from other nonliterate cultures, although I must admit I know of no specific reference to them in Egypt. Still, there was a place for such a wandering minstrel; gathered around the water jar in the village square, in the cool of the evening, the villagers may have listened to just such a story as I am about to relate to you.

Once upon a time there were two brothers. Anubis was the name of the older, and Bata the name of the younger. Anubis had a house, he had a wife, and his younger brother lived with him like a son. It was the younger brother who took care of all the elder's needs. Indeed, the younger brother was a fine lad. There was no one like him in the whole country; the power of a god was in him.

Now one day when he was walking behind the cows, they said to him: "The grass is good over in that place." Bata took them there, and they became very beautiful, and multiplied.

One day when the two brothers were working in the field they ran out of grain, and the elder brother sent Bata home to get more. He found his brother's wife fixing her hair, and when he asked for grain she told him to go and get it himself. He came out of the granary with a sack so huge that the wife realized he was very strong; and she wanted to know him with the knowledge of a man. But when she said, "Come, let us spend an hour sleeping together," Bata became angry. "What is this great abomination which you have said to me?"

Bata went back to the field and worked with his brother, saying nothing. But when the older brother returned to his house in the evening he found the house dark, and his wife lying down very sick, like one who has been beaten. She told him that Bata had made evil suggestions to her, and that, when she recoiled in horror, he beat her and threatened her. So Anubis took his spear and ran out to find his younger brother, who had not yet returned from the field. He hid himself behind the stable door and waited. But when Bata came to the stable with the herd of cows the head cow said, "Watch out! Your brother is there, waiting with his spear to kill you. Run away from him!" The next cow said the same thing, and so did the one after that. At last convinced, Bata looked down and saw his brother's feet under the door. Dropping his burdens, he ran as fast as he could, with his brother after him.

As he ran, Bata prayed to Re to help him, saying: "Thou art he who judges the wicked from the just!" Re heard, and caused a body of water filled with crocodiles to appear between him and his older brother. And his older brother beat his hands together, in a rage at not being able to kill him. Then Bata argued with his brother, telling him what had really happened. And he took a knife and cut off his penis, and threw it into the water.

This dramatic gesture convinced the older brother (as well it might); seeing the boy fainting and in pain, he wept and groaned aloud.

Now up to this point the story is fairly simple, and effective; the Egyptian audience was probably groaning in sympathy, and yearning to see the virtuous and misused young brother rewarded. The complications begin with the story Bata proceeds to tell his remorseful brother as they stand one on either side of the river. He says he is going to the Valley of the Cedar, where he will put his heart in the top of a tree. If his tree is ever cut down, so that his heart falls to the ground, he will be in trouble, and then Anubis must come to his help. He tells Anubis how he will know when the fatality occurs, and then he departs, leaving his brother to return home and deal with his treacherous wife. He kills her and throws her to the dogs. Then he sits down and weeps for his younger brother.

Now we switch to Bata in the Valley of the Cedar. He manages well enough until the gods decide he needs a wife. They make one for him, a girl more beautiful than any girl in the land, and Bata falls in love with her. It is obvious that Bata's self-mutilation in the first part of the story is blandly ignored by the storyteller; perhaps it is assumed that the gods took care of that little matter too. Like any infatuated bridegroom, Bata tells his wife all about his heart, up in the pine tree. He also warns her not to go out, for fear of the Sea-god.

As we might expect, the girl ignores the warning. The Sea-god rolls up in pursuit as soon as she goes out; she makes good her escape, but leaves a lock of her hair, which the god takes to Egypt. So wonderfully fragrant is this beautiful hair that when the washermen of Pharaoh come down to wash his royal clothes, the perfume from the hair impregnates them. Vexed, the chief washerman goes down to the bank to find out where the perfume is coming from. He finds the lock of hair and takes it to the king, who consults his magicians about it. They tell him where the girl is living, and advise him to send for her.

But the messengers sent by Pharaoh are killed by Bata, all but one, whom he sends back to tell the king what has happened. Next time the king sends soldiers in great number—and, more cannily, a lady chaperone, "whose hands were filled with all sorts of beautiful women's adornments." That does the trick. The girl goes back to Egypt with the escort (we must assume that Bata was out hunting that day) and, preferring the position of royal favorite to a dull life in the Valley of the Cedar, she betrays the secret of Bata's heart to the king. Down goes the tree, down goes Bata's heart; and one day, Anubis (I hope you have not forgotten the remorseful older brother) sees that his pot of beer has gone bad. Knowing this for the sign, he snatches stick and sandals, clothes and weapons, and sets off for the Valley of the Cedar. After a long and arduous search he finds Bata's heart and gets it back inside Bata, whom he has discovered lying dead on his bed.

Bata is himself again, but he must revenge himself on his wife. Turning himself into a magnificent bull, he has Anubis take him to Egypt where the king welcomes him as a sacred animal; but the worthless girl tricks the monarch into killing the beast. Next Bata becomes a pair of trees. The girl again works his destruction, but before the trees are cut down a seed from one of them falls into the girl's mouth. She becomes pregnant—with Bata himself, who, as the king's supposed son, eventually succeeds to the throne. Bata's first act as pharaoh is to drag his wife-mother before the magistrates, who unanimously condemn her to death. He then appoints his elder brother Anubis as heir to the throne, and everybody lives happily ever after.

I like this story, despite its misogynist attitude. I like its sublime indifference to motivation, its easily identified heroes and villainesses, and the rich inventiveness of episodes which defy logical sequence. As in the case of "The Doomed Prince," the "Tale of Two Brothers" has several familiar motifs—the hero's transformations, the talking animals, the wonderful lock of hair, and the stock hero figure of the "younger son," who overcomes numerous tribulations to become king. The first part of the story has been compared to the tale of Joseph and Potiphar's wife, while Bata's temporary death and self-castration are as harmless as the poisoning of Snow White and the Sleeping Beauty, since they can be cured by magic.

Not all Egyptian amusements were as indolent as the ones we have described. Hunting was a popular activity and, as practiced by noblemen and kings, its purpose was pleasure, not the production of food. Fowling expeditions, as we have seen, had some of the aspects of a family Sunday in the country. In the reliefs this sport was pursued in marshy regions, where the reeds grew higher than the hunter's head. He poled his light boat (made of papyrus stalks bound together) through the shallow water until he reached a spot where the birds might be hiding. If he used bow and arrow to bring them down, the arrows were blunt, designed to stun rather than kill. The throw sticks and boomerangs used in this sport were equally nonlethal; since they could be wielded by one hand the hunter might hold a decoy in the other—a live duck which obligingly flapped and squawked to alert its wild fellows as the hunter clutched it by the feet.

Obviously it took some skill to hunt successfully with these missile weapons. It was their archery, however, in which the

Egyptians took the greatest pride. The bow was used in warfare, but also in hunting, and boys practiced assiduously to gain skill in this art. They were perhaps the first of the great bowmen of history, and, if we can believe the boasts they recorded, Robin Hood might never have won the golden arrow had Amenhotep II been present at the match in Nottingham Town. The Egyptian records suggest, however, that force in shooting was as important as accuracy. Amenhotep's chief pride was that he could shoot an arrow through a metal target three inches thick. "There is no one who could draw his bow," says one inscription, "not among his own army, among the rulers of foreign countries, or among the princes of Retenu—because his strength is so much greater than [that of] any king who ever lived."

The Egyptians hunted wild cattle, ibex, gazelle, and the like, but the royal prey was the lion. It took courage to hunt a lion with bow and arrow, even mounted, as the king was, in a chariot. The flimsy vehicles could easily be overturned by an enraged beast, and although the king was accompanied by attendants, there was always the chance that the lion might catch the king. Thutmose III almost lost his life on one hunt, not to a lion, but an elephant; he was saved by one of his soldiers, who stepped in under the nose of the charging beast and drove a spear into it. Thutmose encountered his elephant on one of his Asiatic expeditions; they were not to be found in Egypt.

When he got home, exhausted and perspiring after his hunt, an Egyptian gentleman might relax with a quiet game of senet. Several board games of this type were played, and they look so intriguing that I regret that I am unable to tell the reader how to play them. You can see game boards in many museums; some Egyptians were so addicted to them that they took the game along with them into their tombs, and a few have been carefully mended, after being worn out by frequent use. The handiest of the boards are made in the shape of flat rectangular boxes, with the layout for senet on one side and another game on the other; a drawer in the box held the pieces.

The senet board had thirty squares, in three rows of ten; the pieces were little cone-shaped affairs, six to each player, and the moves were determined by the fall of a set of carved wands,

Board and pieces for the game of *senet*. The hieroglyphs show that some squares had a special importance; the water sign on the fourth square from the right may be a hazard or penalty, while the next square to the left bears the triple hieroglyph meaning "goodness"— an advantageous square. *The Metropolitan Museum of Art, Gift of Egypt Exploration Fund, 1901.*

thrown like "pick-up sticks." Senet was more like parcheesi than chess; the aim was not to take the opponent's pieces, but to progress through them back to the starting point, or to the opposite end of the board. Unfortunately we will never be able to play the game unless we can determine one essential point—how the fall of the sticks determined the moves. No treatise on "How to Win at Senet" has ever been found, and it is not likely that it ever will be, because the Egyptians seldom wrote textbooks.

There is one other Egyptian habit, possibly to be classed as an amusement, which I cannot resist describing, because it seems, offhand, so improbable. They went sight-seeing. Not abroad, however; not if they could avoid it. A good many Egyptians did get to see the world, as royal envoys, or soldiers, or couriers, but the literary evidence suggests that they hated every minute of it. Wenamon, who went through a series of humiliating adventures when he sailed to Byblos in search of cedar, had good reason to dislike Dor, where he was robbed, and Byblos, where the prince insulted him and his country, and Cyprus, where the inhabitants tried to kill him. But an earlier story, that of Sinuhe, who won fame and fortune among the Bedouin, has the same attitude; riches and reputation notwithstanding, Sinuhe continued to long for home and as soon as he received a summons from Pharaoh he dropped his Bedouin wife, children, and noble rank to hurry back to Egypt.

Although they were home-loving people, who enjoyed the quiet of their walled gardens, some Egyptians traveled a good deal within Egypt. Clerks, officials, merchants, farmers taking produce to market—all made use of that cheap and convenient road, the Nile. And when their business in Memphis or Thebes was concluded, they did what many another weary businessman has done —they went sight-seeing.

It is not surprising that the Egyptians should have been interested in their own antiquities. To an Egyptian of the Middle Kingdom the pyramids of Giza and Dahshur were as far removed in time as the oldest medieval castles are for us. And by Saite times, in the seventh century B.C., the Egyptian tourists were viewing relics that had stood for two millennia—relics that were older, for them, than the Colosseum and the Roman Forum are for us.

There are inscriptions—we call them graffiti—scribbled all over the walls of the pyramid temples of the Fourth Dynasty by the sightseers of later periods. The pyramid at Medum was a popular spot; Eighteenth Dynasty visitors left their names, and the date, and one added the comment that he found the temple "as though heaven were within it, and the sun rising in it." The private tombs were also visited, and some Saite tourists found the paintings and reliefs so admirable that they had them copied, down to the last detail, in their own tombs. But the case that intrigues me most is that of a tomb found at Deir el Bahri and excavated in 1925 by a Metropolitan Museum expedition under Herbert Winlock.

I have quoted extensively from Mr. Winlock, here and elsewhere—to the neglect, it might seem, of equally worthy scholars—because he wrote a book which is, for me, one of the most delightful works on archaeology ever composed. It has the forbidding title, "Excavations at Deir el Bahri," and it is the season-by-season report of the Metropolitan Museum's excavations at that site. It was written for a "lay" audience; most of it is drawn from the reports written for the Museum's Bulletin. The noteworthy thing about this book is not the absence of technical language, but the addition of such elements as humor, personal reactions, and imagination. To judge from his writing, Winlock was an unusually sensitive and perceptive human being, but he was not necessarily unique. Flashes of sympathy and charm show up even in technical works—Ludwig Borchardt's reaction to the sculptor's workshop at Amarna, George Reisner's lines on the pitiful skeletons of the servants buried alive in the Sudan—and many others. The trouble is, most excavators are so busy that they barely have time enough to turn out the technical reports demanded by the profession, let alone write charming stories for non-archaeologists. The difference between technical reports and popular articles is immense, and it lies in the attitude, not the talent, of the writer. William Flinders Petrie, who wrote a fascinating autobiography, turned out excavation reports of superb dullness. I am not decrying the technical report, but I do think it is a pity more archaeologists don't write autobiographies. They would be much more interesting than the insipid life stories of actors and criminals which seem to be in vogue today—and they wouldn't have to be ghost-written either, because many excavators write extremely well.

But back to Deir el Bahri. The big monuments at that site are the temples of Hatshepsut and of Mentuhotep. In the 1924–25 season (expeditions in Egypt work from the fall of one year to the spring of the next, since the summer climate is frightful), the Egyptian Government decided to restore the façade of Hatshepsut's temple. It had been known since the days of Mariette that there was a tomb under the temple, the tomb of a queen named Neferu, but it had never been cleared, and to visit it, it was necessary to crawl "like one of the snakes one feared to meet" (Winlock) over nasty heaps of rubbish through pitchblack underground passages. Another factor that might have deterred modern visitors was the heap of dismembered, half-burned Roman mummies that filled the tomb chapel from floor to ceiling.

When the front of the temple was cleared, the excavators found the brick façade of the queen's tomb, with the corridor leading down to the chapel. They carried out the unpleasant job of cleaning chapel and corridor, but found nothing there to reward them for their labors. Hundreds of years after the queen had been buried, the chapel had become a factory for limestone dishes, made out of the blocks that lined the walls. Only tiny fragments of the original reliefs were discovered.

From the chapel another corridor led down to the tomb chamber. This had been walled up in ancient times—fruitlessly, since robbers had penetrated the burial chamber and taken everything in it. The excavators were intrigued, not by the all-too-common evidences of theft, but by indications that the chapel had been a popular tourist spot anciently. On the small scraps of stone littering the floor, the remnants of the once beautiful reliefs, were the names of visiting tourists, whose admiration for the sculpture evidently did not inhibit them from scribbling all over them.

Queen Neferu lived during the Eleventh Dynasty. Since Hatshepsut built her temple over and across the original entrance, blocking the tomb, it was assumed that the visitors who left their names must have come during the period between the Eleventh and Eighteenth Dynasties, before the temple was built. But the excavations of 1925 brought out a surprise—a narrow tunnel, built at the same time as the Eighteenth Dynasty temple, which led north from the upper temple court to the door of the tomb. There is only one plausible reason for the construction of this tunnel—to allow access to the tomb after its old entrance had been closed by the temple terrace of a later and greater queen than Neferu. Someone wanted the masterpieces of ancient relief to remain accessible. Was it Senmut, the supposed architect of Deir el Bahri, or the queen herself, moved by some antiquarian bent? Or was it simply the demands of the "tourist trade"—despised by modern intellectuals, but prompted, in ancient Egypt as today, by the love of beauty and the sense of wonder?

# VII

## Be a Scribe, Put It in Thy Heart

### *Education*

LET us return to the little Egyptian boy whom we left, some ages back, just entering into manhood. Candor compels me to admit, against my feminist inclinations, that Egyptian culture as we know it was primarily the product of these grown-up boys—artists, sculptors, administrators, kings, scribes, carpenters, goldsmiths. . . . Name almost any profession whose products have survived, and they will be professions staffed by men, not by women.

We have already discussed some of the trades, and others will fall into place as we proceed. Now it is time we took a look at the professions. If a boy wanted professional status, and prestige higher than that of a mere craftsman, his career might end in a number of different ways, but it almost had to begin in one place —the scribal school.

Sometimes we talk about scribes as if they constituted a separate profession, but they were really the raw materials out of which most of the professions were formed. At the top of the ladder were administrators, courtiers, high-ranking priests and soldiers. On the lower rungs were army scribes, court scribes, temple scribes—the secretaries and clerks and white collar work-

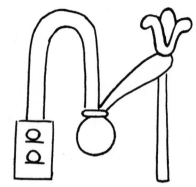

*Hieroglyph for scribe's implements*

ers who kept the machinery of the state running smoothly. Professor John A. Wilson has coined the term "white kilt" workers for this group; it is a very neat and apposite expression, which would have made sense to the Egyptians. The scribe's clean white clothes were prestige symbols, like the long fingernails of Chinese nobles; they meant that he did not have to do manual labor.

The boy whose father came of this "white kilt" class, and the boy whose ambitious father wanted to raise him into it, attended a school of some sort where he was taught to read and write. We know very little about such schools. Were they run by the temples, or by the state, or by private teachers? At what age did the boys start school? Did girls ever attend? How long did the course take? Were there postgraduate courses in foreign languages or accounting? We can guess at some of the answers, but we don't really know.

There were no little mud-brick schoolhouses in Egypt—at least none have ever been found. Some of the boys may have been taught in the nearby temple. Others might go to a school run by a local scribe in one room of his house. Wealthy and noble youths, one may reasonably surmise, would have had private tutors. The equipment for a schoolroom was simple; there were no little desks or blackboards to survive to gladden the eye of a future archaeologist. There were no schoolbooks either. Basic exercises consisted of dictation. The boys only needed writing equipment: the equivalent of pen and ink, plus a pile of ostraca—smooth fragments of broken pottery or stone, which they used as slates. Beginning students didn't use papyrus; it was too expensive.

The scribe's outfit is well known, from actual examples and from drawings. The so-called palette was a narrow rectangular piece of wood with a slot down the center to hold the pens, and depressions for cakes of ink. The pens were slender rushes pounded or chewed at one end to form a fine brush; when not in use they were kept in a pen case, which was often made in the shape of a pretty, rounded column with a flower capital. The ink came in solid form; the black was usually some kind of soot, and the red, made of red ochre, was used for rubrics, or headings. The scribe needed water to moisten his ink cakes; it was kept in a small shell or pot. One of the common hieroglyphic signs shows the scribe's outfit—the little water pot in between the long palette, with its two rounded ink cakes, and the pen holder. To complete his equipment a scribe might have a burnisher for smoothing out rough spots in the papyrus, a grinder for preparing his ink, a ball of linen thread to tie around the papyrus roll when it was finished, and a rag for rubbing out mistakes. The most convenient eraser, however, was a quick swipe of the tongue.

The scribe wrote sitting on the ground, with his legs crossed; the front of his kilt, pulled taut across his knees, provided a sort of writing desk on which he could unroll his papyrus. The pot of water was on the ground at his right, the palette in his left hand; he dipped his pen into the water, rubbed it on the cake of ink, and he was ready to take dictation.

Papyrus used to grow lavishly in the swampy parts of Egypt. It is almost nonexistent today—the curious tourist can see some growing in a carefully tended plot outside the Cairo Museum—which is a pity, because it is a pretty plant, with tall slender stalks and a feathery green tuft on top. The art of making papyrus is not lost; it has been made in modern times by the experts of the British Museum, among others. The papyrus must be fresh. It is cut low down, just above water level; the lower part of the stem makes the best writing material. It is cut into lengths, and the outer rind removed. The inner pith can then be cut or separated into strips one-eighth to one-fourth inches thick. The strips are placed on some absorbent material, parallel to one another and slightly overlapping; another lot of strips goes on top, also over-lapping, and at right angles to the bottom layer. The papyrus maker then pounds the whole business with a wooden mallet. It takes an hour or more of steady pounding, in case any reader is considering the experiment. The material can be put in a press later, but the initial pounding is essential. The result is a sheet of thin "paper" whose surface can be burnished with a stone. The juices of the papyrus weld the strips together without the need of any other adhesive, but glue was used to fasten separate sheets together into the rolls the Egyptians used instead of books.

Though papyrus was comparatively cheap, it was not cheap enough to be used for the first bumbling efforts of little school-boys; and anyone who has supplied a first-grader with notebooks can understand why Egyptian parents refused to buy papyrus for their beginners. Hence the ostraca, an ample supply of which was available in any town, free for the taking. The sweating children had to learn at least two types of writing, the pretty picture hieroglyphs and the cursive hieratic script. Later a third form of writing, demotic, came into use. Considering that there are hun-dreds of different hieroglyphic signs, the task of the budding scribe was not easy, but at least he wrote the same language, essen-tially, in all three scripts. Once the boys had learned the signs, and had acquired some vocabulary, they wrote texts from the teacher's dictation, and then the teacher corrected them. Some of the texts were fun—stories and tales—but others were less entertaining. Like most human beings, the Egyptian schoolteachers were un-able to resist inculcating a moral when they had the chance. The most popular moral was the superiority of the scribal profes-sion over all others. One text points out the spiritual advantages:

> A man is perished, his corpse is dust, all his contemporaries have gone to dust; but it is writing which causes him to be remem-bered in the mouth of him who utters [the prayers for the dead]. More beneficial is writing than the house of a builder, or tombs in the West. It is better than an established castle, or a stela in the temple.

The text goes on, in a similarly lofty tone, to mention the names of great scribes of the past, whose tombs have been forgotten and whose houses have crumbled into dust, but whose names are remembered because of their writings. It must be emphasized that the Egyptians did not want to have their names remembered for sentimental reasons; the survival of the name, even in someone's memory, implied the survival of the personality after death.

Other texts with a related theme are less exalted. They describe, with ghoulish relish, the horrors of other occupations. The metalworker has fingers like a crocodile's hide, and stinks worse than fish roe. The craftsman is so tired at night he can hardly move, the barber is still shaving when night falls. The contractor is dirtier than a pig from carrying mud, the weaver has to sit in his shop all day, breathing stale air, with his knees jammed up against his belly. And so it goes, through embalmers, cobblers, bird-catchers, and every conceivable activity. But the scribe! He never goes hungry; he reaches the halls of the magistrates. Most important of all—"there is no profession free of a boss, except for that of the scribe—*he* is the boss!"

The boys copied all sorts of things—hoary advice from antique sages, stories, long tedious lists of nouns, poems, business letters. They did not always copy them correctly, and since some of our only copies of important literary texts come from these schoolboy exercises we have good reason to deplore the students' lack of skill. Egyptian is not the easiest language in the world to read, particularly when it is being elegant and literary; if we have to correct the grammar and spelling of the ancient schoolboys as well, we do not have an easy time of it.

Since there are no textbooks, we assume that most of the instruction was oral. How far this instruction went we cannot know. Egyptian grammar has been analyzed according to modern rules, derived, in part, from the model of Latin grammar, so our Egyptian textbooks take up nouns and verbs and adjectives, and tell the student what forms of a verb express futurity, participial action, and so on. The commoner hieroglyphic signs have been classified according to function as well as shape and origin. To generalize, we might say that some signs express sounds, others ideograms or whole words, and still others the class of objects to which the word belongs. The last category consists of signs called determinatives, which are added to the "spelled-out" word to clarify its meaning; they have no sound value. For example, the word *sesh*, written with the hieroglyph of the scribe's palette, could be a verb, "write," or a noun, "scribe." (It could mean other things, too, but let's not confuse the issue.) If the word in question was supposed to be "write," the determinative indicating the class of abstractions was added to the palette sign. If it was "writer, scribe," the man determinative was used instead.

It is unlikely that Egyptian schoolchildren were treated to lectures on grammar and syntax. They learned the correct forms as children learn to speak their native tongue correctly—by example and practice. I have always suspected, without being able to prove it, that Egyptian scribes may have been aware of the functions of such things as determinatives, and that they might have had a few simple verbal rules for their use. In its most obvious form, the determinative principle is one a harassed schoolboy might have worked out for himself. Suppose he encounters the word "scribe" in dictation for the first time. He knows how to spell the verb "write," and with other examples in mind, and the cold eye of the teacher upon him, he might extrapolate, and write "scribe" as "write" minus the abstract determinative, and plus the man determinative. He was stimulated to do his best by a principle succinctly expressed by the Egyptians: "A boy's ears are on his back, and he listens best when he is beaten."

Reading and writing were the main subjects, but some scribes had to acquire other specializations. Arithmetic must have been a basic course, for whether he ended up as an army scribe calculating rations or a temple scribe in charge of the god's property, or a court scribe concerned with architecture and construction work, the scribe usually had to be able to do simple arithmetic. The subject was certainly taught, but how, and by whom, we don't know.

Another specialty which became important after the beginning of the New Kingdom was foreign languages. Even if we had no evidence we would suspect that at a wealthy cosmopolitan court there would have to be some men who knew enough foreign tongues to deal with traders, envoys, and messengers from other countries. The Amarna tablets, found at that site, show that Egyptian kings of this period carried on constant correspondence with their representatives in the conquered cities of Syria-Palestine, and also with brother kings in the great empires of Mitanni, Hatti, and Babylonia. The "Foreign Ministry" scribes did not need to learn all the languages of these areas, for the diplomatic *lingua franca* of the period was Akkadian, just as Latin was an international language in the Middle Ages. There must have been a group of scribes at the royal court who could read Akkadian and press the little wedge-shaped characters onto the clay tablets on which they were commonly written.

The boys would absorb some history (or the Egyptian equivalent) and some literature, rhetoric and ethics, through the texts they copied. We will probably never know what other subjects, if any, were imparted straight from the mouth of the teacher into the heads of the boys. They had a formidable task just with reading and writing; the happiest moment of the day must have been lunchtime, when their mothers appeared with their bread and beer. But when they graduated from the schoolroom they had, in their knowledge of the "writings," the key to advancement. It could lead to high office, or, more commonly, to a comfortable, respectable post in the entourage of king, god, or noble.

## The Hekanakhte Letters

On the veranda of his house, a youngish man named Mersu relaxed after the noonday meal. It was a day in July or August, somewhere in the neighborhood of 2000 B.C. The sun beat down on the dusty earth of the courtyard; from the women's quarters at the rear of the house came the shrill voice of Mersu's wife, trying to collect the children for their afternoon rest. The noise did not disturb Mersu; he was used to it. He was just about to close his eyes and drift off into slumber when the sight of a man—a newcomer—passing through the gates brought him upright in his chair. The man was a messenger; in one hand he carried a roll of papyrus. Mersu clasped both hands over his belly; there it was again, that odd little pain that had bothered him lately, especially after eating. Then he stood up to receive the letter from his father.

Mersu's father, Hekanakhte, was *ka*-priest of a vizier named Ipi, who lived and died during the First Intermediate Period. When this great man was buried in his tomb near Thebes, he left estates in that area whose produce was to be spent on the upkeep of his tomb and the ceremonies necessary to keep his spirit alive and well nourished. Hekanakhte was the man in charge of the funerary arrangements in behalf of the vizier; his own salary came out of the produce of the estates. He lived in a little village called Nebsyt, a few miles from Thebes and the tomb he tended. His sizable family included his five sons—Mersu the eldest, Sinebnut and Sihathor, both grown men, and the younger boys Anubis and Snefru. The older sons were married, and their families lived with Hekanakhte. In addition, there were various unattached women: Hekanakhte's old mother, a poor relation called Hetepet, and a woman who may have been a widowed daughter. An important member of the group, though not a member of the family, was Hekanakhte's assistant Heti. It was a big family and, as one might suspect, not always a harmonious one.

From time to time Hekanakhte had to leave home in order to visit the other property which was under his supervision. He stayed away on these trips for many months, leaving Mersu in charge of things; but though he was gone he was not forgotten. He bombarded Mersu with letters, and Mersu, who was trying to manage his father's obstreperous household as well as carry out his priestly duties, used to take these lengthy epistles up to an empty tomb near the bigger tomb of Ipi, where he could ponder their words of wisdom in peace. When the empty tomb was ready to be occupied, the workers swept the accumulated debris, including the letters—which Mersu evidently discarded after reading them— into a hole in the floor, and covered them up. There they stayed until they were discovered by archaeologists in 1922. They form one of the most fascinating pictures of family life from any ancient culture. One of the people intrigued by them was Miss Agatha Christie, who used the characters, though not under the same names, as the basis for her story of murder in ancient Egypt, *Death Comes As the End*.

I always picture Hekanakhte as a skinny little old man, somewhat flabby around the middle, but active as a cricket. In my mental image he has no hair on top of his head, only a fringe of gray over his ears. When he remembers to do so he slaps a dusty black wig on his head. He carries a long staff, which he uses like a pole-vaulter's pole to turn his shuffling walk into a series of quick hops. His face is wrinkled and his nose is beaky, but his black eyes are bright and alert, peering suspiciously out at the world from under lowering brows.

The letter Mersu received that afternoon in summer asked him to send his father five bushels of wheat and as much barley as he could scrape together, plus any food that was not needed for the family. The inundation was about to begin, and Hekanakhte's letter includes the following ominous remarks: "As for any flooding on our land, it is you who are cultivating it, and I shall hold you responsible. Be very active in cultivating, and be very careful. Guard the produce of my grain! Guard everything of mine; for I shall hold you responsible for it. And if my land floods—too bad for you!"

Several other letters followed this one, but Mersu did not save any until the next summer, during which time Hekanakhte remained away. Conditions in Egypt were bad; the inundation had been low, and crop failures had caused near-famines in many areas. Hekanakhte's letter says that he has managed to find some food and plans to send it to the family. Evidently it was not an abundant supply, for the old man meticulously lists the shares due each member of the family. "Now you must not be angry about this," he insists. "See, the whole household, as well as the children, are dependent on me, and everything is mine." Then he quotes a pair of hoary proverbs: "The hungry must hunger," and "Half life is better than dying altogether"; and proceeds, working himself up into quite a passion: "Why, here they have begun to eat men and women! There are none anywhere else to whom such food is given. You must give this food to my people only while they are working. Mind this! Make the most of my land, strive to the uttermost, dig the ground with your noses. See, if you are industrious, men will praise God for you. Lucky that I can support you! And if any one of the men or women spurn the food, let him come here to me, and stay with me, and live as I live! Not," he concludes self-pityingly, "that there is anyone who will come here to me."

Between lectures on general behavior, Hekanakhte gave ex-

plicit directions for the management of the property in Thebes—
what field to sow with what seed, the names of men to whom land
was to be rented, and so on. Hekanakhte was worried for fear
someone would get more than his due, and he warned his harassed
son that if anyone was overpaid, the excess would be deducted
from Mersu's own share. It seems that Mersu had everything to
lose and nothing to gain; when there were losses he had to make
them good, but Hekanakhte never offered to reward him for gains
made by his good management. One of the letters found in the
cache had never been opened until the modern excavators broke
its seal; it was full of helpful hints on business, and one cannot
resist the suspicion that Mersu, driven to distraction, dropped it
unread into the handy hole in the floor, and went on to do his
work in his own way.

One surprising factor about life at this period is the amount of
letter-writing which must have been carried on. We have only
Hekanakhte's letters to Mersu, but from what he says it is evident
that he was getting letters, not only from Mersu, but from other
relatives, all complaining, tattling on one another, and going behind Mersu's back to report their animosities to the absent father
of the family. Hekanakhte threw himself into all the quarrels with
relish. The poor relation Hetepet was evidently unpopular; in
one letter Hekanakhte says irritably, "I have already told you, do
not keep a woman friend of Hetepet's away from her. Take great
care of her, although of course you don't want her with you." The
two youngest boys were also a trial to their elder brother. Anubis
wrote to the old father complaining that Mersu had taken some of
his things, and Hekanakhte shot right back with "Give back to
him any article of Anubis' that you have, and whatever is missing,
pay him back for it. Don't make me write to you about it again! I
have already written to you twice about it!" The youngest boy,
Snefru, was his father's spoiled darling, and Hekanakhte constantly nagged Mersu to be sure the brat was kept happy. "I have
been told that (Snefru) is unhappy. Take great care of him, and
give him food, and salute him from (me) a thousand times, a
million times! Take great care of him and send him off to me
directly after you have cultivated." But Snefru refused his father's
invitation, and the following year Hekanakhte wrote feebly, "And

if Snefru wants to look after the bulls, then put him to looking after them. He doesn't want to be running up and down cultivating with you, nor does he wish to come here with me. Indeed, whatever he wants, you must let him enjoy it."

One would think that Hekanakhte had troubles enough with his quarrelsome brood of children and dependents, but he did not know when to leave well enough alone. He never mentions a wife, so presumably he was a widower. In a burst of elderly vigor he decided to take a concubine, and this damsel destroyed what little peace was left in the house. She had not been there long before Hekanakhte was writing: "What am I supporting you for, you five boys, and what can my concubine do to you? As to doing any harm to my concubine, take warning! You aren't associated with me as my partner! If you would shut up, it would be a very good thing," he concludes vulgarly.

The concubine, Iutenheb, managed to irritate everybody. Hekanakhte ordered his son to fire one maid who had threatened or offended the girl; he warned Mersu against the third son, Sihathor, too. There was also trouble with a tenant named Ip. In despair the old man finally instructed Mersu to send the charming bone of contention to him; this letter is full of sententious complaints like "how can I ever live with you in one establishment, if you will not respect a concubine for my sake?"

It is no wonder that Miss Christie, the expert on murder, saw violent potentialities in the Hekanakhte household. But perhaps they were no worse than they are in a lot of families, particularly those which are complicated by poor relations, grandmothers, and the equivalent of a stepmother living with grown sons. (Just what was Sihathor doing to the concubine, one wonders?) It is certainly an amusing and nearly unique picture of daily life—the daily activities, quarrels and resentments of an average "white kilt" family of the second millennium B.C. We do not get such periscopes into the past very often, and it is amazing how effective this one is, and what a clear picture we are given of the personalities involved. Hekanakhte is more than a personality, he is a "character" in the full slang sense of the word, with his fussy "now mind this" and "pay attention to what I say" larding every letter, and his constant prickling reminders that the whole family is dependent on *him*. When I see the eldest son Mersu, I see him as rather timid, balding prematurely, and with an incipient ulcer. Let us hope that when his crotchety old father died he left the property to the son who had worked so hard to maintain it, and that Mersu was able to get his contentious relatives in order.

## The Scribe and the Bureaucracy

One of the significant aspects of Egyptian life which is brought out by the Hekanakhte letters is the combination in one man of functions which we would consider incompatible, or at least divergent. Hekanakhte's "job" was that of *ka*-priest to the deceased vizier, which meant that he was supposed to make the offerings to the dead man's soul at such times as the mortuary contract stated. We would define this as a priestly function. However, Hekanakhte's letters show that he spent a lot of time administering the lands left by the vizier to supply his tomb offerings. He was more of a bailiff than a priest.

The higher the position in the bureaucracy, the greater the variety of the official's responsibilities. There was considerable division of labor in the Egyptian economy, and craftsmen were real specialists in their own lines. We know of sandal-makers, bakers, carpenters, bird-catchers, beekeepers, janitors, matmakers, incense molders, goldsmiths and coppersmiths, fishermen, and dozens of others. But when we get to the upper echelons of high officials, we find that they could turn their hands to just about anything.

The career of Senmut, Hatshepsut's favorite, is a good example. He was a prophet of both Montu and Amon (priesthood); chief steward of Amon and overseer of the god's storehouses, orchards and other property (temple administration); chief steward of the king (civil administration); overseer of works (construction, engineering, architecture); father-tutor of the queen's daughter and steward of her estates, prince and count, sole companion, wearer of the royal seal; and, at one point in his active life, he may also have been a soldier. It is true that many of these offices could have been rewards for a particular talent for administration. The president of a big modern corporation may have under him artists, machinists, truck drivers, engineers, and so on; in the Egyptian sense he could be described as overseer of truck drivers, chief artist, and supervisor of engineers. Perhaps some of the talents which we ascribe to these Egyptian jacks-of-all-trades may have been supervisory only. Even so, it is evident that some of our modern categories are not applicable. The president of the corporation would not preach sermons from the pulpit on alternate Sundays, nor be sent as a field officer to lead an army on a campaign, as one Fourth Dynasty official was.

An Egyptian official would have been baffled by the suggestion that he render unto Caesar those things which were Caesar's, and unto God those things which were His. Caesar *was* God—or at least god—and there was no functional difference between church and state. At some periods a single man might hold both the vizierate and the high priesthood of Amon, the supreme civil and sacerdotal positions. This concept explains, to some extent, the apparent overlapping of functions which we find in so many official careers.

However, we must also take into account the attitude of the ancients toward aptitude and talent and professional training. Parents did not worry about selecting a career for their boy which would employ his highest abilities, or suit his fancy. Undoubtedly there were men of genius who followed their proper bent, and boys of ambition and talent who raised themselves out of obscure backgrounds to the rank of "prince and count." Except for the scribal schools, however, training must have been by the apprentice system, and a boy's best teacher was his father, who could not only teach him the tricks of the trade but could bequeath to him the tools and the goodwill which he had acquired. Even the high administrative offices, though theoretically bestowed by the king, tended to run in certain families. When the king's faithful old vizier died, his logical successor was the son who had so long profited from his father's wisdom and experience.

At the top of the ladder, of course, was the king. Actually, he was not really on the ladder; he sat suspended in air several feet above it. The notion of the divinity of the king has been questioned, but not seriously shaken; by dogma he certainly was a god, and if his subjects, singly or en masse, ever regarded him as less than sacred such a viewpoint never got into an official publication. He owned the land and its people; he bestowed all offices, heard all complaints, led all armies, and was high priest of every god. Obviously there was a gap between dogma and practice; the king could not be in a hundred places at once. His religious functions were delegated, and his executive activities were supported by the vizier and by a whole cabinet of officials.

The vizier was the highest of all officials, the deputy of the king in all the affairs of state. In the Old Kingdom the office was usually held by a prince of the royal blood, as were other important positions. Later, commoners could aspire to the job.

The vizier's responsibilities were awesome. He was in charge of just about everything. Though many of his duties were delegated, the office apparently got too complicated for a single occupant, and by the Eighteenth Dynasty there were two viziers, one for Upper and one for Lower Egypt. This was Egypt's imperial age, and as one might expect the bureaucracy expanded with the empire. It isn't always easy for us to understand the table of organization, since the Egyptians didn't use the same categories we do. The Ministry of Works, for example, involved viziers, treasurers, and priests. However, from the inscriptions of the period it is possible to get a general idea of how the system worked.

Under each vizier was an Overseer of the Treasury, who kept track of taxes and tribute. The Overseers of the Granaries and of Cattle worked closely with the Treasurer, since much of the national wealth consisted of produce rather than cash. The king's personal officials included the Steward, who administered the vast royal estates, the Chamberlain, in charge of the domestic details of the palace, and the First Herald, who supervised the palace guard and did a lot of other things we wouldn't consider consistent with that semi-military post. The army had its own organization, as did the temples, but these categories were not mutually exclusive; a man might hold the supreme priestly office at the same time he occupied a high administrative position. The highest office was not always the one that wielded the greatest power; Senmut, Steward of Amon under Hatshepsut, was certainly one of her most influential officials, though he was technically subordinate to several other men. This phenomenon is not entirely unknown in modern times.

There were literally dozens of other titles—Fanbearer on the Right of the King, Overseer of the Harem, Pages and Scribes of this and that, Overseers, Accountants and Herdsmen. The title of Judge is known, but justice was apparently one of those categories which the Egyptians didn't consider a separate department, as we do. The king was supreme judge, of course; the vizier was instructed, when he assumed office, that the administration of justice was in his hands; but actual courts of law, that of the vizier as well as local courts, varied in composition from case to case, and were presided over by priests and soldiers as well as by different officials. However, court records were meticulously kept, and impartiality was the ideal, if not always the fact.

At the bottom of the heap, the base of the social pyramid, were the peasants—illiterate, unorganized, and probably unsanitary. It has been said that the life of the fellahin, as the Egyptian peasant farmers are called, was much the same in the nineteenth century B.C. as in the nineteenth century of our own era.

Slavery, as a widely practiced institution, cannot be definitely proved in Egypt before the Eighteenth Dynasty, but it certainly existed then. Most of the slaves were foreigners, captured in war. Many were owned by the state—which includes the temples—but private persons, some of them pretty low in the social scale themselves, might also have a slave or two. Although these unfortunates could be bought and sold, or rented out like any other piece of property, they were in some ways better off than the ordinary peasant. They were entitled to food and lodging, clothes and ointment, and those who worked in great households might rise to positions of considerable importance. We know that some were emancipated, and others even married into the families of their owners.

The poor farmer on his little plot of land might well envy the well dressed, plump slaves of the great noble. Technically he was a free man, but in actual fact he was not much more than a serf. He was harassed by numerous obligations to the state and to his immediate superiors, and he spent most of his waking hours at work in his fields—when he was not hauling stones for pyramids and other buildings, or "chastising" various enemies of Egypt. Yet he had his pleasures, and if we can believe the reliefs in which he sometimes appeared, he was a cheerful fellow, singing at his work and exchanging quips with other laborers. We know very little about them, these men and women who made up the great majority of "the Egyptians." From our viewpoint it seems unfair that we should have less information on the long generations of "common folk" than on any of the better known pharaohs. Yet not one of the mighty rulers of Egypt—not even Akhenaton— seems quite as real as the fussy old man named Hekanakhte, who was only an insignificant *ka*-priest of an unimportant vizier named Ipi.

# VIII
## "I Fought Incredibly"

### *The Army*

AT some point in his life almost every little boy wants to be a soldier. These days he can be a Roman soldier, complete with plastic greaves and breastplate, an intergalactic trooper, or a knight in armor, but these are merely variations on the basic theme—a love for legitimized mayhem, which is a congenital characteristic of all human males. The little Egyptian boy was no different. Since there were no toy manufacturers to influence his tastes, his choice was obvious: He wanted to be an Egyptian soldier.

Among the texts which schoolboys had to copy were several which might be subtitled, "Why Not to Choose a Military Career." Here is one of them:

Come, let me tell thee of the woes of the soldier! He is awakened when an hour has passed, and he is driven like an ass. He works till the sun sets. He is hungry, his body is exhausted, he is dead while yet alive.

He is called up for Syria. His marchings are high up in the mountains. He drinks water every three days and it is foul with the taste of salt. His body is broken with dysentery. The enemy comes,

135

and surrounds him with arrows, and life is far away from him. They say, "Hasten on, brave soldier—win a good name for yourself!"—but he is barely conscious, his knee is weak and his face hurts him.

When the victory comes, His Majesty hands over the captives to be taken down into Egypt. The foreign woman is faint with marching, so she is placed on the neck of the soldier. His knapsack falls and others take it while he is loaded down with the Syrian woman. His wife and children are in their village, but he dies and never reaches it.

Frightful, isn't it? I have had to prune this text considerably, for it goes on at great length. We might suspect that the glamour of the military life was great, since the schoolmaster had to conjure up such horrific pictures to combat it. We may also wonder whether budding scribes had any choice in the matter. There was a form of military conscription; was there also such a thing as student exemptions from the draft?

The text I have quoted dates from a later period, when soldiering could be a profession. In the Old Kingdom, under the pyramid builders, there was probably no large standing army. When trouble arose with the Libyans or the Nubians, the king ordered his local governors, or nomarchs, to levy troops. This may have resulted in a situation resembling the press gangs of eighteenth-century England, with the nomarch's men dragging reluctant heroes out of pretended sick beds, or caves in the hills, or

*Soldier*

local taverns. One gets the impression that the Egyptians were never keen on fighting. "The army," if one can give that name to a big disorganized militia, was not only called up for military campaigns. Under regular military commanders it was also employed for state work projects—quarrying, digging canals, and perhaps building pyramids.

Professor R. O. Faulkner, author of a definitive article on Egyptian military organization, thought that there must have been some sort of professional, standing army, even in the Old Kingdom. He assumes that the king had sense enough to realize the danger of relying on troops who owed their immediate loyalty to the local prince who had called them up. This is a reasonable assumption. However, there is no sign of a big group of household troops. Perhaps the core of the king's own army was the royal bodyguard, whose members could officer an amateur army in case of war. Although there is mention of a rank called "army commander," possibly the equivalent of "general," one of the most famous of the Old Kingdom campaigns was led by a man who held no military rank. His name was Uni, and he served under the kings of the Sixth Dynasty. When it was necessary to chastise the Sand-Dwellers, Uni, a mere Overseer of the Tenants of the Palace, was placed at the head of the army, although there were many men of high rank available. He was chosen, he says, because he could manage the men better than anyone else.

Uni's military career is an example, not of royal favoritism, but of the "Lord High Everything Else" tendencies of Egyptian officials which we discussed in the preceding chapter. Once again it is a question of administrative ability; and, really, what other talent would be needed to manage an army? For the Egyptains, there was no such thing as military science. You just got your men out to where the enemy soldiers were standing, and then they shot arrows at one another and whacked each other with clubs and axes until one side got tired of it all and ran away. Some famous battles of the later period, when standing armies were the rule and kings prided themselves on their role as warriors, indicate a degree of ineptness and lack of common sense—let alone military strategy— that is astounding. So there was no reason why a judge and overseer like Uni couldn't have been sent to chastise an enemy, and done it—as he claims—successfully. Even in modern wars, the best soldiers are not always graduates of military academies.

After the Sixth Dynasty the dangers that worried Professor Faulkner—and, we hope, the king—actually occurred. The local rulers used their local troops for their own purposes, set themselves up as independent princelings, and dared the king to do something about it. One nobleman bragged that he had resisted the Royal House when it attacked him. Nobody, including Professor Faulkner, claims that the downfall of the united monarchy was caused by feudalistic military organization. It may have been the other way around—the nomarchs took advantage of a situation which they would never have dared to exploit when the monarchy was strong.

When forceful centralized government was restored, in the Middle Kingdom, the powerful nobles still maintained their own armies. Probably they didn't get away with it for long. Senusert III, the great warrior-king of the Twelfth Dynasty, seems to have subdued his proud nobles just as he subdued the Nubians. By this time the army had become a more regularized institution. It was recruited (perhaps this is a polite word for conscripted) by the army scribes, who got quotas from various districts. Perhaps most of the conscripts—the "young men," as they are called—served for a specified time and then went home, but other troops, whose name we translate as "warriors," seem to have been real professionals. Another possibility is that "young men" was the designation of the raw recruits, and "warrior" a rank equivalent to the Pfc. of the American Army. Then there were the "shock troops," who may have been seasoned veterans.

An elite corps was formed by the "retainers," who seem to have been young men of rank chosen to go into battle with the king. They were not the same as the royal bodyguard, though some of them seem to have been selected from it. In any case, it was an honor to be a "retainer."

At the head of the whole business was the "great overseer of troops," or the commander-in-chief. He had generals under him; some of them were no more than overseers in charge of quarrying operations, some actually led troops in the field, and others commanded the forts of Nubia. There was a host of army scribes, responsible for everything from recruiting to supply. One title has always fascinated me: "Master of the Secrets of the King in the Army." Professor Faulkner thinks he may have been a military adviser. As a constant reader of Eric Ambler, I am struck by another possibility. If the Egyptians did not use secret agents, the people they fought may have done so; there is a wonderful story of the great Ramses being deluded, on the eve of battle, by two men who pretended to be deserters from the opposing army in order to assure the king that most of the enemy forces were far away from the town. They were actually creeping up on Ramses at that very moment, and his credulity lost him the battle, and almost lost him his life.

We do not know how much actual training, if any, a young recruit had before he was marched out to fight the Nubians. However, young Egyptian boys probably learned to use the throw stick and the bow in hunting. Weapons were very simple during this period; bows were just lengths of springy wood, and war arrows might be made of hardened wood, without even stone points. Archery was a skill in which the Egyptians took some pride, and they probably started practicing when they were still young.

The bowmen made up one group among the soldiers. Others carried axes. The actual weapons which have been found include slings, spears, daggers and clubs. Presumably a battle began with the archers and slingers softening up the enemy from a distance, but it ended in hand-to-hand combat with axes and clubs. I have always had the feeling that there would not be many wounded after these battles—that if a man went down everybody jumped on him. However, one of the medical treatises deals with wounds, particularly with fractures of the skull, and this last would no doubt be a common casualty in a battle fought with clubs. Nobody wore armor, although soldiers did carry big shields covered with hide.

The Hyksos, that mysterious people from Asia who invaded Egypt after the fall of the Middle Kingdom, seem to have been responsible for a host of innovations in the art of war—if it can be called an art. We are constantly being forced to modify the statements we make about the Hyksos; the name itself may be incorrect, as applied to the whole mass of invaders, and some of the

A chariot, found in a Theban tomb of the Eighteenth Dynasty. The front of such chariots might be closed in by panels of wood or woven material. *The Archaeological Museum, Florence. Photo by Alinari.*

artifacts ascribed to them have been seriously questioned. It is undeniable, however, that there was a drastic change in the Egyptian arsenal, and in the Egyptian attitude toward war, after the Hyksos.

The Hyksos are usually given the credit for introducing the horse and chariot to Egypt. The skeleton of a horse was found recently at an Egyptian fort at Buhen, in Nubia, in a level which is definitely pre-Hyksos, but this does not invalidate the theory, since neither horses nor chariots have been found in Egypt itself before the Hyksos came.

We have several Egyptian chariots, from the tomb of Tutankhamon and from the tomb of his presumed ancestor Yuya, whom we mentioned back in the first chapter. Yuya was a captain of chariotry, so naturally he would want to take his chariot with him. At first glance, these vehicles seem to be mostly wheels—two big ones, with four spokes per wheel and leather tires around the wooden rims. Between the wheels was the body of the chariot, floored with woven leather strips and partially surrounded by a

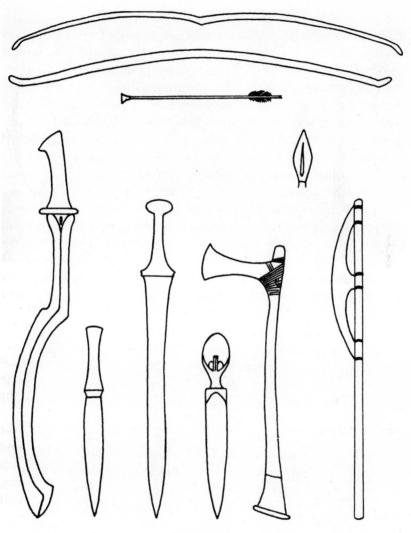

### Weapons

Above, compound (top) and regular (below) bows, with arrow. Below, left to right: khepesh scimitar, post-Hyksos dagger, long-sword, pre-Hyksos type dagger, axes; Scale is 4:1 except for the bows, which are 6:1.

curved railing. The back was usually left open. They look like light, flimsy vehicles, with a tendency to tip; but to make them as stable as possible the axle was put at the very back of the carriage body, while the pole went under the floor and then bent up at an angle to join the collar which went around the horse's neck. The chariots had to be light, if they were to be pulled by the little horses then in use. In warfare two horses might be used to each chariot, but they had to pull two men, the driver and the warrior. In some of the reliefs the valiant king is shown all alone in the chariot, with the reins tied behind his waist so that he can wield his bow. It's a good trick if you can do it.

Egyptian weapons changed significantly at this same period. Copper arrowheads became common; a new variety of dagger appeared, cast all in one piece to lessen the strain between handle and blade. Perhaps these were used for overhand, stabbing blows, wherein the dagger was held at right angles to the length of the arm. The older daggers may have been held in such a way as to continue the line of the forearm, and used to slash upward; the strain on the joint of the hilt would not be so great as it was in stabbing. Sometimes the dagger was strapped to the upper left arm, otherwise it was stuck through the warrior's belt. Swords were used, and there are a few with a long grip which may have been used two-handed; they are sharp on both sides but relatively dull at the point, which means they must have been used like a saber rather than a rapier. There was no art of fencing, which is not surprising when we consider that even in the Middle Ages sword fights simply consisted of hitting the other fellow as hard and as often as you could. One curious and romantic-looking Egyptian sword was a sort of scimitar with a curved blade. The old clubs and axes still continued in use along with the new weapons. So did the bow, but it had undergone a considerable change. Instead of being a single piece of flexible wood, the new compound bow was built up of several layers of tough springy wood, or alternate layers of wood and horn, glued together and covered with bark. It was curved in the reverse direction from that in which it was to be shot, to give it greater power.

By the middle of the Eighteenth Dynasty body armor was beginning to be used, at least by that most important soldier, the king. It consisted of a linen or leather shirt covered with overlapping metal scales. The king's blue battle helmet, of stiffened leather, probably began its career as a head protector in battle, although it soon became one of the ceremonial crowns. Charioteers carried big shields, to protect themselves and the warrior they drove, and even the horses wore heavy blankets that covered most of their backs. The little mare buried with Senmut, Queen Hatshepsut's favorite, had such a blanket of quilted leather lined with linen to prevent chafing.

The army that carried this arsenal into battle was a different thing altogether from the conscript armies of the Old Kingdom. We can give some of the credit for this—if credit it is—to the Hyksos again, since it was the effort of driving these foreigners out of Egypt that began the habit of campaigning which ended in imperial conquest. Beginning with Ahmose, who pushed the Hyksos out of Egypt into Palestine, and culminating in Thutmose III, who brought Syria-Palestine under Egyptian control and defeated the powerful kingdom of Mitanni, the kings of the Eighteenth Dynasty were seasoned campaigners. Under Thutmose III the army went out to fight in Asia every year for almost twenty years; it must have been an annual occurrence as predictable as the inundation. The men who survived these campaigns were no longer amateur soldiers.

The army of the Eighteenth–Twentieth Dynasties was divided into groups of about 5,000 men, each division being named after the god whose standard it bore. These standards are fascinating objects—images of gold or gilded wood, carried on high poles so that they could be seen above the dust of battle and, presumably, spur their defenders on to greater valor. Each division consisted of 25 "regiments" of 200 men each, and these regiments also had their standards. Some were simple painted squares of wood, others bore designs like the one that showed two men wrestling. The royal marines carried standards shaped like ships. The literature of war contains no noble high-sounding references to these standards or to the soldier's honor which was attached to similar devices in Roman times; but it is not farfetched to suppose that the standards came to have some such significance to the men who marched under them.

Most of the men did march, although each division had a chariot section. Chariotry was the elite branch of the service; it led the charge, to clear the way for the foot soldiers behind. The infantry was made up of several types of soldiery, called by different names, the meaning of which is not always clear to us. There seems to have been a distinction between veterans and new recruits, and perhaps also between volunteers (career army types) and conscripts. The "Braves of the King" sounds like a select group, and in at least one case their commander led the attack on the besieged city. Then there were military specialists: the heralds, who may have acted as dispatch runners, carrying the general's orders to various parts of the field; the scouts, mounted on horseback (there was no cavalry, as such); and a whole battery of scribes. Thutmose III had an officer who was responsible for the royal quarters at night when the army was on the march, and presumably transport, supplies, communications and other support groups were also organized.

Some of the male slaves captured in the Asiatic and Nubian wars were allowed to serve as soldiers, and as time went on such mercenaries became an important part of the military forces. Another originally foreign group of soldiers were never slaves; they became, not only thoroughly Egyptianized, but an elite corps. These men were Nubians, of mixed Hamitic and Negro blood, perhaps related to the warlike C people who gave the Middle Kingdom pharaohs such a hard time during their conquest of Cush. A delightful group of model soldiers found in an Eleventh Dynasty tomb shows that by that period they were already an integral part of the armed forces; the black men are as well armed and bear themselves as proudly as their Egyptian counterparts from the same tomb. During the Second Intermediate Period a large group of this warlike people moved into Upper Egypt. The hated Hyksos occupied northern Egypt at this time, and the rebellious princes of Thebes were preparing for the war of independence, which eventually drove out the Asiatics—with, it is now believed, the active assistance of Nubian troops. However, it was not long before the Nubians ceased to be a separate ethnic entity. Their distinctive graves, some so shallow that they have given the name "pan-grave people" to this group, soon disappear—not because the Nubians left the country, but because they adopted the customs of their new nation. The round Nubian huts became Egyptian houses, the graves turned into tombs, and the "pangrave people" became the famous Medjay, who served Egypt for centuries as soldiers, policemen and guards. After a few generations they would be assimilated physically as well as culturally, for the Egyptians, whatever their other sins, were never stupid enough to discriminate against people on the basis of skin color. The Medjay were first-rate fighting men, and that was what counted with Egypt's warlike pharaohs of Dynasty Eighteen.

We have fairly detailed descriptions of two ancient battles and, as I said, neither indicates much foresight on the part of the Egyptian general who was, at least normally, the king. In both cases the assault was to be made on a walled town, and in both cases the enemy did not wait to be assaulted, but sallied forth to meet the Egyptians. Thutmose III, who was attacking Megiddo, had the nerve to lead his army along the most direct path to the city, which happened to be a narrow mountain road over a pass. The obvious idea of an ambush does not seem to have occurred to the enemy; or possibly the road was not as dangerous as Thutmose's official report makes out, since its aim is to show the king's daring contrasted with the cautious timidity of his staff. And, of course, a rash act that succeeds is daring, while one that fails is just stupid.

Ramses II, at the battle of Kadesh, did something equally rash, but in his case it turned out to be stupid. In the first place he took the unsupported word of two casual passersby, who may have been enemy agents, that the main enemy force was a long way off. He then strung his army out, leading the van, so that half of it was too far behind to be of any use to him in case of trouble—which he promptly found. The activities of the enemy commander suggest that elementary notions of strategy (or is it tactics?) were not unknown, although they were not practiced by the Egyptians. If he did send out the enterprising liars who told Ramses the fairy tale about his whereabouts, he was an exceedingly canny man. He followed it up by leading his troops out behind the opposite side of the city, hidden from the approaching Egyptians; he swung them around in a circle and hit, not the first division, which was closest to the city, but the second. This division, that of Re, was caught completely unawares, and the enemy commander destroyed it. From that point on the story becomes a trifle misty; the Egyptian version attributes the survival of the king to his own valor in holding off, single-handed, the whole enemy army until the two divisions he had carelessly outstripped came up to his rescue. Ramses II has never inspired much confidence in me, so I have my doubts about this version.

Thutmose III was luckier, perhaps because his opponent was not so good a strategist as Ramses'. Thutmose got his army out of the pass without incident and thus was able to conduct his battle in approved style. The enemy was waiting, and both armies proceeded to arrange themselves in battle order, on a wide plain which gave everybody room to spread out. The trumpeters then sounded the charge (there are some attractive war trumpets in museum collections), and off went the chariotry, led by Thutmose, at a mad gallop, kicking up stones and dust and making a considerable racket—springs crackling, wheels rattling, and everybody yelling. The mounted archers began to shoot, though how they could have expected to hit anything I don't know; I suppose if the enemy was thickly massed they were bound to hit something. The enemy front line also consisted of chariotry, at least in the Asiatic territories; the two sets of chariots engaged, or one swept the other away; at any rate, the field was now cleared for the infantry, who came running up waving their axes, clubs, swords and daggers. Eventually, in the Egyptian narrative, the enemy broke and fled—to their city, if they had one close at hand. A siege usually followed, and it was sometimes maintained until the enemy was starved out. Thutmose III, who was a busy man and had a lot of cities to conquer, took some of them by storm. Judging from his accounts, clemency was the order of the day, not a brutal sack of the conquered city. Since it now belonged to Pharaoh, with all its people and their possessions, the common soldiers could not be allowed to loot it.

Some of the conquered peoples were chosen to serve the conquerors as soldiers rather than slaves. No doubt the Egyptians were glad to have mercenaries doing their fighting for them. The armies of the late period came to be made up more and more of foreign mercenaries. Such men had served Pharaoh at an earlier time; the famous Medjay, a Libyan tribe, became the royal bodyguard and the capital police. But not until the later Empire was a majority, perhaps, of the army made up of men whose only loyalty to Egypt came through their pay. What, if anything, this had to do with Egypt's later failures on the field of battle no one can say for sure, but it may have had its effect.

The army *coup d'état* is a familiar occurrence in some areas of the world; as far back as the Year of Four Emperors, when the Roman legions nominated their own Caesars, the army has been regarded as an entity capable of wielding political power. It is only natural that we should look for the same thing in Egypt after the rise of the professional army, and, since we are looking for it, naturally we find it. At the end of the Eighteenth Dynasty, after the fall of the royal house of Amarna, the throne of Egypt was held successively by two men who had, among other titles, that of "general." Harmhab served under Tutankhamon and perhaps under Akhenaton as well. By the time he assumed the Double Crown there was probably no man alive who had a legitimate claim, by birth and blood, to the kingship, but this does not explain why it was Harmhab, and not some other commoner, who won it. Harmhab had no sons, and his successor was another army man—if the identification of Ramses I with General Paramses is correct. It's all very confusing, but confusion is compounded by the fact that both Harmhab and Ramses were other things besides generals.

A similar case occurred at the end of the Twentieth Dynasty, when a man named Herihor turned up in Thebes with the resounding titles of Vizier of Upper Egypt and High Priest of Amon and removed—rather politely—the reins of power from the last of the feeble Ramesside kings. So for a long time the history books reported that the increasing power of the priesthood of Amon culminated in a theocracy which ruled at least part of Egypt. Then somebody noticed that before Herihor got to be High Priest he was Viceroy of Nubia and Commander of the Army. The religious coup became a military coup, and once again as in the case of Harmhab the army got the credit for controlling the state.

With all deference to the distinguished scholars who have

supported this interpretation, I cannot help but feel that it over-simplifies the ancient Egyptian scene, and forces modern view-points on a culture to which they were not applicable. The army, the bureaucracy, the church and the state—these categories were not as clear-cut in Egypt as they are today. We do not know how Herihor and Harmhab seized power, or which of their many titles conceals the real source of a strength great enough to enable them to mount the throne of the Two Lands. Their success may have been owing to their control of the army, or their high rank—or, for all we know, to their beautiful brown eyes.

## The Forts

We can't leave the subject of the army without mentioning forts. The best place to look for the ruins of fortresses is Nubia; eleven of them were built in a fifty-mile stretch near the Second Cataract of the Nile, during the Middle Kingdom. Perhaps the most impressive of the ruins are those at Semna, where the Nile passes, narrowly constricted, through a region of hard rock. Two forts, one on either side of the river, controlled traffic north and south. Semna West is the bigger of the two; Semna East, also called Kummeh, is opposite. These two have been excavated, but a third fort, Semna South, turned out to be impracticable for the expedition, under George Reisner, which worked on the other two forts. It seems that once a herdsman brought his two camels into the ruins of the fort to graze. He decided to take a nap, and when he awoke, groggy with sleep, he saw a white gazelle bound-ing along in front of him. He snatched his rifle and fired; and then discovered that the gazelle was really one of his own camels. This was not a small financial loss, it was a catastrophe, and the herdsman decided he must have offended some powerful spirit to be so afflicted. The ruined fort thus acquired a taboo, and none of the natives would work there. At least that was the story they told Reisner.

The three forts of Semna, plus another one three miles away, formed an administrative unit under the commander of Semna West, the biggest of the group. The excavator calculated that the four forts could have held at least 300 men, and perhaps twice that number, in view of the ability of the ancients to live in spaces we would consider impossibly cramped. Thus the commander could send out a force of from 150 to 200 men against local raiding parties, which would be the usual problem he had to contend with. In case of a serious widespread revolt, the Egyptians sat tight inside their walls and waited for reinforcements from home.

The forts were built to command the river, which was the main artery of traffic, military and commercial. The north-south road ran through the west fort at Semna so that the commander could keep an eye on land traffic as well. There were magazines and storehouses inside the fort, and it had a covered stair, protected by thick walls, leading down to the river so that water was obtainable even under siege. Semna would have been a hard place to take; the brick walls, six to eight meters thick and perhaps ten meters high, were bonded with heavy timbers to make them stronger. Square bastions projected at intervals, with towers on each corner; the reconstructions of such forts look amazingly like certain medieval castles. The tops of the walls have not survived, but we assume there was a walkway on top. Around the fort, except on the riverside, where it perched on top of the Nile cliffs, ran a wide ditch, the outer face revetted with dry masonry.

Inside the fort was a small town, complete with temple and a house for the commander. Some of the soldiers—the officers, perhaps—had their families with them. Assignment to one of these forts must have been received with hearty groans; at best it was dull duty, in an arid, unfriendly region. And there was always the chance that the wretched Cushites might annihilate the whole garrison.

All in all, perhaps the teachers of the scribal schools were right. The chances of booty and promotion were slight, and the "woes of the soldier" were great.

# IX

## Wielders of the Chisel and the Brush

### *Painting and Sculpture*

I WILL never forget my first sight of the late Professor Henri Frankfort, the day he walked into a classroom to begin a series of lectures on Near Eastern art and archeology. Physically he was not a big man, but his erect carriage and expressive features made him a dominant figure in any group. My most vivid memory of that day, however, is of the reading list and course outline which he passed out to us students. We had expected the usual names— Erman, Schäfer, Breasted, Capart. . . . They were there. Also on the list were Otto's *The Idea of the Holy,* van der Leeuw's *Religion in Essence and Manifestation,* and a number of other terrifying titles which seemed, offhand, to have absolutely no connection with Near Eastern archaeology.

Professor Frankfort's background should have prepared us for that reading list. Although he began as an excavator, in Egypt and in other parts of the Near East, and did excellent work in the more conventional aspects of fieldwork, he soon became interested in broader areas of study. He wrote on art and on religion, and in both he constantly stressed the necessity for Egyptologists to consult authorities outside their own necessarily limited field.

Over the years Egyptology had become a full-time job for a scholar. To an outsider it may seem very narrow; yet it is so complex that no living Egyptologist would claim to be a universal expert. New discoveries are constantly being made, new theories published; the language itself, like the ability to play the piano, requires daily practice in order to maintain proficiency. The result is specialization within specialization; if you approach one Egyptologist to ask his opinion on a scarab you bought in Egypt, he may pass you on to a colleague with the remark that "my field is plant ornament; so-and-so, at the Boston Museum, is the man for scarabs."

This being the case within Egyptology itself, you may imagine how wary Egyptologists are of venturing into other fields such as classical archaeology or anthropology. Yet most Egyptologists agree that it must be done. No field of history is isolated, and the broader one's background the more easily one may be able to see specific meanings. Some attempts have been made to solve the dilemma of specialization vs. generalization through symposia or conferences, where historians and scholars from other fields sit around a table sipping water and giving talks to one another. Despite the fact that the people who participate in these conferences are often brilliant scholars, I have yet to see one which I thought produced results, in the form of a genuine synthesis of ideas. Even in a symposium, scholars tend to talk in narrow terms about their own fields (which is natural enough, with a battery of experts waiting for the first mistake), and the scholars who listen to them can usually think of too many exceptions, in terms of *their* specialities, to allow of generalization. The ideal solution, which perhaps can never be realized, is to find one man who is a specialist in many fields at once.

If Henri Frankfort was not such a man, many of his admiring students thought he was. In recognizing the need for a broader approach, he did no more than many Egyptologists have done. But in trying, himself, to achieve some of the needed syntheses, he did something which few scholars are brave enough to do. His premature death deprived Egyptology of a talent which is sorely needed and whose absence is, perhaps, already being felt.

My motive for talking about Professor Frankfort is, in part, to offer a small and humble tribute to a great scholar, and also to prepare the reader for some of my prejudices in regard to Egyptian art. Any discussion of the subject is, inevitably, nonobjective, unless we restrict ourselves to a prosaic catalogue of Great Works; and anyone who has studied under an outstanding teacher is, inescapably, stamped forever afterwards with the impress of that teacher's ideas. Consciously I disagree with many of Frankfort's interpretations, but I will never be able to talk about ancient art without echoing him.

One other name must certainly be mentioned, however: that of Heinrich Schäfer. His book, *Von Ägyptischer Kunst*, is one of the basic works—perhaps *the* basic work—for anyone who wants to study Egyptian art as more than a catalogue of pretty pictures. The earlier editions of this book were printed in the old Gothic type which, together with Schäfer's extremely erudite German, made the perusal of his theories an arduous intellectual exercise. A new edition has appeared, in standard type; but it is a pity that such an important volume has not been translated.

Frankfort acknowledged his debt to Schäfer, but the two parted company on a basic point. Schäfer believed that in order to understand Egyptian art it was necessary to steep oneself in the culture, to probe deeply into Egyptian spiritual and ethical thought. The form of the art could not be understood without studying its content. A similar approach is followed by many art historians and art critics, not to mention critics of literature and music; a corollary is the biographical method, in which it is maintained that the artist's work cannot be apprehended without a knowledge of his life. Another critical school, however, argues that the artist's motives, his childhood experiences, and his cultural background are extraneous to a study of the work of art. Its form can have sufficient meaning in itself.

Frankfort believed that both approaches were necessary, but that the study of form must come first. He himself admitted one obvious difficulty—that while form and content can be separated in theory, it is not so easy to keep them apart in actual practice. I couldn't agree more.

Take a look at the illustration which shows the Egyptian style of drawing a walled garden with a pool. Above the Egyptian pool we have a modern perspective drawing of the same object, which should make clear to the reader, more conveniently than words could do, how the Egyptian style of representation differed from our own. The reality of the Egyptian drawing is not visual reality, yet no one would deny that it is reality, of a kind. All the parts of the garden are there: pool, trees, doors in the wall, duck in the pool. Not all these elements are visible in the perspective drawing, which is thus inferior to the Egyptian version with regard to the complete and accurate rendering of an object in all its parts.

One obvious characteristic of Egyptian two-dimensional art, which can be seen in our example, is the absence of foreshortening. This is brought out by the Egyptian way of drawing the human figure. Suppose you—and by "you" I mean an untrained, not particularly talented artist, like myself—suppose you want to draw a man. If you show him in front view you will run into several problems of foreshortening. Unless you are satisfied with a sort of blob, you, the untrained artist, cannot draw a nose that looks like a nose. Feet are even worse; they will look like wooden blocks. So you decide to draw your man in profile. Now the nose looks like a nose, and the feet have a certain resemblance to feet. But what are you going to do with the shoulders?

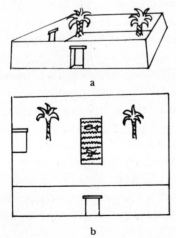

a

b

*Walled garden with pool*
a. modern perspective drawing; b. Egyptian version

What the Egyptians did was to combine two points of view—profile and front view. The face was drawn in profile with the eye in front view; the shoulders were again in front view and the feet in profile, but in between the body was gradually turned so that there was no abrupt change in point of view. The drawing of the garden combines the two points of view less ingeniously. It is really a combination of what we would call plan and elevation.

We may tend to be a little patronizing about the Egyptian style of drawing, considering it inferior to a style which understands and uses perspective. Schäfer was one of the people who pointed out that perspective drawing, instead of being the "right" way of drawing, is actually uncommon. It was discovered once, and only once—in Greece, in the fifth century B.C.; and only those cultures which came in contact, directly or indirectly, with Greek art learned to draw this way. This is Schäfer's interpretation; I repeat it for what it is worth without being able to prove it. But his main point is certainly correct; perspective drawing *is* unusual in those parts of the world which have no cultural connections with ancient Greece.

We do not find the use of perspective in two-dimensional art in any of the ancient cultures of the Near East. This does not mean that they were unaware of its effects. Their eyes were constructed just the way ours are, and they could see perfectly well that the farther away an object is from the beholder the smaller it is, and the higher it is. Then why didn't they draw things that way?

Perhaps because it was easier to draw things their way, without perspective? I find it easier; I can produce an acceptable Egyptian painting much more easily than I can produce a copy of da Vinci or Dürer. But surely this is an impossible answer, particularly for a civilization which built the Pyramids without mechanical power or iron tools.

It is at this point, I think, that the formal approach fails us. We can describe what we see in Egyptian paintings; but what we see is really meaningless unless we know why the particular forms were chosen. There are aesthetes who rhapsodize over Egyptian painting because of its purely formal qualities; and certainly it has many appeals. The colors are pretty, the drawing has the crisp assurance of long-established and accepted technique, some details appeal to the eye or to the emotions. But there is, I think, a touch of that condescension I mentioned earlier in these evaluations, a suggestion of "how quaint these primitives were!" Egyptian painting was not quaint, and it was not primitive. The rules of style, the "canon," were established by the middle of the second millennium B.C. and they were not altered until after the end of Egypt's existence as a distinct cultural entity. We may speak glibly about the static quality of Egyptian culture to explain this remarkable continuity; but the fact remains, that these rules would not have been followed for so long unless they had satisfied the demands of the society. What those demands were we must now try to investigate.

To begin with, we must remember that a good deal of Egyptian art was funerary, and thus utilitarian, not aesthetic, in function. The tomb paintings were not meant to make the place look pretty. They insured that the dead man would be provided with all the objects and all the pleasures which the paintings depicted. Primitive art in general is thought to have had its origin in magic. The wonderful cave paintings of European prehistory, like those at Lascaux, were not made by a Neanderthal Pinturicchio, commissioned by Ug the chief to adorn his mansion. Many of them are stuck away in dark, unfrequented corners. Experts believe that by depicting the animals desired for food the prehistoric artists were invoking magical laws which promised them a successful hunt.

Now if magic is at the basis of art, including Egyptian art, it is important that the object be shown as complete and whole, so that nothing vital is missing when the spiritual similacrum is given to the soul of the deceased. As we saw in the drawings of the garden, the Egyptian version shows the whole garden, with the pool. The perspective drawing cannot show the pool, and so the spiritual garden of the dead man, in the land of the West, might lack this desirable feature.

This is the conventional explanation for the "why" of Egyptian painting. There are two objections to it: one is the old quibble, that we can never be sure that our analyses of the motives of dead and dust aliens are correct; the other is that the magical thesis does not explain all the eccentricities of Egyptian two-dimensional art. If you want to draw a "whole" man, and make sure that no essential part of him will be missing when he is reborn into eternal life, you do not show his head in profile. The Egyptian version gives a man two shoulders, two arms, two legs, and a body; but it deprives him of one eye and one ear. The Egyptians could draw heads in front view; one of the common hieroglyphs takes this form, and the little god Bes is always depicted from the front, face and all. So perhaps the theory of magical utility is only a partial answer to our "why."

I ought to apologize for muddying up a neat clear explanation with objections, but it is vitally important, I think, to see that history is not a series of questions and answers. It is a series of questions, to which there are sometimes answers, sometimes other questions, and sometimes just a despairing shrug of the shoulders. The whole point of historical research is to put something in the place of those shrugs. Someday someone will come up with an answer to all the problems of Egyptian art. In the meantime, the notion of magical utility does give us a clue, if not a complete explanation.

The magical approach can be applied to the study of sculpture as well as of painting. Some of the statues of gods and kings in our museums come from temples, but the others, particularly statues of private persons, were meant for the tombs. The utility of a tomb statue is easy to explain in magical terms; in a culture which put so much stress on the preservation of the body, we may reasonably assume that some sort of physical representation of the dead man was a prerequisite for eternal life. If the mummy were damaged or destroyed, a handsome statue could be an acceptable substitute.

Whether they were primarily magical or not, Egyptian works of art were more than just utilitarian; they were also beautiful. Many people find the sculpture of ancient Egypt easier to enjoy than the painting, since it was not affected by the absence of perspective which distorts—for our eyes—the two-dimensional art. There was a canon for sculpture as well as for painting; both were set early in Egyptian history, and both were followed for two thousand years. The essential quality of Egyptian sculpture, which strikes most beholders at once, is its squareness. When you look at a statue you can almost see the block it was cut out of. The Law of Frontality applies, since most statues were set up against a wall, and were meant to be seen—if they were seen at all—from the front; but a statue may be subject to this law and still not be "square." In Egyptian statues almost all the lines are right angles or parallels. A seated statue—one of the most popular poses—was particularly "square." Right angles at hips and knees, straight legs, rigid back and stiff neck—there is never any twisting of the torso or turning of the head. It is all straight up and down.

Another general remark which applies to Egyptian sculpture in the round of all periods is that the body is not treated in detail. Musculature is barely indicated; the torso is a series of smooth planes, the legs and arms are shaped columns. Even when, in the late period, an attempt was made to show musculature, it was as formalized and lifeless as the Assyrian sculpture of approximately the same period. It is hard to find the right word for this phenomenon, because the terms we might be tempted to use have misleading connotations. Some scholars say Egyptian sculpture is abstract; this always makes me think of the blocks of concrete filled with holes, called "Woman Nursing Child" or "Aspiration," which may be found in modern art museums. Egyptian sculpture is too close to reality to be called abstract. We can't call this treatment "sketchy," either; it is too complete and too finished. It is better to avoid such labels altogether.

My own personal impression of these statues is that they are lifeless. They are not dead, but frozen, caught in a single moment of eternity. There are bones under the smooth polished skin, but no nerves, no tendons, and only a few big muscles. The muscles are in a timeless repose; they do not function. In form, the torsos and limbs of most of the statues might have been turned out of the same mold. When variation does occur, it tends to become standardized: three rolls of fat around the middle to indicate plumpness, and so on.

If this is true of the bodies—for me at least—what about the heads? I have already hinted at my own prejudice in regard to the question of portraiture in ancient Egyptian art; I do not believe that exact likeness was an essential aim of Egyptian "portrait"

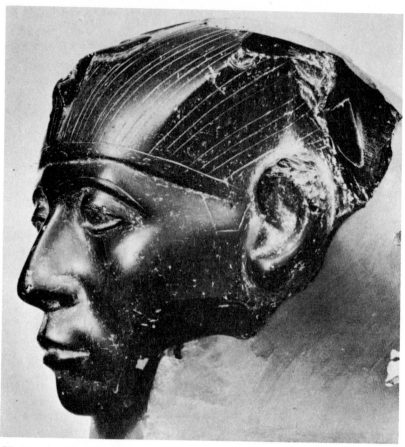

Head of a Twelfth Dynasty King (Senusert III?). *Fundação Calouste Gulbenkian, Lisbon.*

sculpture. To some extent that interpretation is subjective; but I cannot resist the opportunity of reproducing, for the reaction of the reader, two so-called "portrait" heads from two different cultures. The Egyptian head shown is that of a Middle Kingdom ruler, unidentified by inscriptional evidence. The other photograph is a bust of the Roman emperor Caracalla. To my eye there is a great deal of difference between these two "portraits"; I have the feeling that if I met Caracalla's bust attached to a body and strolling down the street I would recognize the fellow at once. Even the trunkless stone heads have unique identities as they balance on their necks on the shelves of Roman museums; the merest

Caracalla. *The National Museum of Naples. Photo by Alinari.*

amateur soon learns to recognize the chill beauty of Augustus, the wide-eyed glare of Caracalla, and the pudgy, narrow-lipped face of Vespasian.

The Egyptians? Perhaps we might know some of them. I think I would recognize Akhenaton; for one thing, he doesn't look like any other pharaoh. But what did he really look like? In the flesh? Like the strange Karnak colossus, with its elongated face and diabolic mouth, or the sensitive, melancholy miniature from the Louvre?

Some Egyptologists feel that they can recognize their friends the pharaohs, and they confidently label statues, or fragments thereof, with specific royal names on the basis of resemblance to other, known statues. Perhaps these scholars have a more skilled eye than mine; long experience gives an expert a feeling for relationships and resemblances which may be valid even though it cannot always be made explicit. Yet this sort of scholarship can be treacherous; fancied resemblances have been used as the basis for elaborate theories of family connections, usurpations, invasions, and conquests for which there is no textual evidence. The eye is easily misled by the unfortunate tendency to see, not what is actually there, but what it wishes or expects to see. Any parent of a newborn infant knows, for instance, that the poor child may be identified as the "spitting image" of half a dozen different, doting relatives.

Although I am willing to admit that the experts may be right and I may be wrong, I think there is more evidence in favor of my prejudice than in favor of theirs. Egyptian sculpture can be classified into periods with distinctive stylistic attributes. The heads of Old Kingdom monarchs suggest the divinity of kingship: calm, assured, inhumanly regal, the finely cut features might be those of a god. The Middle Kingdom Senuserts and Amenemhats have lined, careworn faces. In the New Kingdom there is a softening, not necessarily of purpose, but of contour, a greater smoothness and sophistication. It does not require an expert to tell an Old Kingdom head from one made in the Nineteenth Dynasty. But this very difference tends to obscure the fact that heads of the same period look a great deal alike.

In point of fact, even the experts often fail to agree on the identity of a particular head unless it is inscribed. No one could possibly mistake a bust of Tiberius for a portrait of Augustus; but the same head has been identified by different scholars as a portrait of Akhenaton, his successor Smenkhkare, and his wife Nefertiti.

One point which supports our contention that exact resemblance between a statue and its owner was not important is the frequency of usurpation of statues. If one king wanted to "borrow" the statue of one of his predecessors he did not—as the Romans did in reliefs—remodel the features of the head. He simply cut his name over that of the original owner.

This brings us to our final argument—the special efficacy of the name as a means of identification. The spoken and written word had magical power. A man's name was more than a handy label, it was an integral part of himself, carrying a spark of his own essence. To have one's name remembered was a necessity for survival after death; if only the name survived, something of the man lived on. The inscription of a statue with this magic spell, the name, gave the stone not only identity, but a sort of animation. The necessity for portraiture, for likeness, was not so strong.

And yet, says the informed reader, there are genuine portrait sculptures from ancient Egypt. They *look* like portraits. Some, though uninscribed, are identified beyond any reasonable doubt—Nefertiti, Queen Ti, Amenemhat III. . . .

There are exceptions. There are sculptured heads which certainly look like portraits—the Sheikh el Beled, Queen Ti, perhaps a dozen others. It would be ridiculous to claim that Egypt never produced a single portrait statue; whatever the canon and its requirements, the talents and tastes of individual artists varied widely. From time to time a skillful sculptor did produce a work of art which suggests portraiture, in the strictest sense of the word. The trouble is, we don't know *whom* the heads are portraits *of*. In the case of Queen Ti, to take only one example, we can be fairly sure of the general period to which the head should be dated. But a few scholars think the lady in question is not Ti, but rather her daughter, Sitamon. The features do bear a vague resemblance to other so-called portraits of Ti, which are identified by name; but then Sitamon may have resembled her mother.

162 *Red Land, Black Land*

I think the reader would be surprised to learn how shaky many of the accepted identifications of sculptured heads really are. Unless they are inscribed, the ones that are "certain" ought to be labeled with a question mark, and the ones that have question marks probably should not have names at all. Many of these latter cases are Amarna heads; scholars who are reasonably rational about other periods seem to go all to pieces over Akhenaton and his family. An example that I find particularly vexing is that of a little female figure which forms part of one of Tutankhamon's elaborate ornaments. The object is a boat, carrying a female dwarf and the little woman in question. She is a dainty, decorative person, slim and naked, kneeling in the prow of the boat. There is no reason to suppose that she was ever meant to be an individual rather than an ornament, much less a member of the royal family. Yet you will sometimes find her labeled *Mutnedjmet, the sister of Nefertiti (?)*. The question mark seems to be regarded as a magic sign which legitimizes a wild guess and turns it into a scholarly theory. The same magic sign is applied to many of the Amarna heads which were found in a sculptor's abandoned workshop. Not a single piece bears a name or an inscription, yet some scholars claim they can recognize almost all the members of the royal family. I admire the enthusiasm of these historians, but I remain unconvinced by their labels, even with question marks.

All this debate about portraiture is fun, but it is not really important; a head need not be a portrait to be great art, and some of the Egyptian statues are truly great art.

I have said that there are changes in style over a period of time, and this is true. Yet we talk about an art form which covered two millennia as a unity. This is oversimplification, of course, but I am sure that even this cursory discussion will seem complicated to a non-Egyptologist who only wants to learn enough to identify the art works he sees in museums. Yet in one sense we are justified in oversimplifying, for, although details varied from century to century, the basic rules did not change. These rules—or canons—fixed not only the form of sculpture and painting, but the poses and postures as well. The canon applied most rigidly to persons of rank. The lower the individual in the social scale, the more freely he could be portrayed; children and animals were just about at

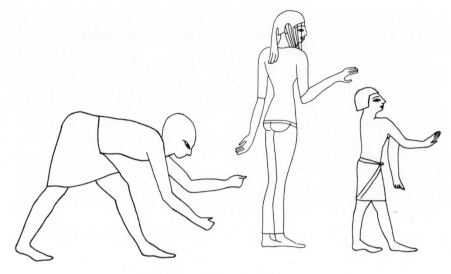

*Deviations from the canon*

the bottom of the scale, and that is one reason why Egyptian animals and birds are particularly charming. They could fly and prance and crawl and flutter without injuring a dignity they did not possess. Servants were fairly undignified, so they could be shown indulging in activities which were not proper for the nobility. The small tomb models of the First Intermediate Period show bakers and butchers and weavers animatedly engaged in various aspects of their work, and tomb paintings include quite a variety of poses, including wrestling, dancing and acrobatics. Our illustration shows a few such deviations from the canonical rules; some are really delightful, and they indicate that Egyptian artists were not as limited as one might think. Other attempts were not so successful.

While the servants work and cavort, the nobleman and his wife sit or stand in stiff aloofness, removed from the reality of the scene. The seated and standing postures were the most popular for persons of dignity, but they were also allowed to kneel, before the gods or the king. The king, being more dignified than anyone else, only knelt to the gods. Another favorite pose during certain periods was that of the "seated scribe"—a man sitting cross-legged with his kilt drawn taut across his knees and his shoulders slightly bowed. There are few recumbent Egyptians in our artistic representations, except dead ones. The mummy, of course, lies flat, and the anthropoid coffin itself might be regarded as a sculptured, supine figure. Limited as they are, these poses are eminently satisfactory—dignified, stately, and sometimes graceful.

If the canon applied rigidly to the pose of the kings, it was equally inflexible about the royal physique. The divine ruler was supposed to be handsome, with a body as shapely as that of an Apollo. This is the form of the king's statues—almost always.

### Amarna Art

Inflexible as they were, the formal rules of art relaxed during certain periods. During the First Intermediate Period, a time of political anarchy, one finds greater freedom—as well as clumsier technique—in the poses allowed to lesser beings. But the period of innovation par excellence is the age of Akhenaton, the heretic, or monotheist, or whatever he may be called. We refer to the art of this period as Amarna art, and it is sufficiently different from the canonical style to require detailed commentary.

The most shocking change, perhaps, is the collapse of the king's physique. If we stroll through the halls of the Cairo Museum contemplating kings—Menkaure, the Senuserts, the Thutmoses—we see them all as similar in shape—broad-shouldered, slim of waist and hip, straight and strong. Then—we come upon Akhenaton, with his pot belly, his sagging breasts, his elongated skull and spindly shanks! Carrying tact to an unnecessary extreme, the nobility of his court asked to be represented in the same way, so the tomb reliefs of the period teem with oddly shaped people. Postures too are radically different in Amarna art. Tutankhamon is shown leaning on his staff or slouching—in the royal throne! Akhenaton kisses his wife and bounces his children. There is an overall relaxation of the older rigidity, a greater use of curved lines in the representation of the human figure and in plant forms, one might even say a loosening of rules, which may be interpreted as charming freedom or dreadful decadence, depending on one's general attitude toward Akhenaton and his new ideas.

Here again we must do some delving in the historical and cultural background in order to understand what is going on. The answer can only be tentative; but the clue probably lies in the word *ma'at*, usually translated as "truth," which was the *leitmotiv* of Akhenaton's reign. He lived by truth, and honored truth; and if we only knew what he meant by "truth," we would know a lot more than we do about the motives and the psychology of one of the most dramatic figures in all Egyptian history. Unfortunately, *ma'at*, like our own "truth," means a lot of different things. Most Egyptologists deny that Akhenaton's *ma'at* had a profound ethical or philosophical meaning; it was not that eternal truth which makes men free, it was probably not even justice. Usually, in the Amarna context, it is taken to mean "candor." As applied to the new art forms, it meant an increased effort to show the world as it really looked.

Assuming that the word *ma'at* is the key to an understanding of Amarna art, we are still a long way from knowing how to use that key. Schäfer saw in Amarna art an increased emotional content, an expressiveness—not, please, expressionism—of feeling. Frankfort admitted the expressiveness, but viewed it as a secondary result—the result of the *ma'at*, "candor," which demanded a more literal rendering of reality.

Both these interpretations leave me slightly dissatisfied; but I lean toward Schäfer because, in fact, Amarna art never really challenged the basic canons of formal art. Grotesque as the forms may be, unusual as the poses may appear, they are distortions, not violations, of the old forms and the old poses. Sculpture is softer, and more rounded; but it is still frontal and still, despite the deceptive suggestion of curves, essentially straight up and down. Painting and relief give the human body in the familiar combination of profile and front view, house and palace plans are the same confusing blend of plan and elevation. Of course the court artists were used to working in this style, and most of them would have found it utterly impossible to break away from it, but I cannot help suspecting, particularly in view of earlier successful, if spasmodic, attempts at deviation from the canon, that a talented young painter could have made a closer approximation to visual reality if that had been what the king was demanding. Akhenaton wanted something different from the old formal style, assuredly; but what he wanted we may never know until we know more about the man and his time.

Amarna art may, in some cases, strike a modern viewer as less pleasing than the canonical style. The plant and animal forms attract us because of their increased freedom; but the human figure still has the disadvantages of the unfamiliar perspective (or lack of it), plus the new distortions which rob the body, male or female, of its grace. The two little Amarna princesses, who are often reproduced and admired, are really horrors. Their bodies are boneless, their arms and legs have a rubbery flaccidity, and their long, naked skulls suggest a pair of extraterrestrials out of H. G. Wells. I take exception, also, to the admirers of this work who claim that it represents childhood successfully. Like most artists, including the immortal Greeks, the Egyptians depicted children as miniature adults. The proportions of babies are nonhuman; their heads are too big and their stomachs stick out. In some reliefs all the Amarna people look like children, for the exaggeration of head size is an oft-encountered facet of this art form, and Akhenaton's protruding abdomen, copied by his fawning courtiers, also gives these people a superficially childlike appearance. The Amarna princesses are not children, they are Amarna people, and they look like unhealthy people at that. I must end my diatribe on the little princesses by mentioning that this is one of my favorite Egyptian paintings. I have an enormous copy of it, in color, and the only reason why it is not on my wall is because the other members of my family cannot abide it.

In both painting and sculpture Amarna art went through several distinct stages of development, even in its brief lifetime. The softening of forms began before Akhenaton's reign; one statue of his father, Amenhotep III, shows a flabby corpulent body wrapped in a thin pleated robe which shows its unkingly physique only too clearly. This little statue probably does involve an attempt at visual reality; it looks like the body (the head is, unfortunately, missing) of an elderly man who has lived too well. By the first years of Akhenaton's reign, this "candor," if we want to

Two princesses. Fragment of a relief from Tell el Amarna. In the original the little girls were shown sitting at the feet of their parents, Akhenaton and Nefertiti. *The Department of Antiquities, Ashmolean Museum, Oxford.*

call it that, has turned into something which could almost be termed caricature. The most striking examples are a group of colossal statues which Akhenaton had made for a temple at Thebes. His face is impossibly elongated, with a hanging chin and a disturbing smile; his body shows what seems to be a pathological condition, in extreme form. While they are ugly, these statues are extremely evocative, and it may be that they appeal to some people as great art. Perhaps the reason why they strike most Egyptologists as grotesque is that they are in Osirid form, and the contrast between the classic, sacred image of the god and the brutal violation of his traditional shape is almost painful to the trained eye.

As we all know, Akhenaton soon shook the dust of Thebes off his sandals and built a new capital city in a virgin spot where his cherished god could be worshiped in peace. There at Amarna the

Headless statue bearing the name of Amenhotep III. Note the fringed robe and pleated over-mantle. *The Metropolitan Museum of Art, The Theodore M. Davis Collection. Bequest of Theodore M. Davis, 1915.*

distinctive art developed forms of great beauty without the exaggeration of the earliest efforts. Tell el Amarna has been excavated by several groups, but it was Ludwig Borchardt, working under the auspices of the Deutsche Orient-Gesellschaft, who turned up the most exciting object found in the ruins of Akhenaton's short-lived capital. (Exciting does not mean important; the Amarna letters must claim that second distinction.) He found it in the debris of what had been the workshop of a sculptor named Thutmose.

Thutmose lived and worked in the same house, perhaps using one room as a storeroom or display chamber. He was still living at Amarna when Akhenaton died. Within a few years the exodus from the doomed city began. At first the inhabitants thought the removal back to Thebes was only temporary. They followed the court, locking up their houses and taking with them only personal possessions. Later it became evident that the city which had enshrined Akhenaton's jealous god would never be tolerated by the followers of Amon-Re. Some of the house-owners returned to Amarna and cleared away all their possessions, even carrying off door frames and columns to use in the new houses they were building in Thebes. In other cases, possibly scavengers cleared the houses of the rich; very little in the way of furniture, jewelry, or personal possessions has been found at the site. But for some reason or other Thutmose's workshop was not completely cleared. The German archaeologists surmised that Thutmose may have gathered together all the unclaimed or unfinished pieces he had on hand, and then locked up the house and left them.

Among these abandoned pieces of sculpture was the great bust of Queen Nefertiti, which has been reproduced in every medium from postcards to dress material. She really is beautiful, with her long, arched throat and faintly smiling face, tinted with the colors of life. When she made her first appearance in the Berlin Museum a loud shout of admiration arose from all the world. One voice in the general clamor, however, did not express admiration. It came from the Egyptian Government, and it said, in essence: "How did she get there?"

Ever since Mariette's time there have been strict laws in Egypt regarding the export of antiquities. Foreign archaeological expeditions are supposed to spread out their finds, at the end of the working season, for the inspection of a man from the Department of Antiquities. He makes his selection, and the expedition gets only what he chooses to give them, unless other arrangements are made in advance. The general rule is that the Egyptian Government keeps the unique objects and shares the rest.

In the case of Nefertiti, the Egyptian Government maintained that it never would, never could, let such a unique treasure out of the country. This is probably true. I have heard several stories about the escape (or kidnapping) of Nefertiti, and it is hard to make out precisely what did happen. The archaeologists of the Deutsche Orient-Gesselschaft insisted that the whole thing had been open and aboveboard. By the terms of their agreement with the Antiquities Department they were entitled to all artworks recognized as models or pattern pieces. Nefertiti was there, on the table with all the rest of the objects; her unique beauty was obviously not recognized by the participants in the final reckoning, and she was passed on to the excavators with the other models.

Seeing Nefertiti as she is today, it is hard to believe that an inspector could have failed to recognize her as unique unless he was drunk, blind in both eyes, or—but we will not mention a word which might be actionable. However, we must bear in mind that she did not have all her elegant beauty when she was dredged out of the wreckage of Thutmose's studio. Possibly—to be charitable about it—the government inspector was just not very alert. If he really did miss Nefertiti, one could hardly expect the excavators to take him aside and carefully point out that he had overlooked one of the masterpieces of Egyptian sculpture. An archaeologist who did such a thing would merit canonization for inhuman altruism.

The rights and wrongs of the case of Nefertiti cannot easily be determined, especially since they are involved with the larger, and rather touchy, question of the division of antiquities. In most Near Eastern countries the host country claims the right of decision, and if it chooses to keep *all* the objects found, nobody can argue with it. The claims of the host country are indisputable; it owns the land. But what about the claims of the excavator, who contributes time, money, expertise, and elbow grease? *Scientia gratia scientia* is all very well, but the museums which sponsor

Head of Wesir-wer. Egypt, fourth century B.C. *The Brooklyn Museum, Charles Edwin Wilbour Fund.*

archaeological expeditions must have some return for their money. Another important consideration is the availability of the material. For scholars there are certain advantages in a single great collection; they do not have to travel all over the world to see what they want to see. But not everyone can visit the Near East, and there are a lot of people who are interested in Near Eastern archaeology. Dispersal in one sense is a service, since it makes it possible for greater numbers of people to see and enjoy the masterpieces of ancient cultures. The problem is not a simple one; but even if I were sure that someone had kidnapped Nefertiti I would not be inclined to throw stones at him as long as he kidnapped her in order to put her on public display. I don't think I would have been able to resist her either.

After the Amarna heresies were obliterated by the orthodox successors of Tutankhamon, art returned to its old forms. There are suggestions of the Amarna softness in some of the Nineteenth Dynasty pieces, but no more than suggestions. Under the vigorous Cushite kings of the Twenty-Fifth Dynasty a striking new sculptural technique appears alongside the older one. A few heads of this period combine a smooth polished surface with hard, precisely defined facial planes. During the following Saite dynasty this method produced some striking pieces of sculpture, but Saite art is, for the most part, a deliberate imitation of the great periods of the past. Foreign contacts had little effect on art, except in decorative motifs, and the splendid Greek art, even after the conquest of Alexander, produced in Egypt only second-rate provincial Greek imitations or peculiar amalgamations of the two techniques. Perhaps it was impossible for Egyptian art to be influenced by alien styles; when it abandoned its ancient canon, it was no longer Egyptian art.

## The Artist

We have been talking about painting and sculpture in the round exclusively, so that it may seem that we have neglected the elegant Egyptian relief sculpture. However, most of the general

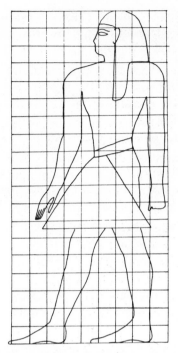

*The human figure, Egyptian style*

remarks we have made about painting apply equally well to relief, since it was also two-dimensional. Most Egyptian relief sculpture is very low relief, and it was usually painted as well. When we admire the wall reliefs in the Old Kingdom tombs, with their delicate rendering of forms, we tend to forget that in many cases the relief sculptor's skill was covered over by that of the artist painter.

Before the sculptor began carving a scene on the wall of a tomb or temple, the surface to be decorated was carefully smoothed, and any cracks or holes were filled with plaster. If the stone being used was of poor quality, the whole wall might be covered with a thin coating of plaster. When the plaster was dry, the outline draftsman—as we translate his title—made his appearance. His task was to draw the outlines of the scene upon the plastered wall. To insure accuracy, and to follow the canon of correct proportions, he used a grid, which was applied directly upon the wall surface before the actual drawing was begun. The intervals between the lines of the grid were measured by means of an instrument similar to a ruler or straight-edge, but the lines themselves were made by a string dipped in red ochre, held taut, and then plucked, like a bowstring. With the same red ochre the artist then drew his figures, using the squares of the grid to guide him. Two of the grids have been found. They differ slightly in their relative proportions, but according to one, a human being was nineteen squares high from soles to crown. Specific parts of the body, such as the foot, forearm, and torso, also had their proper size in terms of grid squares. This was a practical and ingenious technique, for it could be used to draw figures of any magnitude; the artist merely decreased the size of the squares for small figures and enlarged them when an immense king or god was required. Our Figure X shows one of these grids; they can still be seen, by sharp-eyed tourists, on a few Egyptian monuments.

When the outline draftsman had packed up and gone home, the relief sculptor took over. His usual method was to cut away the background, leaving the figures in relief, but sometimes sunken reliefs were made. From time to time an ingenious or lazy sculptor discovered that he could cut away only that part of the background which lay immediately next to the figure and then smooth it out gradually into the wall surface. This saved a lot of time and effort, but the best reliefs were not done that way.

After he had cut out the forms, the sculptor finished the surfaces, indicating details of clothing and musculature, but the real finishing detail was left to the third and last technician, the painter, who may or may not have been the same as the outline draftsman. His palette varied from age to age, but it was always relatively simple, and it was restricted by certain conventions. Clothing was painted white, hair black, human skin red for men or yellow for women. With the humble animals he was allowed a wider scope, and there his ingenuity showed up best. The brilliant birds are among the most delightful characters in Egyptian reliefs; they have been so accurately drawn that the species can be identified, but the colors applied to them were not always those of nature. Attempts to indicate the texture of feathers or fur, and even the rounding of the body, have been discovered in certain animal paintings.

The painter's brush was made out of a length of fibrous wood pounded at one end to separate the fibers into a bristlelike brush. He used different brushes for different colors; these were almost always mineral-based pigments, which is one reason why so much ancient painting has survived so well. The black color was usually carbon; the other popular tints derived from green malachite and red and yellow ochre. The ground minerals were mixed with a vehicle, which was not an oil but an adhesive; Egyptian painting was tempera, not oil painting. The precise adhesive used is uncertain, not because of the mysterious lost art of the Egyptian painter, but because it is hard to analyze a minute proportion of a substance in a minute chunk of paint. One of the adhesives used was certainly beeswax, either mixed with the pigment as a binder or applied over the finished painting as a protective coating. Sometimes varnish was used for the latter purpose; it must have seemed like a good idea at the time, but it has usually turned yellow or brown, obscuring the original brilliant colors.

All sorts of things were painted—boxes, chairs, columns, floors of palaces, walls of temples—but the majority of great Egyptian paintings come from the tombs. So do many, if not most, of the great works of sculpture.

The great majority of Egyptian statues are made of stone, a material which admirably suits the stiff angularity of the style. Unfinished pieces show that the outline of the statue was drawn on all four sides of the block, and the whole figure was roughed out before final details were done. The sculptor's tools were of copper; he used chisels and drills and saws. After the statue was

*Artist at work*

finished, it was polished with an abrasive stone or sand, and then painted. Limestone and other soft stone statues were painted all over, with the usual white for clothing and red or yellow for skin. Statues of hard stone such as granite or basalt, which were prized for the beauty of the texture, were only picked out in paint—eyebrows might be painted black, or the details of a headdress or crown indicated. Sometimes details were added by insets of other materials. The eyes were often inlaid, so well that a certain number of Egyptian statues have quite an unnerving stare.

Other materials were also used for sculpture. Some of the handsomest statues we have from Egypt are of wood; the head of Queen Ti (?) and the Sheikh el Beled are outstanding examples. The metal statues are perhaps less well known than those of wood or stone, and they deserve mention because they represent impressive craftmanship. As early as the Sixth Dynasty, Egyptian metalworkers produced a greater than life size statue of Pepi I, with a smaller one of his son, in copper. It is not certain how this statue was made; it was probably hammered rather than cast. By the Late Period, statues of bronze, and even gold, are found, and these were certainly cast by the well-known *cire perdue* method, in which a wax model is covered with a mold and heated. The wax melts and runs out through a hole left for that purpose, and the metal is poured into the resultant vacant space. Hollow or solid statues can be cast by this method, the former employing a core of some material under the wax; hollow statues, naturally, were cheaper than solid ones. One of the best of the Egyptian bronze statues is that of the lady Takushet of the Twenty-Fifth Dynasty; the designs with which she appears to be tattooed represent the decorations of her elegant robe, and they are inlaid into the copper in silver.

Having discussed the works of art, we ought to say a few words about the artists. The praise that is their due must be given them as a group citation, and anonymously, for few names of individual painters and sculptors have come down to us, and even those few can rarely be connected with a given painting or statue. There is not a single signed work of art from ancient Egypt, unless we view the rough figures of Senmut, hidden behind the sanctuary doors of the temple he is thought to have designed, as equivalents of

The Lady Takushet.
*The National Museum of Athens. Photo by Alinari.*

"Senmut *fecit.*" Tradition, or the circumstances of discovery, sometimes allow us to ascribe names to particular pieces; perhaps Thutmose of el Amarna can claim the beautiful head of Nefertiti as his *chef-d'oeuvre,* but we cannot be sure. Names of other artists have survived, though not in connection with their work. Bak, the sculptor of Akhenaton, "whom His Majesty himself taught," gives us a tantalizing hint about the heretic king; was Akhenaton a dilettante sculptor as well as a religious fanatic? Then there was Iritsen, who lived during the Middle Kingdom and who was, if we can believe his own words, a sculptor of no mean talent:

> I am a craftsman successful in his craft, one who comes out on top through that which he knows. . . . I know the movement of a figure, the stride of a woman . . . the cringing of the solitary captive, how one eye looks at another, how to make frightened the face of the outlaw, the pose of the arm of him who harpoons the hippopotamus, the pace of the runner.

The word craftsman, which Iritsen uses, is important because it describes the status of sculptors and painters. Their trade lacked the semimystical sanctity of the "fine arts"; it was not even a profession, but a craft, on a level with carpentry and jewelry-making. Within the general category of art there were specializations: the painter, the outline draftsman, the relief sculptor, and the sculptor in the round. In the workshops connected with the palace and the temples these craftsmen worked together under the supervision of the chief sculptor and the overseer of craftsmen. There was division of labor; one man might carve a statue and another man paint it. But perhaps there was not strict "union" separation of jobs. A single individual might learn all the aspects of his craft, and be outline draftsman, painter and sculptor in turn, with the hope of working up at last to the supervisory position of overseer of craftsmen. There are several indications that sculptors were regarded as superior to painters; for one thing, the tombs, stelae and other monuments left by successful sculptors far outnumber those left by painters, which implies that they were richer and more prominent.

Most artists, and certainly the best of them, worked for the state. Sometimes the king might order a statue or even a whole tomb to be made for a friend or good servant, as a mark of favor, but there were also artists whose services could be obtained by the private citizen. Were these the state artists, "moonlighting," or was there a class of privately employed artists? We don't know. The same mystery surrounds the training of artists. Since workshops existed it is not unreasonable to suppose that "likely" boys were sent to them for training. I imagine that the boys were chosen because of family connections rather than special talent. In many cases known to us son followed father in the trade, as he did in other trades and professions. It is the apprentice system in operation once again, with the father as the master. Yet some artists obviously took pride in their trade and enjoyed using their talents. Although the canon of art was limiting there was room for the exercise of both skill and imagination; the great works of art surviving from Egypt show that although genius may not have been recognized as such, some ancient Michelangelos did find their way into the trade which was, for them, a genuine calling.

## The Architects

The monumental achievements of Egyptian architects are still dramatically visible along the Nile; of all the aspects of Egyptian culture the temples and tombs perhaps make the greatest impression, and live longest in the memories of visiting tourists.

Evidently building temples was considered a more respectable occupation than carving statues. At any rate, the men who built them mentioned these achievements in their tomb biographies. We can thus attach names to specific structures, which is not the case with statues. The tomb of Thutmose I was constructed by a man named Ineni; the Karnak obelisks of Thutmose III were erected by his official Puemre. Of all the names that have survived, three stand out above the rest; no account of Egyptian architecture would be complete without them.

The first, and perhaps the foremost, was Imhotep, Vizier and Overseer of Works for King Djoser of the remote Third Dynasty. To this man probably belongs the credit for the Step Pyramid,

Djoser's massive tomb, which still dominates the site of Sakkara. Not only was the Step Pyramid a major engineering work, it was, so far as we know, a creative original—the first pyramid, and the first attempt to build on a grandiose scale in stone. Imhotep's talents were not limited to architecture. Later generations of Egyptians honored him as a sage and master physician, and eventually he was worshiped, in this latter capacity, as a veritable god. The Greeks identified him with Aesculapius.

So fabulous were Imhotep's achievements, and so remote the time in which he lived, that some scholars used to doubt his existence. A few years ago a statue base with Imhotep's name, found in the Step Pyramid enclosure, not only solidified him historically but tied him in specifically with the great monument which tradition had long ascribed to him. And for a while it was hoped we were on the brink of a discovery which would give the long-dead genius real identity as a historical personage.

The story of the discovery begins over twenty years ago, when Professor W. B. Emery, the distinguished excavator of the archaic tombs of Sakkara, had a little time left over at the end of his digging season. He had long been interested in a particular part of the site, the westernmost section of the archaic cemetery of North Sakkara. The archaic cemetery contains tombs of the very ancient First to Third Dynasties, and yet, in one place, the surface of the ground was covered with broken bits of pottery which dated from the Graeco-Roman period. As we know, the worship of Imhotep was very popular in Graeco-Roman times; and scholars have long believed that if a tomb of Imhotep existed, it would be in this archaic cemetery, where the other nobles of his period were buried. So, just before closing down his dig in 1956, Emery sunk two test pits in the area. The pits showed Third Dynasty brickwork. They also brought up the remains of sacrificed bulls, and ibis mummies.

The ibis, the long-legged bird sacred to Thoth, was one of the attributes of this god taken over by Imhotep when he attained divine rank. The evidence, then, looked promising. But it was not until 1964 that Professor Emery was able to pursue his investigations. What he found was both unexpected and significant.

The whole area was covered with tombs dating from the

Archaic Period and the Old Kingdom. In Ptolemaic times their walls had been leveled, and the spaces between the tombs filled in, to form a huge flat surface. Why was this done? A reasonable explanation is that the leveled site was the platform for a big building, perhaps a temple. The sacrificed bulls, although they could have been tomb offerings, might have been foundation deposits for such a building.

The excavators proceeded to clear some of the tombs. In the burial shaft of one, thirty-five feet below the ground, they literally fell through into a fantastic underground structure—a vast stone-cut labyrinth, like the Serapeum of Sakkara where the mummies of the sacred bulls were buried. The chambers of Emery's structure also contained mummies—thousands upon thousands of ibis birds, embalmed and placed in pottery jars.

A later season of excavation uncovered galleries of mummified baboons—like the ibis, sacred to Thoth and his godson Imhotep. The baboon burials were those of sacred temple animals; the chests containing the mummies bore short demotic inscriptions giving the animal's name and the date of its burial. Also found were plaster casts of parts of the human body—feet, hands, heads, and so on—which remind us of the votive thank-offerings left by pilgrims who had been cured at shrines of healing—a practice which has continued into the present century.

Professor Emery did not live to complete the Sakkara excavations, but other archaeologists uncovered still more catacombs containing animal mummies, including the burials of the sacred cows who were the mothers of the holy Apis bulls buried in the Serapeum. The restrained scholarly prose of the preliminary excavation reports still manages to convey an astonishing image of a honeycomb of dark convoluted galleries riddling the subterrane of this much excavated area. In Ptolemaic times there was not one but a large complex of temples here, and one of the gods worshiped was certainly Imhotep, whose name has been found on dedicatory stelae. The excavations yielded rich finds of archaeological material, including fragments of the temple archives, which were written in Aramaic and Greek as well as Egyptian.

Yet the burning question remains unanswered. Was one of the battered, vandalized Third Dynasty tombs that of the master architect? Among the largest was a mastaba designated only as number 3517, since no name or other identification was found. The superstructure had been levelled to a height of about a meter and the burial shafts and chambers had been filled with sand. At the head of each shaft Emery found the remains of sacrificed bulls. Were they foundation deposits for a temple built over the tomb, or offerings to the unknown occupant of the tomb? Another mastaba, number 3518, has been dated to the reign of Zoser by means of a jar sealing found nearby. Unlike other tombs in the vicinity, it has precisely the same orientation as the Step Pyramid, and anatomical models—votive offerings—were found outside its entrance.

We will probably never know the answer. Even if the tomb had been found, it is unlikely that it would have given us any useful information. The autobiographical inscriptions which have provided so many fascinating insights into ancient Egyptian life were not written in the tombs of Imhotep's time. Nor is it likely that his tomb would have escaped the depredations of tomb robbers and other vandals. It would have been a thrilling discovery, though, surpassing, in certain ways, the gold of Tutankhamon. Monuments to the triumph of the human intellect are rare enough.

The second great architect, who, like Imhotep, was worshiped as a god long after his death, was born a thousand years or more after his predecessor. He was Amenhotep son of Hapu, and he served the king whose namesake he was—Amenhotep III, of the Eighteenth Dynasty. Some scholars give this man the credit for the Luxor temple, which is one of the most harmonious structures in Egypt. Like Imhotep, Amenhotep son of Hapu was not only an architect, but a wise man of great reputation. He was born of unimportant parents in the Delta town of Athribis, and he started his career as a humble military scribe in charge of recruiting. It was evidently his superior talents which led to the recognition he eventually achieved from the king; not only were statues of him erected in the temple of Karnak, but he had the unprecedented honor of a temple on the west bank of Thebes near that of the king who thought so highly of him. Although he was supposed to have composed a book of wise sayings, no trace of it has ever

Amenhotep son of Hapu. *The Cairo Museum. Photo from The Metropolitan Museum of Art.*

been found. His own inscriptions suggest that he was responsible for the two sole surviving remains of Amenhotep III's mortuary temple. They are prominent remains—two enormous but sadly mutilated statues which rise up out of the cultivated fields across from modern Luxor. They are known today as the Colossi of Memnon.

The career of the third member of our trio of architects contrasts ironically with the honor and respect, culminating in actual divinity, which was granted the other two. Senmut, the parvenu favorite of Queen Hatshepsut, is usually supposed to have constructed her beautiful funerary temple at Deir el Bahri. He was not a popular man. After his royal mistress died, his enemies did their best to obliterate his name and hers from the pages of history; within a few generations of his death, probably his very name was forgotten. William Stevenson Smith has pointed out the most ironic touch of all—in later times a shrine with the names of the deified Amenhotep and the deified Imhotep was erected at the site of Deir el Bahri. There the two were worshiped, while against the very same cliffs stood the building which many people consider the most beautiful temple in all Egypt, with the desecrated, empty tomb of its dishonored builder beneath. Senmut was never buried in the tomb he had impudently constructed under the sacred edifice, but in remote corners of the building small, hastily cut figures of him survived the revengeful destruction of one of his enemies—perhaps Thutmose III, the king he had helped to keep from his birthright for over twenty years.

Now that we have waxed poetical over the names of Imhotep, Amenhotep and Senmut, it is only fair to state that we don't know whether they were architects at all, in our sense of the word. We do not consider the head of the firm of Jones, Smith and Brown the architect of a skyscraper if he orders Jones Junior to draw up the actual plans. We cannot be sure that the Egyptians made the same distinction. There is no Egyptian word for "architecture"; there is not even a title which can be read "architect" with any certainty. Some Egyptologists used the word to translate a title which means "overseer of works," and we still describe men as architects if they say, in their biographical inscriptions, that they erected an obelisk, or built a shrine.

Unlike the artist or the sculptor, the overseer of works was not a craftsman. He was a high official, and he usually had other important titles which gave him noble rank. He must have been the equivalent of the head of the ministry of public works, and he was responsible for building operations from the quarrying of the stone up to the dedication of the finished building. Obviously it was his subordinates who did most of the actual work. Scribes calculated the amount of stone necessary and the loaves of bread per day which would be eaten by the workmen. Foremen managed the gangs of stoneworkers in the quarry, and ships' captains were in charge of the barges on which the stones were loaded. Painters and sculptors did the decorative work and masons fitted the stones. But who drew up the plans?

I wish I knew. I would also like to know *how* they drew up the plans, and *whether* they did. There are a few tattered drawings now in museums which may be architects' sketches. None of them are detailed enough to rank as blueprints, or even reliable plans. Most are drawings of small elements—a doorway, a courtyard planted with trees. One such plan, more comprehensive than the majority is reproduced in our illustration, together with the plan drawn by a modern scholar, Professor S. P. K. Glanville, on the

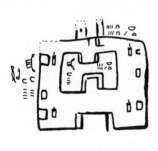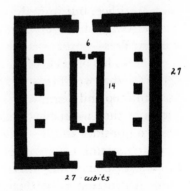

*Plan of a temple*

Left, the original Egyptian sketch with the dimensions given in the small hieroglyphic inscriptions. The squarish shapes on either side are columns, and are in some cases so labeled. Right, the scale plan made by Professor Glanville following the stated dimensions

basis of the measurements given by the Egyptian scribe in the short inscriptions written on his drawing. Obviously the Egyptian version was not a scale drawing; the proportions are all wrong.

Another sketch gives the plan of a tomb. The drawing is accurate enough to enable us to identify the tomb as that of Ramses IV. However, either the architect changed his mind while the work was underway or the plan does not attempt to be precise, since there are several important discrepancies in the measurements. In any case, a rock-cut tomb is a fairly simple structure compared with a temple. It is no more than a series of regularly shaped holes in the rock, the sort of thing an amateur could design without straining his mental equipment: "All right, men, make that room a little longer so the sarcophagus can fit in, and cut a door over there so we can have a storeroom."

Obviously this lighthearted technique would not work with a temple like that of Deir el Bahri, or with any other temple. Deir el Bahri is so lovely, so perfectly proportioned, so harmonious, that it almost demands the existence of a model. The original plan of the temple was altered, but this does not preclude the possibility of an overall plan. Although the Egyptians made model buildings for funerary purposes, no architect's aid has ever been found, with the possible exception of one miniature building. It is an uninspired, rather crude structure, though, and certainly no model, or plan, of any known temple has been discovered.

There are references to an archive of master plans, kept by certain temples. This is not solid proof, but it does support the assumption which the very existence of the architectural masterpieces forces us to make—that either plans or models or both were used to build them. Of course there were full-sized models all over Egypt, the temples of earlier kings. Senmut had such an inspiration close at hand, for there was an Eleventh Dynasty temple at Deir el Bahri itself, and Hatshepsut's structure has some elements in common with the older building. But if Senmut started out by imitating the Eleventh Dynasty temple, he ended by surpassing it.

We still have not answered the essential question: Who actually designed Deir el Bahri and the other gems of Egyptian architecture? There are two tenuous types of argument which may support the assumption, made by many archaeologists, that the overseer of works designed the temples himself. In the first place, there is no known candidate for the position of Royal Architect per se—no man whose name is connected with a given temple in such a manner as to suggest that he, not the overseer of works, drew up the plans for it. Secondly, the design and appearance of a temple were of major importance; they would logically be decided upon by the man who was responsible for the whole operation. That's about the best we can do; it is admittedly unsatisfactory. But until the Egyptian equivalent of Jones Junior appears, claiming to have planned the "beautiful temple of Djeser Djeseru," I am content to give Senmut the credit.

In conclusion, perhaps the best advice I can give anyone who wants to learn to enjoy Egyptian art is to go out and look at it. The best place to go is Egypt, of course; the second best is a museum. For those to whom these goals are impossible, the bookstores and libraries teem these days with picture books on Egypt. Increased photographic skill and new reproductive techniques make some of these books joys to behold. However, despite the weighty apparatus and expensive cameras which are used to prepare these new books, the finest reproductions ever made of Egyptian paintings were made by painters—a husband and wife team, Nina and Norman de Garis Davies. It is hard to find examples of their work, since most of it was produced for museums or other scholarly institutions; it is thus published in rare, expensive volumes. But it is perfectly wonderful work, reproducing, as no other medium or artist has ever done, the real essence of Egyptian painting.

# X

## Sorcerer, Scientist and Priest

### Magic, Science and Religion

THE antiseptic whiteness of a scientist's laboratory; glowing stained glass under the dim arches of a Gothic cathedral; a shabby back room where a man in a preposterous turban bends over a crystal ball. Three different environments and three different systems of thought, as far apart, surely, as the three angles of a triangle.

Up to this point we have been talking about life in ancient Egypt in its more concrete aspects—activities, occupations, objects. This is fine, so far as it goes. But beneath the practical everyday world of food and furniture, funny stories and love songs, lies another stratum—the level of attitudes and ideas. In a culture like that of ancient Egypt these abstractions are seldom explicitly stated; yet they are, rather than the shape of pots or the canon of art, the really significant, and definitive, aspects of the culture. Although the Egyptians sat on chairs and liked to drink beer, their view of the universe was not the same as ours, and one of the basic differences lies in the way they thought about the three categories we are now discussing: magic, science, and religion.

MAGIC: the use of means that are believed to have supernatural power . . . to produce or prevent a particular result believed not obtainable by natural means.

SCIENCE: accumulated and accepted knowledge that has been systematized and formulated with reference to the discovery of general truths or the operation of general laws.

RELIGION: a personal awareness or conviction of the existence of a supreme being or of supernatural powers controlling one's destiny.

Normally, definitions are a good way of beginning a discussion. They nail down the terms to be discussed, and prevent ambiguities. But let us suppose that we are conversing with a Theban priest of the Eighteenth Dynasty. We want him to tell us about Egyptian science; and, in order to explain what we mean, we give him Mr. Webster's definitions.

The priest would not disagree with the definitions; he simply would not know what we were talking about. We would have some difficulty in translation, to begin with, since the ancient Egyptians had no word for "science." They had no word for "religion," either. Magic? There is a word which we translate by that term, but our priest would not apply it to the same things we do. He would gape and scratch his shaven head as we tried to explain the difference between "natural" and "supernatural," and if we finally succeeded in getting across "an organized body of knowledge, systematized . . . and arranged in accord with certain laws," he might very well give us a lecture on the systematized Egyptian pantheon and the rituals used to control the gods.

The point is one which cannot be made too often or too emphatically. To the Egyptians, as to most primitive peoples, the categories which we have distinguished were not mutually exclusive. They were not even separate. If a man came to an Egyptian doctor with a broken leg, the physician might apply a splint, rub it with a mixture of honey and herbs, pronounce a magical incantation, and hang an amulet, like a religious medal, around the sufferer's neck. We would say that he had employed several different methods of healing, only one of which could be considered effective. But the Egyptian patient would have been highly indignant if his medical adviser had only used the splint.

It would be an oversimplification to say that the difference between an Egyptian doctor and a modern M.D. is that the former believed in magic. We have two problem words: "magic" and "believe." What does magic suggest to us? A series of kaleidoscopic images—Swami Hassan with his turban and crystal ball, a cute little Merlin out of Walt Disney, damned Faustus and the pale shade of Helen. Magic . . . one of the most evocative words in the language, ranging from glamour to horror, from the glimmer of Titania's wings in the moonlight to the old women screaming in the fires of the Inquisition. Magic to primitive man was something altogether different. We will try, in this chapter, to get some idea of what he did have in mind.

But first we must examine our second problem word, "believe." Primitive man believed in magic. The sophisticated reader, versed in anthropology and ethnology, may find this statement obvious to the point of tedium. He already knows that.

The sophisticated reader may think he accepts primitive man's faith in magic. He probably does not. This is one of the great difficulties facing historians, archaeologists and ethnologists—the difficulty of really accepting a theorem which is, we like to think, so alien to our own point of view. Of course it is impossible to get inside another man's skin and think the way he does. When we interpret a culture as different from our own as that of ancient Egypt, we are translating. We cannot even break down the facets of culture into chapters suitable for a book without violating the essential unity of the lives of these other people; and everything we say about them is said in our words, each of which has a backlog of associations and meanings which are not those of the culture in question. We cannot solve this problem; we can only remember, constantly, that we are translating, and that something is always lost in translation.

I have accused my sophisticated reader of not really believing that which he thinks he does believe. I will prove my point by citing an example.

There once appeared, in a learned Egyptological journal, an article by a learned Egyptologist on the harem conspiracy under Ramses III, of the Nineteenth Dynasty. The plot itself was the sort of thing one expects from an irregular institution like a harem: one of the ladies had decided that her son ought to be the next king instead of the legitimate heir. In order to insure this desirable goal it was necessary for the old king, Ramses III, to be sent to join his father the Sun somewhat ahead of schedule. The lady succeeded in interesting a number of important officials in her project, but it failed in at least one of its aims. Owing to the ambiguity of the official record, we do not know whether Ramses III actually was murdered by the conspirators or not; but the legitimate crown prince, later Ramses IV, discovered the plot in time to save his throne and his own neck. The plotters were tried and, we presume, executed—although the record merely states, with that almost Victorian squeamishness which the Egyptians sometimes exhibited, that the criminals were "overtaken by their sentence." Some, the most highly placed, were allowed to commit suicide.

One passage in the text is particularly interesting. In order to seize power and reach the inner precincts of the palace, the conspirators had made writings "for enchanting, for banishing, for confusing—because some gods were made of wax, and some men also."

The most reasonable interpretation of this passage is that the plotters used magic. The waxen images are magicians' props, known from all over the world. The written spells controlled the will of the loyal guards and courtiers who protected the king.

This is the accepted explanation. However, the author of the article I mentioned does not believe that the plotters used magic at all. His counter arguments deal with the passage I have quoted, and necessitate new and hitherto unknown translations of such words as "enchanting" and "gods." Egyptian is a good language for this sort of argument, because its vocabulary is still not completely fixed; new meanings do turn up, now and then, for known words. As for the significant phrase "made out of wax," the author wants to make it a figure of speech, not a figure of magic. Anyone who has ever studied a foreign language has probably noticed the infuriating propensity of prepositions in other tongues to mean almost anything. The preposition we translate "out of" can, by some stretching, be made to mean "into!" Things which are made "into wax" are made malleable, susceptible to influence.

These arguments are plausible, although the figure of speech is an English idiom rather than one the Egyptians would have used. But the philologist who tampers with established vocabulary must have motives purer than Caesar's wife. He cannot invent new meanings in order to support a preconceived theory. The author of the article states his theory quite candidly:

"The conspirators were in too risky a situation to entrust the outcome of their plot to magical procedures."

The reader can see, I am sure, the point of this discussion. The author of the article on the harem conspiracy does not "believe" that the Egyptians believed in magic. He "knows" that they did; Egyptian culture is full of examples. But when he comes right down to a specific case, one in which *he* would certainly not have trusted to magic, he wants to give his friends the Egyptians credit for an equally enlightened approach.

I have gone into this at some length, not to pick the bones of Scholar X, but to show that if he can commit such a basic blunder, the rest of us had better beware of complacency. Of course it was in just such a risky situation that the Egyptians *would* have used magic. Magic was not a game, or the last resort of the incompetent. It was a tool—possibly the most important tool of all.

In terms of Mr. Webster's definitions, pyramidology and psychic research can be called "sciences." In case the reader is unfamiliar with pyramidology, let me beg, in the names of Breasted, Petrie, Erman and Champollion, that he will never, ever, confuse it with Egyptology. Pyramidology is the study of the mystic and prophetic import of the Egyptian pyramids. No one who has read the volumes published by pyramidologists (or pyramidalists) can deny that the subject is organized, accumulated (only too much so), accepted (by many people), systematized, and based on what its followers claim are general truths. Possibly some of them *are* general truths. But it is certainly not a science. Nor would I include psychic research in that category, although its tenets have been formulated, and a formidable mass of documentation has been collected by its numerous adherents.

Obviously there is something wrong with our definitions. They do not really distinguish between the three categories we are discussing, even in our terms, and they certainly have given us no insight into primitive magic. Let us tackle the problem in another way; let us take our categories in pairs, and try to distinguish the essential differences between them.

Magic and science are not diametrically opposed. They have much more in common than one might suppose. Several eminent anthropologists have pointed out the similarities. Like science, primitive magic was an attempt to formulate principles through which the forces affecting man could be understood and manipulated. These principles had to be based on assumptions about the world. When the assumptions were false, primitive man got magical principles; when they were correct, he had science. In this sense magic might be called a bastard, or pseudo, science, for primitive man had no way of telling false assumptions from true assumptions.

This interpretation of magic as a pseudo science has been challenged, naturally; what scholarly theory has not? The challengers maintain that primitive man knew quite well the difference between magic and the rational techniques which may be called primitive science. When a Trobriand Islander plants a garden he is careful to weed and water and protect his plants. He uses magic, too; but, says Dr. Bronislaw Malinowski, he would smile if you suggested he grow crops by magic alone, without water, or weeding, or seeds.

Much as I admire Dr. Malinowski, I am not sure that he is making a significant point. His Trobriand Islander might smile if it were suggested that he grew crops by rational methods alone, without magic. To the people who believe in it, magic is just as important as the water or the seed.

It might be claimed that primitive men used practical techniques, primitive science, whenever they could, and only resorted to magic to cover areas in which unpredictable factors—luck or chance—might affect the results. But magic was not used in garden magic only to ward off destructive storms, or kill pests; often the spell covered the whole process: "Make this corn grow!" Furthermore, this distinction assumes the impossible: that primitive man's definitions of the predictable and the unpredictable were the same as ours, and that he made our distinction between the natural and the supernatural. In one sense all of his life was supernatural, shaped by powerful forces which acted directly on his fragile body and his few possessions. He did the best he could, with his seeds and his watering can, and then he plastered the whole process over with a thick, protective coating of magic. To assume that he recognized a qualitative difference between his rational and nonrational techniques is to make an assumption which the evidence does not justify.

One of the differences between magic and science, then, lies in the validity of the assumptions which underlie their structures. However, it is not always easy to distinguish between false and true assumptions. The best way of recognizing a true assumption is to see whether it actually works out, in practice. It is an ironic fact that when magic works, it is no longer magic, but science. Hypnotism, once an adjunct of the black art, is now semirespectable and unglamorous; the beginnings of the physician's craft are to be found in the hex bag of the tribal witch doctor. The experiments of such men as Dr. Rhine, in extrasensory perception, may end in reducing this magical phenomenon to a science. At the rate Dr. Rhine was progressing, this end admittedly looks to be a long way off; but we cannot afford to be dogmatic about states of knowledge.

Let us consider a theoretical case in order to see how plausible such false assumptions may appear. Imagine that you are a Neanderthaler whose mate has been taken away by a bigger, fiercer Neanderthaler. Even a caveman had sense enough to avoid combat with someone who could tear him limb from limb; still, our caveman resents the theft. Now he has no one to gather firewood, and toast his chunk of mammoth over the coals, and carry his baggage when the tribe shifts hunting grounds. He has to do all these menial chores himself. It upsets him. Standing well out of his rival's sight, so that his behavior will not be interpreted as a challenge, he has a temper tantrum. He stamps up and down; he bellows; he waves his pointed stick and pretends to thrust it into the body of his enemy; if he knows any bad words, he swears. After he has exhausted himself and his store of invective he collapses onto the ground and wipes his perspiring brow. And then, of course, he feels much better. Who wouldn't, after such an enjoyable release?

The performance in which our Neanderthal man imaginatively thrashes an opponent who is too big to be thrashed otherwise has an immediate, practical result. It relieves him. Suppose something else happens. Suppose, next time the hated rival goes hunting, the mammoth catches him, instead of vice versa, and rams a horn into him. One need not rely too heavily upon coincidence to assume that this happened now and then; life was hard in those far-off days. Now what is our hero to think? A rudimentary sense of sequence, reinforced by hatred and a desire for revenge, may enable him to connect his fit of rage, which was followed by a strong emotional reaction, and the subsequent accident. He has killed his enemy! He knew at the time that something important had happened; he felt so good!

Now this is one of the places at which magic and science part company. Sequence is not causality, although it is easily mistaken for it. One morning, about 4 A.M., I may put on a flowing yellow robe and do a dance on the balcony. An hour or two later the sun rises. Here we have not only sequence, but intent, and a contrived similarity between the "cause" and the "effect"—the yellow robe and the graceful bounding leaps with which I will, no doubt, imitate the rising of the solar orb. Did I make the sun rise? You may laugh, intelligent reader, but if I went about it properly I could probably collect a few people, even in our day and age, who *would* believe it. We talk very glibly, many of us, about cause and effect, but most of the time we are talking about something which does not exist. In the complex, everyday world, the causes of particular phenomena are not easy to isolate. What causes two people to fall in love, to conceive a child? What causes a plant to grow, a bird to fly, a child to catch measles? What is the cause of war or of a Mozart symphony? What makes my geraniums die while my neighbors' plants flourish? Even when we can pick out a single "cause" it has to be qualified. I suppose a child catches measles because it picks up a measles germ; but it may wallow in germs without contracting the disease if it has natural immunity, or if it has had measles before—or for other reasons which as yet elude us. Let us make allowances for our primitive ancestors. It is not surprising that they could not tell good causes from bad causes, when some modern logicians wonder whether they exist at all.

But back to our Neanderthal hero, flushed with success and triumph. If he has enough imagination to make the connection between his tantrum and his enemy's death, he will also see the implications. This is a great discovery! Perhaps he is noble and altruistic, à la Rousseau; if so, he will rush home after the hunt and explain his new invention to all the neighbors, so that they too can influence men and mammoths. Chances are, though, that he will not. Chances are that he will tell them about it, and then explain that he is the only one clever enough to do the job. So he becomes a witch doctor, or shaman, or warlock—the first of a long line of workers in magic, who lived for countless ages on the credulity of their fellows.

We have already established the fact that it is not easy to distinguish a true "cause" from something which is not a cause at all. Still, a genuine cause should consistently produce the same result. Would not the patrons of a magician notice that he could not always get results from his spells?

No, they wouldn't. People don't see the things they don't want to see; they have selective imaginations. A success is remembered, a failure forgotten, just as pleasure remains longer and more vividly in the memory than does pain. Furthermore, the magicians were men of superior intelligence and craft; if they were not, they probably didn't last long. This is another of the symptoms of magic that distinguishes it from science—that much of its effectiveness depends on the personality of the magician. The scientist who eventually discovers the cause of cancer may be an unpleasant fellow personally, but his character will have no effect on the cancer virus, or whatever it turns out to be. A good magician, however, must have a lot of personality, or that quality called "charisma"—the ability to move men.

There is no profession in which charisma is more useful than in magic—unless it is politics. Take the field of medicine, which was, in primitive times, riddled with magical techniques. The "psychosomatic" ailments, which may include everything from backache to blindness, are not affected by modern surgery or medicine; but imagine the effect upon them of a powerful assertive personality, reinforced by the patient's belief in magic. Certainly the sufferer would be relieved. Even the pain of physical ailments would be alleviated. "Yes, Doc, I do feel better!" Today the doctor's bedside manner may help or hinder his patients. In primitive medicine the bedside manner was 90 percent of the battle.

A really clever shaman could also experiment with herbs and drugs, the proper use of which would increase his percentage of cures. The practical application of the magician's intelligence could thus bring under control certain aspects of a given magical problem, which would make him much more effective. Take hate-magic—spells designed to defeat or cripple or kill an enemy—one of the most important sub-fields of the black art. The use of poison as an aid to witchcraft is well known, even in comparatively recent European history. The man who pays the magician his fee is satisfied with results; he doesn't know or care whether it was incantations or arsenic that laid his enemy low.

An experienced poisoner, then, could set up a respectable practice in "spelling" people to death. In love-magic some practical auxiliaries might also help—anything from bribery and blackmail to advice to the lovelorn: "Comb your hair once a week and file your teeth to sharper points." Even in weather-magic, where charisma is admittedly limited in effect, the shaman could employ his superior intelligence to observe phenomena which his duller-witted contemporaries might miss. If he could not produce rain on call, he might be able to predict it ahead of time, from cloud formations or recollections of seasonal variations. If he were called upon to stop an eclipse, all he needed to do was to keep on waving his arms and chanting until the shadow over the sun passed away. And, in the last extremity, if all his efforts resulted in crashing failure—*he could talk his way out of it.* Adverse magic from some rival sorcerer, failure of a supporter in observing the necessary rituals—any such argument, if emphatically pressed, might convince his hearers. Being a cynic, I am inclined to agree with those anthropologists who believe that the most successful magicians may have been men who didn't believe in their own spells. An honest man, overcome by failure, might admit that he didn't know what had happened to thwart his spells. In some primitive cultures he would not survive such an admission very long.

Another reason why magic seemed to work was because it did work; it worked because people believed in it, and they believed in it because it seemed to work. This is not as paradoxical as it sounds. Expressed hostility and malevolent intent can certainly cause anxiety and fear, nervous indigestion, and illness. A curse can kill—if the victim believes in it. Conversely, a potent protective charm may act as a psychological prop, increasing a man's self-confidence and, consequently, his effectiveness. No—it is no wonder people used to believe in magic. The real wonder is that we no longer do so—if we don't.

How many of us really understand the principles of such a common household device as the telephone? We know it works by scientific laws, not by magic, because various authorities, from our teachers to *Popular Science* Magazine, assure us that this is so. But if, starting next week, the teachers and *Popular Science* said that the messages are carried by little fairies who run along the wires from town to town, a lot of us would be just as happy to accept that explanation. And if the right people told us that human blood makes the corn grow taller, some of us would go right out and sprinkle the corn. Not believe in magic? Who, us? We have our faith healers and our demagogues, and magicians who sell us spells entitled "positive thinking" and "how to win friends and influence people." Surely there is a sound psychological basis to such spells; so was there to much primitive magic. We are science-minded, modern men; but there are those among us who refuse to have children inoculated and who deny themselves blood transfusions, on the ground that such acts are contrary to the will of God—although I do not recall that He has ever expressed Himself on either of these subjects. And for sheer irrationality, the doctrines of racial purity and racial supremacy are on a level with sprinkling the corn with blood. Most of us are not science-minded; we are not even rational. We live in an intellectual climate which accepts "science" as a vague general principle, but we "believe" in science just as uncritically as the Egyptians believed in magic. It is not because we are more rational than our remote ancestors that we find it hard to understand their system of thought. It is only because our kind of magic is different.

If there is some science in magic, there is also a lot of magic in some religions. Conventionally, magic and religion are distinguished by the means employed to affect the supernatural beings with whom both fields deal. Magicians command and threaten demons; priests adore and beseech gods. Once again, the standard definitions are not very accurate. The priests of some ancient religions seem to have adopted a blackmailing tone more suitable to a shaman than to a humble worshiper: "Either you bring the rain, Great Spirit, or no offerings!" Sometimes primitive magicians invoked the assistance of supernatural beings, gods or demons, but they could, and did, use spells which required no outside aid—spells which, it was believed, worked directly upon the object to be affected, as our caveman's ritual gestures and curses "killed" his enemy. The supernatural beings invoked by ancient magicians were normally divine rather than diabolic, so that the professions of priest and magician often overlapped. Indeed, the notion of magic as a Black Art did not gain real strength until after the spread of the monotheistic religions. Their Gods were jealous gods, and their priests regarded themselves as the only legitimate intermediaries between man and the supernatural. The Egyptians were not so narrow-minded; there was a goddess of magic, and, as we shall see, the Egyptians sought immortality not only through moral rectitude, "which the god desires," but through the crudest of magical trickery—spells which would deceive or control the divine tribunal which judged the soul.

In Egypt, religion and science had their areas of overlap too. The gods were the first scientists—Thoth, who invented numbers, Khnum, the divine potter, Osiris, who taught men the science of agriculture. And some scientists, such as Imhotep, became gods. Church and state were never separated in ancient Egypt, and a learned man served the temple and the king without feeling that he was serving in two different capacities. Architects and physicians were often priests as well. The famous "House of Life" attached to some temples was probably not a university, as is popularly believed, but a *scriptorium*, where scholarly books were written and stored. Medical lore was part of this heritage, and doctors were included among the staff.

Sorcerer, scientist and priest—the three categories were not so far apart after all. If we recognize this, and accept the sincere belief of primitive man in the phenomena we call magic, we will have acquired a key to many of the otherwise baffling beliefs of the ancient Egyptians.

## Egyptian Magic

Since we have just demonstrated, at some length, that we ought to try to look at the world as the Egyptians looked at it, we will have to talk about magic, so far as is possible, in their terms. It is "no fair" to construct an artificial subject called "Egyptian Magic" and dump into it all the activities we would call by that name.

What are these activities? They would certainly include the following: cursing (including killing); curing; erotic magic; agricultural (including weather); divination; resurrection. Since magic and medicine are hard to untangle, and since the Egyptians did not, as a rule, try to untangle them, we will discuss curative magic under medicine. Resurrective magic, designed to reanimate the dead and insure them a happy existence in the hereafter, is perhaps the area about which we have the most information. We would call it magic since, by our system of belief, any attempts to win immortality except the ones set forth in the Judeo-Christian creed are, at best, superstition. This is a little hard on the Egyptians, who probably thought they were being properly religious. So we are going to talk about resurrective magic under mortuary beliefs.

This still leaves us with a respectable body of material. However, not all our categories are represented in ancient Egypt, or else they are represented only by hints or casual allusions. We know very little about weather and agricultural magic, and most of what we do know would have been called religious by the Egyptians—if they had possessed a word for religion. The prosperity and productivity of the country did not depend on rain but on the annual rise of the Nile, whose inundation watered and fertilized the soil. The river itself was a god, named Hapi, and the great mortuary god Osiris was connected, not only with the resurrection of the dead, but with the rebirth of the new grain. Great state rituals, conducted by the king or his representatives, honored these gods and assured the yearly inundation, on which the crops depended. I suspect, from what we know of other societies, that the ancient fellahin of Egypt may have had their own magical ceremonies to make sure the crops were abundant. But nothing is known of this, if it was done.

Spells designed to curse and kill an enemy seem to be pure magic, in that they are normally free of invocations to a god. The cursing texts were written on rough pottery bowls or on figurines, which were then flung down and smashed to bits. The inscriptions name the enemies whose lives are to be broken as the bowls are smashed. Many examples name rulers of cities in Syria or Nubia, so they must have been official state curses. Others name Egyptians: "Ameni shall die, the tutor of Sit-Bastet." These may have been private grudges. With the meticulous thoroughness which I like to consider typically Egyptian, another text curses: "Every evil word, every evil speech, every evil thought, every evil plot, every evil thing, every evil dream," and so on, through a long list of evils. In the cursing ritual, the efficacious elements are two in number: first, the ritual act, which is an application of the principle of imitation—as the bowl is "killed" the enemy is killed; second, the power of the word, which is also twofold. The identity of the enemy with the object to be broken is assured by the writing of his name upon it; the phrase "he shall die" is a homicidal attack, magically speaking.

Some of the "magico-medical" texts also give spells for destroying an enemy; they are more complicated than the quick and easy smashing of an image, but they include the all-important verbal element. The medical texts are full of love charms, too; several, which I find rather sad, are designed to make a man's wife love him. Some of these spells would only work with a wife or concubine, for their successful application depends on the man being on fairly intimate terms with the lady he wishes to encharm. Love charms may be considered a legitimate part of the physician's art; they often involve a prescription to be applied externally or taken internally. Others, surely related to love charms, are designed to "make an old man into a young man," or just to make the old man look young—hair restorers, wrinkle removers, and the like.

It has been argued that divination—attempts to predict the future—and related fields such as astrology are not really magic, because magic involves a conscious act, an attempt to control what is going to happen. This is quibbling, I think; nobody wants to know the future unless he hopes to guide his behavior by that knowledge, if only in a negative way. June is an unlucky month? We abstain from doubtful activities, or even stay home in bed. The tarot cards inform us that a tall dark man will bring trouble and sorrow? We confine ourselves to short blond men. The fatalism which resigns itself to misery, bad luck or illness, without trying to avoid such predictions, would not bother resorting to divination in the first place.

Contrary to popular belief, the Egyptians were not astrologers; they did not have the concept of the Zodiac on which, if I understand the problem correctly, modern astrology is based. But they did have charts of lucky and unlucky days, which remind us of the paragraphs that appear regularly in many newspapers, purporting to tell us how to regulate our conduct according to our horoscopes.

In the Egyptian charts, each day is divided into three parts and marked with signs meaning "good" or signs meaning "bad." Thus, for the fourth day of the month Paophi, we get this: "Bad, good, bad. Under no circumstances go forth from your house this day. He who is born on this day will die of the plague." The next day, the fifth, is consistently dangerous: "Bad, bad, bad. Under no circumstances approach a woman. On this day men shall make offerings to the gods. . . . He who is born on this day shall die of lovemaking." Perhaps some people might not consider this such a bad way to go. Even better is the prediction for the man born on the sixth, which is "good, good, good." He will die drunken.

Another method of foretelling the future was by dream analysis. One papyrus gives over two hundred interpretations of dreams. Here are a few:

If a man sees himself in a dream:

| | |
|---|---|
| seeing a big cat | good; it means a big harvest |
| plunging into the river | good; it means cleansing from all evils |

| seeing his face in a mirror | bad; it means another wife (!) |
| looking into a deep well | bad; it means taking away his property |

These interpretations do not follow the theories of Professor Freud. However, it is possible that the Egyptians did not consider the dream papyrus to be true magic; the symbolic images which kept popping up in their dreams may have had as much rational validity, for them, as the modern interpretations of other dream images have for us. If we want to be certain about what the Egyptians regarded as genuine sorcery, we must refer to their own descriptions. And there is one ancient papyrus which gives us some excellent examples.

The protagonist of the tale is no less a personage than the great King Khufu of the Fourth Dynasty. One day he called his sons to him and asked them to amuse him with tales of wonderful events. Thereupon the first son related how a magician punished his unfaithful wife. He made a waxen image of a crocodile. When it was thrown into the river it came to life, growing to normal crocodile size, and when the wife's lover came to the water to bathe, the crocodile seized him. The adulterous wife was burned.

The second story told by the princes described an equally talented magician who folded up a lake, leaving the bottom dry so that one of the royal ladies could retrieve an ornament she had dropped into the water. The greatest magician of all, however, was one who lived during Khufu's reign; and when his younger son told the king about this man, Khufu ordered that he be summoned to court to display his spells. The old man, whose name was Djedi, had the best trick of all. He could put back a head which had been cut off. Khufu asked him to do it and offered a criminal, condemned to death, for the experiment. But the wise man replied, "Not a man, O sovereign, my lord!" and used a goose instead. I have always liked this story because its spirit is so unlike that of many later Oriental fairy tales. Even a condemned criminal is rejected by the old magician; for to work magic on men, the "cattle of the gods," that is forbidden.

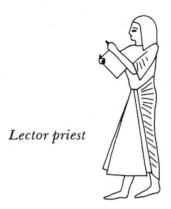

*Lector priest*

These tricks, then, are real magic, regarded by the Egyptians themselves as marvels. Other examples can be found in other stories, such as the ones we have quoted earlier in this book. The crocodile image is particularly interesting because it is a very ancient example of a type of sorcery which has flourished until modern times, in many parts of the world. It also confirms our theory that such waxen images were used by the conspirators in the plot against Ramses III.

The talented wonder-workers in the tales related to King Khufu were not called magicians; in the text they have the title "lector priest." This title designated one of the classes of priests who served the temples, and who specialized in a knowledge of the sacred writings; they were, perhaps, the scholars of the hierarchy, and they were often skilled in magic. Doctors were part-time magicians, too; as everyone knew, illness could be caused by demons or by the spirits of the dead, and a physician had to know how to deal with them. But the greatest of all the practitioners of magic, old Djedi, was neither a priest nor a physician. Not only could he restore the dead to life; he knew the numbers of the secret chambers of the sanctuary of Thoth, the key to powerful magic, and he could foretell the future. Knowledge of the magic art was not restricted to priests; there was a profession of "magician," and another title which has been translated as "amulet-man." The amulet-men sometimes formed part of the staff of royal expeditions sent into the deserts for copper or stone, and we suppose that they supplied the workers with the little charms which could protect them against some of the dangers of the barren, waterless waste.

No, magic was not a toy or a parlor game. The wrinkled, balding official who paid a doctor for a prescription to make himself young—in order, perhaps, to win the heart of a foolish girl who preferred good looks to wealth—was not playing games. Magicians were on the royal payroll; and magic could be, as in the case of the cursing texts, a tool of international relations—we can hardly call it "diplomacy."

# XI

# "The Useful Things That Are Established Forever"

HAVING proved that the terms "magic, science and religion" have no real meaning, we will begin our study of Egyptian science in the same negative manner, by stating that there really was no such thing. The Egyptians were skilled at a number of practical crafts, many of which involved the application of scientific laws. But these laws were seldom, if ever, explicitly stated. We can have, as we had in Egypt, technology without science: knowing how to do something without knowing why it works.

### *Mathematics*

Perhaps the nearest thing in Egypt to a pure science was mathematics. The Egyptians used a decimal system in which a single stroke represented *one*. Two strokes stood for *two*, and so on, up through *nine. Ten* rated a separate sign, like a croquet hoop. From *eleven* to *nineteen* the figures were formed by adding the requisite number of strokes to the *ten* symbol. *Twenty* was two croquet hoops, *twenty-one* was two hoops and a stroke. Besides *ten* and *one*, the only other numerals that had separate signs were *one hundred, one thousand, ten thousand, one hundred thousand* and *one million.* There was no zero.

This system is even more cumbersome than Roman numerals. The Romans could write "1965" with only six signs. The Egyptians needed twenty-one separate symbols to express the same figure. Just on the basis of the Egyptian numerals we might reasonably suspect that Egyptian arithmetic was a tedious process. It was.

Egyptologists seem to take a grisly delight in disillusioning people who believe the Egyptians were masters of sciences lost to the modern world. If they were, they were masters of sciences so obscure that we have no evidence of them. In all the known sciences they were not remarkably advanced; they are admirable, not because of their wisdom, but because of what they were able to

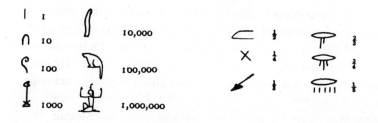

*Egyptian numerals*

accomplish with the knowledge they did have. Egyptian mathematics was no more advanced than any of the other sciences. Indeed, the Egyptian method may not even deserve to be called mathematics; it was hardly more than simple arithmetic.

Their arithmetic was essentially additive. Even multiplication and division were done by an additive process. To take an example, let us multiply eight by sixteen, as the Egyptians would have done it.

| | |
|---|---|
| 1 | 8 |
| 2 | 16 |
| 4 | 32 |
| 8 | 64 |
| 16 | 128 |

What we have done is to double each side of the table until we reach the desired answer. If our problem is one that does not work out evenly by such a process, we simply add the two factors necessary for the required sum. Ten times eight, using the above table, is the sum of eight times eight and two times eight—sixty-four plus sixteen, or eighty.

Division was done by the same method, only backwards. To divide ninety-six by eight, we would double eight (the right-hand column of the above table) until we obtain two figures which can be added to make ninety-six. Thirty-two and sixty-four meet this requirement. The corresponding numbers on the left-hand side of the table, which we have, of course, doubled as we doubled the right-hand column, are eight and four. Eight plus four equals twelve—the answer.

Sometimes the doubling method did not give the exact answer. Thirteen divided by three ends up as four threes with one left over. How did the Egyptians deal with the leftovers?

Egyptian fractions are lovely objects. They were expressed by the word "r," "part," written over a number. "R" over *five* was one-fifth, "r" over a croquet hoop and four strokes was one-fourteenth, and so on. There are separate signs in hieroglyphs and in hieratic for one-half, one-fourth, two-thirds, and, rarely, three-fourths. But in ordinary computation, the only kinds of fractions the Egyptians could express were unit fractions, in which the numerator is *one*.

But, says the reader, with such a limitation one cannot *do* arithmetic! As soon as you add or multiply a fraction—almost any old fraction—you get an answer in which the numerator is more than one. The Egyptian method of doubling would work with fractions in which the denominator was an even number; twice one-fourth equals two-fourths, which can immediately be reduced to the unit fraction one-half. Twice one-third equals two-thirds, and the Egyptians had a sign for that fraction. But twice one-fifth, or twice one-seventh, gives a result which the Egyptians could not express at all.

They did express it; but not as two-fifths or two-sevenths. Instead of two-fifths, they wrote one-third plus one-fifteenth—which is the same thing, if you work it out, expressed in the necessary unit fractions.

Admittedly this is not a simple procedure, and it would have taken a scribe some time to work out the necessary unit fractions for every fractional computation. Hence the Egyptians developed tables of such problems, presumably for reference, so that when a scribe had to double one-ninth, he merely looked at his table and found that the answer was one-sixth plus one-eighteenth. Our illustration gives excerpts from such a table which presents solutions to problems of addition of fractions.

We are told by a specialist in pre-Greek science, Professor Otto Neugebauer, that "experience teaches one very soon to operate quite rapidly within this framework." I am sure it has taught him to do so, but it would take more than experience to let most of us "operate" easily with fractions like these! However, we are handicapped by the knowledge of our own framework. If we had been taught arithmetic by the Egyptian method from the beginning, presumably we would find it easy too.

We don't know for sure how the Egyptians worked out these tables. They had no algebra. They did have geometry; they could calculate areas of triangles, trapezoids, rectangles, and circles, and there were problems for similar elementary volumes, including a correct computation of the volume of a truncated pyramid. This last was the most impressive achievement of Egyptian mathematics; equally admirable, perhaps, was their value 3.16 for *pi*, which is reasonably accurate. It has been claimed that the Moscow mathematical papyrus gives a solution for calculating the area of a hemisphere, but Professor Neugebauer thought a simpler interpretation of the problem is more likely.

Not only was mathematics, the basic tool of the sciences, fairly primitive, but it was also completely pragmatic. The mathematical texts from which we derive our knowledge contain tables and sample problems of the type a working temple or court scribe would have to be able to do—finding the area of a field, or the number of bricks needed to build a ramp of a given size. The Greeks had nothing much to learn from the wisdom of the Egyptians in mathematics; in many ways the Babylonians were far ahead of their contemporaries down south.

### *Astronomy*

The Egyptians have a certain reputation as astronomers; this may derive from their invention of a good calendar, since they have no other claim to fame in that field. Their calendar is the distant ancestor of our own, with its twelve months of thirty days each, plus an extra five days, to make the total of 365. The year is longer than 365 days, of course, but it was a long time before anyone figured out how to work in the extra one-fourth (and a fraction) day per year. The Egyptian calendar did not take the extra into account and, as a result, it soon got out of step with the real solar year. Still, it was a decided improvement over the flexible lunar calendars used by other peoples.

Our twelvefold division of day and night is also Egyptian in origin. The sixty-minute and sixty-second divisions are not; in fact, hours of fixed length probably did not appear until the invention of mechanical clocks. Egyptian hours varied in length depending on the season of the year. An hour was the twelfth part of the time from sunrise to sunset, for day, and from sunset to sunrise, for night. In winter the night hours would be longer than the day hours and in summer the reverse would be true.

The hour divisions can hardly be called "astronomical," however, and it is doubtful whether the Egyptian calendar owed anything to astronomy. It may have come from observations of the annual Nile rise, which culminated in the vital inundation. This phenomenon, in turn, was at some point connected with the reappearance on the horizon, after a period of invisibility, of the star Sirius. But it is yet to be proved that we owe our calendar to the astronomical talents of the ancient Egyptians.

What, then, did they accomplish in this field? Surprisingly little. Not until Hellenistic times, when Egyptian thought was influenced by ideas from Greece and Babylonia, do we find any texts involving mathematical calculations of astronomical phenomena. The only things which could possibly be called astronomical from pharaonic Egypt are the decan charts.

The decans are constellations whose risings, or transits, fall ten days apart (hence "decans") and which may be used to tell time during the night. On coffin lids of the Middle Kingdom and on ceilings of later tombs we find representations of the night sky with the decanal constellations inscribed thereon. The most elaborate of these are the ceilings of the tomb of Senmut, the architect of Queen Hatshepsut, and of the cenotaph of King Seti I at Abydos. At first glance, Senmut's ceiling looks as if it ought to mean something. There are circles subdivided into pie-shaped wedges, stars, mysterious deities, and short identifying inscriptions.

Unfortunately, with a few exceptions, it has thus far proved impossible to identify Senmut's stars with known constellations. Part of the difficulty may lie in the Egyptians' willingness to subjugate accuracy to neatness, and reality to an artificial order. There are indications in Senmut's ceiling that the original sketch was redrawn, possibly to make it look more artistic. Obviously we cannot hope for accurate drawings under those circumstances. Another consideration which may have affected accuracy was the mechanical copying of older texts, which were no longer accurate for the later period, and which may not have been copied correctly. Religious requirements—for each hour was under the guidance of a particular god—may have inspired further deviations. In this last consideration we see the working of the now-

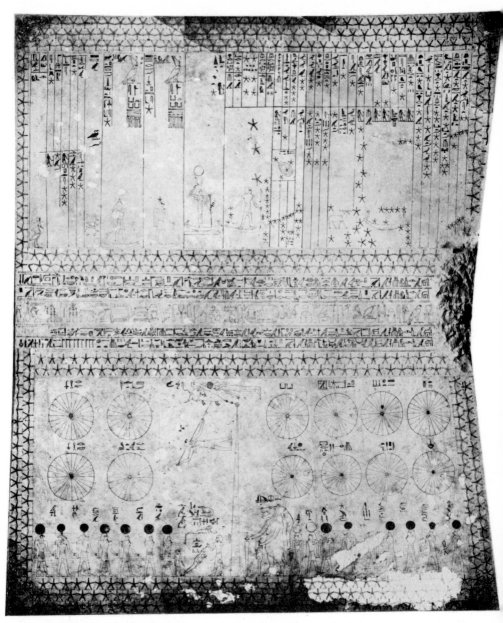

Ceiling of Senmut tomb. *The Metropolitan Museum of Art, photo by Egyptian Expedition.*

familiar principle—the impossibility of separating science from the other categories which we call religion and magic. The so-called astronomical texts are usually found in tombs or in coffins; their functions was not scientific, but religious, and they were probably altered, as necessary, to best serve that function. The decans had some effect on astrology, but they never had an influence on the development of astronomy.

## How to Build a Pyramid

The Egyptians could not calculate the volume of a hemisphere or predict an eclipse, but they do not seem to have been disturbed about this. They got along; and they did some surprising things with the knowledge they did possess.

We have already mentioned a few of the technological processes at which the Egyptians excelled, such as metalwork, papyrus-making, weaving, beer- and wine-making, faience, glass and pottery. Eventually, we will discuss mummification, which, in Egypt, can be viewed as a technical skill. Perhaps the best way of studying Egyptian technology is to take a specific example and see how it was done. I have chosen to examine the Great Pyramid for several reasons; in the first place, the construction of a pyramid involved a number of different technical problems, and in the second place, Khufu's pyramid has been analyzed, measured, described and discussed at greater length than has any other structure in Egypt.

The Great Pyramid is the largest of the three pyramids of Giza, and the tomb of King Khufu (Cheops in Greek) of the Fourth Dynasty—around 2600 B.C. I have already been taken to task by several friendly pyramidologists for refusing to admit that Khufu's tomb is the Master Plan of the Universe, and a monumental prophecy in stone; but at the risk of incurring further correspondence I must cling to my narrow-minded opinion. The Great Pyramid was a tomb, and that is all it was.

The Great Pyramid is impressive. It is impressive to look at, and quite overwhelming when you consider the statistics. The more than two million blocks of which it is composed average about two tons apiece in weight; the biggest blocks weighed fifteen tons. The four sides measure approximately 755 feet each. No two are exactly the same length, although the difference between the longest and shortest sides is only 7.9 inches. The structure was, when completed, 481.4 feet high. The area covered by the base is 13.1 acres.

Even more amazing than the size of the pyramid is the accuracy with which it was put together. The sides are oriented almost exactly in line with true north, south, east and west, the greatest error being on the east side, which was only 5'30" west of north. The angles are almost perfect right angles: 90, 3, 2; 89, 59, 58; 89, 56, 27; 90, 0, 33. The casing blocks which covered the exterior were fitted together with joints of one-fiftieth of an inch—so small that you can hardly get a pin into them, so small that the jointure cannot be seen until you get your nose right up against them. And the whole massive building rests on a dressed-rock platform which had a deviation from true level of only 0.004 percent.

It is no wonder that generations of travelers have been moved to extravagant speculations about this pyramid. All sorts of wild theories, from djinns to "unknown lost sciences," have been invented to account for its existence. But there is no need for such fantasies. The Great Pyramid and its smaller relations could have been built with the simplest of tools and technology.

Before the actual hauling of stones began, the Egyptian architect had to meet two separate problems. The first was the leveling

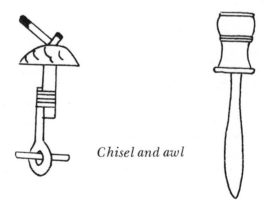

*Chisel and awl*

of the plateau; the second, the plotting of the angles and the orientation of the building.

Once the sand and gravel had been removed, down to bedrock, the area to be leveled was surrounded with low walls of brick and then flooded. By measuring down from a number of points on the surface of the water, a network of trenches of equal depth could be cut. The water was then released, and the areas between the trenches leveled to the same depth. The Egyptians had a long history of experience with flooded fields, irrigation trenches, and the like; this method would have come naturally to them. That it was actually used, as most authorities believe, is suggested by a curious fact—that when the prevalent north wind of the Cairo area is blowing, it would cause precisely the error from true level, on the water surface, that is actually found on the Great Pyramid plateau. In the case of this particular pyramid, the platform was not completely leveled. A core of rock was left in the middle, to be built into the structure.

For some reason or other a pyramid had to be made so that its sides faced the four cardinal points. We know, from later reliefs, that temples were oriented by "looking at the sky, observing the stars, and turning [one's] gaze toward the Great Bear." However, simple observation, even of so prominent a star as the North Star, would not give results commensurate with the remarkably accurate orientation of the pyramids. So it has been suggested that the Egyptians might have found true north by sighting on a star in the northern sky and then bisecting the angle formed by its rising and setting positions, and by the position of the observer. In order to do this accurately it is necessary to have an artificial horizon—a wall, in other words, which is perfectly level and which is high enough to cut off everything but sky from the view of the observer. Said observer stations himself behind his wall and waits for the chosen star to appear. Following his directions, an assistant marks the spot on the "horizon" wall where the star is first visible. A second mark is made at the point on the wall where the star sets, or disappears from the sight of the observer. Plumb lines are then dropped down from the top of the wall and marks made on the ground, immediately below the marks on the wall. Lines drawn from the observer's position to the two marks on the ground form an angle, whose middle line gives true north. The other compass points are found by constructing right angles to the line of true north.

While the pyramid plateau was being cleared and leveled, stoneworkers were already busy in the quarries, cutting out the first of those two million blocks of stone. The material used for the bulk of the Great Pyramid was a kind of limestone, the same stone of which the pyramid plateau itself is composed, and it was cut right on the spot. The casing stones, which gave a smooth covering to the structure, were of a different, finer-grained limestone. They must have been brought from the well-known Tura quarries just across the river from Giza, in the Arabian hills near modern Cairo. Now limestone counts as a soft stone—soft as stones go—and it can be cut with copper tools, like the ones the Egyptians had. With copper chisels the workers cut the desired block free on all sides except the bottom; it was detached from its base by wedges.

Not all the stone used in the Great Pyramid was soft stone. The pavements of the mortuary temple next to the pyramid were of basalt (dolerite), a decidedly hard stone. The great sarcophagus in which the king was buried was made of granite; so were the walls of the King's, or Burial, Chamber, and the plugs which were meant to block the passage leading to the royal mummy. Granite was used for casing parts of the Second and Third Pyramids at Giza; in the Third Pyramid probably the greater part of the casing was of this hard-to-work stone.

Granite and basalt are hard stones. They cannot be cut with copper chisels. One of the happiest of the claims made for the ancient Egyptians is that they must have had steel—two thousand years before they had iron in any quantity—in order to cut such difficult materials. An alternative theory is that they had some method of tempering copper to make it fantastically hard. So far, there is no evidence for either of these notions, except for the undeniable fact that these hard stones *were* cut. But there are simpler, if not easier, ways of accomplishing this feat.

One method of quarrying granite, which was certainly used later in Egypt, was to pound it out with heavy dolerite balls—a tedious, heartbreaking job, certainly, but so is building a pyramid. Another possibility is the use of copper saws and/or drills.

Saw marks have been found on the granite sarcophagus from the Great Pyramid, and on the basalt pavement blocks from the temple of that pyramid, and drills were certainly used for hard stone statues and vases. It is true that cutting basalt with a plain copper saw would be somewhat difficult. Nowadays we sometimes cut hard stones by using points of even harder stones which are set into a drill or saw. The use of diamond points in industry is well known. Diamond ranks 10 on a measuring device known as the Mohs scale; it can cut just about anything, including quartzite, the hardest stone the Egyptians ever quarried (7 on the Mohs scale). But, sad to say, the Egyptians did not have diamonds. Neither did they have topaz (8) or rubies and sapphires (9) or even beryl (8) before the Greek period. We must conclude, then, that the Egyptians did not use hard stone points, or teeth, to cut their granite and quartz.

There is another method of cutting hard stone: with an abrasive powder. Diamond dust is used to cut diamonds. Having no diamonds, the Egyptians had no diamond dust, either, nor, so far as we can tell, did they use pumice or emery powder. They did have quartz sand. If diamond dust can cut diamonds, presumably quartz sand can cut quartz. In one case, sand was found at the bottom of a drill hole in a piece of alabaster; so it is possible that some such abrasive powder, used with copper drills and saws, answers the important question of how the Egyptians cut such stones as granite and basalt.

Once the blocks were cut, they had to be transported to the pyramid plateau. The limestone used was either from Giza or from quarries across the river. The dolerite probably came from the Fayum, not too far away, but the granite was cut at Assuan, six hundred miles south of Giza. All the stones were transported, as far as possible, by water, being floated across the river from Tura to Giza in the case of the limestone, and carried by boat downstream from Assuan in the case of the granite. Probably the transport was done during the period of high water, when much of the valley lay under the inundation and the stones could be floated right up to the base of the plateau. The hardest part of the job was the distance from the bottom of the plateau up to the pyramid site.

Although we have no description or drawing of stones being

dragged up to a pyramid site, there is an interesting scene in a Twelfth Dynasty tomb which depicts the transport of a colossal statue. The colossus rests on a sledge without wheels, which is pulled by 172 men. Perched precariously on the knee of the statue the overseer claps his hands to set the rhythm for the "heave-ho" chant which still accompanies heavy labor in the Near East. Another man, on the front part of the sledge, pours water onto the ground to lubricate the track. This colossus must have weighed fifty or sixty tons. The blocks for the pyramid ranged from a mere two tons to a possible, staggering, 200 tons (in the temple of the Third Pyramid). But there is no doubt that they were pulled, just as the statue was, without assistance from wheels or engines.

Now we have the stone and the site all prepared. It remains only to build the pyramid.

Archaeologists are still debating the details of pyramid building, just as they disagree about a number of other things relating to ancient Egypt. There is little disagreement, though, about the main point: that these mammoth structures, and all the other colossal building works of Egypt, were constructed without motive power other than that of human muscle, and with the simplest of machines. It has been claimed that the Egyptians had pulleys. Maybe so, but the theory is not widely accepted. The conventional view is that the stones of the pyramids must have been dragged into place, just as they were dragged across the land between the river and the pyramid site. Ramps are the only possible method, and ramps must have been used.

If you put two Egyptologists into a room together and mention a subject—any subject—connected with ancient Egypt, you will probably get two different theories. A ramp is a simple affair, and most Egyptologists agree that ramps must have been used. Nevertheless, there are two different ramp theories. According to one, a main ramp was built straight out at right angles to the face of the pyramid, with subsidiary ramps or scaffolds on the other three sides. The alternate theory suggests that there were four ramps, one starting at each corner, resting on the rough outer surface of the casing stones and rising parallel to the faces of the pyramid. If the reader really cares about the problem he may refer to the Bibliography and read the arguments of the opposing schools; they are too long to mention here. The important thing is: no pulleys, no hoists, only muscle power and ramps.

Naturally no ramps were needed for the first layer of stones; they were hauled up to the leveled site and shoved into their designated places. Then the ramp was built. It would be raised for each new level, and the next layer of stones would be dragged up and positioned. The process was not quite that casual; you can build a pyramid by piling blocks on top of other blocks, but the result will not be very stable unless each block goes into the right place. In many pyramids additional stability was given by internal casings, or accretion faces (see diagram). The blocks of these inner casings, made of the finer Tura limestone, were built into the core of the pyramid as it went up.

Something else was built in—the "substructure," here located in the heart of the pyramid—mortuary chambers, ramps and passages. Even the huge granite sarcophagus was lowered into the burial chamber before it was roofed over. One of the pyramid mystics' favorite arguments has been the fact that the sarcophagus is bigger around than the passage leading up to the burial chamber. I don't know what this could possibly prove (djinns?) except the obvious—that the sarcophagus was put in from up above before the roofing blocks of the chamber were added.

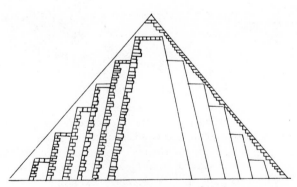

*Diagram showing accretion faces*
*and facing stones of pyramid*

Although the external design of the pyramid was probably established from the beginning, the interior underwent several changes of plan. There is an entrance in the north face, some fifty feet above the ground, and about twenty-five feet east of the center of that side. From here a corridor led down at an angle of approximately twenty-five degrees, through the pyramid and down into the rock of the plateau. The entrance was probably masked by casing blocks which looked like all the other casing blocks, and the passage itself is less than four feet high; it was not designed for the convenience of inquisitive tourists. The descending passage goes along for 345 feet and levels off, ending in a small, uncompleted chamber. On the far side of this chamber the passage continues for a little way before ending abruptly.

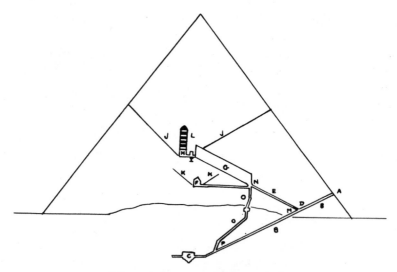

*Plan of Great Pyramid of Giza*

a. entrance; b. descending passage; c. incomplete burial chamber of first stage; d. entrance to ascending passage; e. ascending passage; f. "Queen's Chamber"; g. grand gallery; h. burial chamber; i. antechamber; j. air passages (?) from King's Chamber; k. same from Queen's Chamber; l. relieving chambers; m. plugs blocking ascending passage; n. entrance to well; o. well; p. connection of well with descending passage

This chamber and passage were probably part of the original interior plan, which called for a burial chamber under rather than in, the pyramid. Subterranean burial chambers are found in other pyramids, including both the other Giza tombs. But later on, Khufu changed his mind. By that time the pyramid itself was partly built, so the workers had to cut a passage up through the roof of the descending corridor at a point about sixty feet from the entrance. The new, ascending passage ran up through the blocks of the pyramid core, going up at the same angle as the older corridor went down. It was about 130 feet long. Then it leveled off, and at the end of the level stretch, right in the middle of the pyramid, a chamber was built. It is the so-called "Queen's Chamber," although it was not meant for a queen, but was the king's burial chamber in this second stage of design. The corridor leading to it is so low that present-day tourists have a choice of two equally awkward positions: hands and knees, or an angle, at the waist, of ninety degrees.

Before the Queen's Chamber was finished, Khufu changed his mind again. We don't know why. He went back to the top of the ascending corridor and built the Grand Gallery. It goes on up at the same angle as the ascending corridor, but instead of being only a few feet high its ceiling is 28 feet above the floor. The walls are only 7 and a half feet high, and above them there is a corbel vault of astounding size—some 153 feet long. It is still one of the most imposing sights in Egypt, in spite of the naked light bulbs and the crude iron stairs which have been constructed to aid weak tourists in reaching the Burial Chamber.

This, the "King's Chamber," was the third and final burial chamber. It was lined with granite blocks and it is rectangular in size, measuring about 34 by 17 feet, and 19 feet in height. It does not open directly off the Grand Gallery, but is reached through a low passage and an antechamber. The King's Chamber is perfectly plain—no paintings, no inscriptions, no reliefs. The walls are smooth except for two curious breaks—shafts, which start from the north and south walls and go all the way through the pyramid at angles of thirty-one and forty-five degrees respectively. We don't know why these shafts were built; they are too small for anything bigger than a mouse. The most obvious suggestion is that they were for ventilation; not so absurd as it sounds, since the king was not really dead. However, it is doubtful that the Egyptians realized the healthful value of fresh air. They provided no such shafts in later tombs. Possibly there was a religious reason which is yet unknown. The Queen's Chamber has similar shafts, but they were never finished.

Although the King's Chamber has a flat ceiling, it is only the base of a remarkable architectural element. Above the ceiling there are five small rooms or compartments, one above the other. The lower four have flat roofs, and the highest has a pointed roof. All these little chambers were invaded by modern searchers looking for hidden treasure, but it is unlikely that anything was ever concealed in them. They were meant to relieve some of the strain on the ceiling of the burial chamber; and it was quite some strain, we must admit. Modern calculations suggest that there was, in fact, no necessity for such elaborate safeguards. The Egyptian engineer may have overcompensated for a pressure which certainly was present, but no one can deny that overcompensation is better than not enough.

Among the objects which were inserted into the heart of the pyramid while it was being built were several huge granite stones. Their function was to plug up the ascending passage after the funeral and keep out (Khufu hoped) ambitious tomb robbers. Three of them were actually found at the bottom of the passage.

Several minor, but intriguing points are raised by these stone plugs. In the first place, they really *are* plugs, being less than half an inch narrower than the width of the corridor, and only about an inch less in height. Maneuvering these huge blocks into position *up* a sloping passage would have been a tricky job even for the Egyptians. How, for instance, could they keep the first block from sliding back down and braining them while they pushed numbers two and three in behind number one?

The answer is that they didn't. The entrance to the ascending passage is an inch narrower than the plugs; they couldn't have been shoved into it from below, via the descending passage. Therefore they must have been put into the pyramid from above, and stored in some spot above the ascending passage until it was time to use them. Measurements show that the only space big enough for them was the Grand Gallery. After Khufu's coffin had been deposited in the huge granite sarcophagus, amid the lamentations of his women and the solemn prayers of the priests, the funeral cortege departed, leaving a crew of workmen in the Grand Gallery. These men levered up the stones which had been stored there and slid them down into the ascending passage, one after the other; they continued to slide until they reached the lower end, whose mouth was too small to let them pass. There they piled up, forming a very effective barricade between the dead king and the outside world.

But what about the workers? Their situation looks bad; they are barricaded from the outside world too. Have we another example of barbaric sacrifice for the benefit of the dead?

Look at the plan of the pyramid. At point N you will see a long well, or shaft, leading down from the Grand Gallery to the lower part of the descending corridor, near the abandoned burial chamber of the first stage. After the entombed workers had lowered themselves down the shaft, all they had to do was walk up the descending corridor, bypassing the plugs in the ascending corridor, and go out. The entrance (A) was the last part to be blocked. It has been suggested, somewhat absurdly, that the workmen put in some strenuous overtime on this escape shaft, without official permission. There is no reason to suppose that Khufu planned to share his tomb with a group of motley workers; this sort of thing was not done during the Fourth Dynasty. Nor is it likely that a work of such magnitude could have been carried out unbeknownst to the official powers.

By the time the interior of the pyramid was finished, the exterior resembled a high flat platform whose sides were hidden by ramps and embankments. Up the main ramp a sweating, chanting gang of workers pulled the stones for the next course of masonry. These stones had already been flattened on the bottom—the bedding joint—and the masons had smoothed the top of the previously laid course to receive the new stones. When the fill, or core, stones had been positioned, the casing blocks of fine Tura limestone were hauled up. Masons had prepared them while they were still on the ground, cutting the jointing sides and the bottom level, and planing the outer surface to approximately the correct slant. Before the stones were slid into place a thin layer of mortar was spread over the bedding joint and the other faces. This was not so much for adhesion, since the weight of the huge stones made them stable enough, but to facilitate movement and make final adjustments easier. The casing stones were then levered into position, using the bosses left in place for that purpose; and then, while the masons smoothed the tops of the stones in the new course, the ramp was raised and lengthened—to preserve the original angle—in preparation for the next course of stone. The very top of the pyramid, 481 feet off the ground, was finished off with a pointed pyramidion, a miniature pyramid of hard stone, sometimes plated with gold.

Then the workers started to demolish the ramp. As it went down, masons swarmed over the face of the structure, smoothing the face of the casing stones so that each block matched neatly with its neighbors. The Egyptians used scaffolding in later periods, so presumably they would have employed it for this purpose. As the ramp descended, the masons worked down, finishing their work by smoothing the lowest course of stones, and the pyramid stood in all its glory, smooth and shining, tipped with gold.

How long would it take to build something this size? Herodotus, the energetic Greek traveler, gawked at the mass of the Great Pyramid as thousands of later tourists have done and, like them, he asked his guides for statistics. He reports that it took twenty years to finish the work, employing 100,000 men "for periods of three months" on the transport of the stone. This makes 400,000 men a year. Probably the estimate is too large. Petrie calculated that 100,000 men might have been employed in a given year, and a modern investigator, Dows Dunham, believes that no more than 2,500 men could have worked on the actual face under construction at a single time.

Herodotus describes how a pyramid was built, but there is no point in quoting him since he did not know as much about it as we do. One sentence, however, is worth repeating: "The upper part of the pyramid was finished first, then the middle, and finally the part which was lowest and nearest to the ground." Obviously Herodotus is—correctly—describing the final polishing and finishing of the casing blocks, but I will never forget the first, wonderful image that popped into my mind when I read this sentence: the top third of the pyramid hanging unsupported in the middle of the air, while the workers shove the middle part under it, and then put the bottom under the middle.

Often when I think about pyramids, and the workers straining to drag the monumental blocks, I remember a scene from a film, one of those day-long, wide-screen, technicolor extravaganzas about the Hebrews. The Hebrews were, in this scene, dragging stones for a temple. Watching the work was Moses, dressed in kilt and collar, which costume showed off his admirable physique. As the sweating slaves groaned and staggered along, one old lady got the hem of her flowing robe (an admirable uniform for stone dragging) caught under the block she was helping to haul. Moses did not know that the old lady was really his mother. Being the hero of the film, however, he tried to get the overseer to stop the block and let the old lady disentangle herself. The cruel overseer refused. The next ten minutes of the film were very exciting. First we saw Moses, rushing frantically around the plateau trying to find someone with enough authority to stop the wicked overseer. Then we flashed to the stone, grinding remorselessly onward, and the elderly female tugging weakly at her skirt—which must have been woven of iron. Back to Moses; back to the old lady. Nobody in the theatre laughed—except me—so apparently it did not strike the audience as incongruous that the Egyptians would employ feeble old ladies for such heavy labor, or that the old lady would prefer a messy death to the immodesty of taking off her dress, or that nobody in the vicinity thought of whacking off the tail of her robe with a knife, or that the overseer would rather run her down than get on with his work. True, a modern automobile is not much deflected when it hits a human being, but a monolithic stone on wooden rollers would probably come to a grinding halt. None of the reliefs show women engaged in work of this sort—masons, stonecutters, laborers, are all men. An old lady wouldn't be worth her bread and onions. I suppose no one enjoys films about ancient Egypt more than Egyptologists; it gives them the generally popular opportunity, rare in their specialized profession, of sneering at someone else's ignorance.

We are also inclined to sneer, I am afraid, at the pyramidologists who, in defiance of all the evidence, persist in believing in the occult properties of the Great Pyramid. It was built, they say, by supermen of ancient times (Anglo-Saxons, usually), and if you know how to read its message, it mentions all the important events of world history—most of which were future events for the pyramid builders, who were thus not only supermen but prophets.

It is easy to understand why people are driven into such beliefs. The pyramid itself promotes extravagant theories; it really is hard to believe that it could have been built by people as poorly equipped as the Egyptians. Another motive which probably prompts the pyramid mystics is the rather pathetic desire to find answers to questions which never can and never will be answerable in terms of feet and inches. I can understand them, but they irritate me nonetheless because their views cheapen a rather impressive accomplishment. We need not ask whether the Great Pyramid was worth the effort. The Egyptians, or some of them, thought it was, and their opinion carries more weight than ours. Whatever the reasons and whatever their moral value, the fact remains that a structure like the Great Pyramid shows what people can do if they want to badly enough. Without iron, without machines, with only human muscle power and human will, they quarried these monumental stones and put them into place. There is more wonder in this than in any marvels of magical lore.

## Boats

We could describe a number of other examples of Egyptian technology, but, for lack of space, we will have to restrict ourselves to only one more. I want to talk about boats.

There are few other countries in which boats have been as important as they were in ancient Egypt. Not only was the river the most convenient form of transportation, flowing straight and navigable for almost six hundred miles, but it split all of Upper Egypt into two halves. Constant communication between the east and west banks was necessary, particularly when a city was built

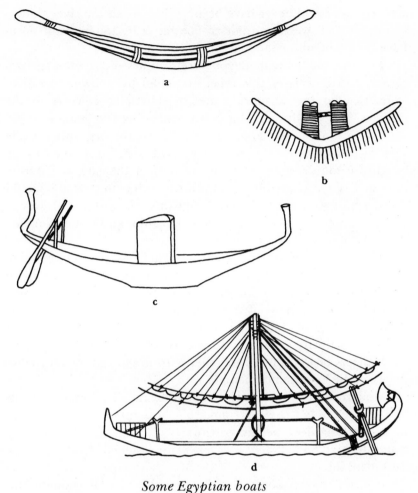

*Some Egyptian boats*
a. reed float; b. predynastic boat; c. funerary boat; d. sea-
going ship of 18th Dynasty

on the east side and its cemetery, as dogma preferred, on the west.
Without boats, it would have been a long walk around. The
Delta, with its many small streams and canals, found water
transportation equally convenient. Some places could only be
reached by water, and boats were a lot more comfortable than
donkeyback or shank's mare. Perhaps the pyramids and the mas-

sive temples could never have been built without the river; blocks of stone which were transported 600 miles by water could never have been hauled the same distance.

The earliest boats in Egypt were bundles of papyrus tied together. Little skiffs of this type, propelled by poles or paddled, were used far into dynastic times by sportsmen fowling in the marshes, and all through Egyptian history by the peasants, who could afford no more elaborate craft. Before the beginning of the First Dynasty, however, fancier boats had been built. We can see rough outline drawings of them on pots of the late predynastic period. I don't know how accurate these drawings are; I would think a boat so sharply curved would sink like a stone. However, we can assume that such boats had twin cabins and were propelled by banks of oars.

These oared predynastic boats must have been made of wood, as were later boats. The Egyptians had a serious problem with regard to wood, since none of their native trees produced good long planks. The boats of the king and the gods were sometimes fashioned of cedar, imported all the way from the Lebanon, but the great majority of craft were patchwork affairs, made of many small pieces of wood fitted together with the matchless skill early displayed by Egyptian carpenters.

Modern boats have a keel, with closely set ribs. Egyptian boats had no keel, only a shell or framework of planks with light ribs at intervals. The deck beams, or thwarts, did not interlock on the frame to give added strength, but were fastened directly to the hull planking.

In calm waters, boats like these would do well enough. But heavy seas, such as might be encountered on voyages to Punt or Asia, could break the back of such a frail structure. Some sort of additional strengthening, to compensate for the absence of a keel, was desirable. The Egyptians did not use nails. Their boats were pegged together, or laced with rope, and they used rope to give added strength to the hull. Some of our examples show heavy cables wrapped around the hull at bow and stern; attached to these was another stout cable which passed fore and aft, over crutches, along the length of the ship.

Oars or paddles like the ones on the predynastic ships were used throughout Egyptian history. When boats sailed downstream with the current, against the prevailing north wind, or when bends in the river made the wind ineffective, the oarsmen got to work. When boats went upstream, with the wind, the sails were raised. Since sails were only useful part of the time, masts were built so that they could be unstepped or, as I would say, taken down. They were then laid on high crutches so as to be out of the way of the steering gear and the rowers. The sails were made of linen, and were square. The earliest sails had only a single yard; they were "loose-footed," and flapped. Later sails had two yards, so that the sail could be used to maximum advantage. Sails also got bigger as time went on, until some were enormous affairs, wider than they were high.

The steering apparatus was simple at first—two or three large paddles, without tiller or rudder post. At the end of the Old Kingdom there was a technological breakthrough in steering; rudder post and tiller were added, and the steering oars were reduced to one. The helmsman followed the directions of an officer who stood in the bow with his eyes wide open and his sounding pole ready. In certain stretches of the river, such as the narrows we referred to in the first chapter, he had to be on his toes.

The Middle Kingdom is the period of models—houses, workers, shops—and boats. We have a number of model craft, all of them quite charming with their little crews and ornaments, including the owner, lounging in a chair and sniffing a flower. Wealthy noblemen of this period may have owned a whole fleet of boats. One of them, at least, had twelve models of various types placed in his tomb.

The standard riverboat might be thirty to forty feet long. Some traveling boats belonging to nobles were extremely elegant, with big cabins made of leather over a wooden framework. The busy official could carry his trunks, his servants, and even a minstrel to sing to him while he sat in the shade, under a canopy, and watched his crew of eighteen ply the oars. When he got hungry, he headed for the banks and had the mooring stake pounded in;

up bustled his kitchen boat, which had been following at a respectful distance. From the small utility cabin of this boat, joints of meat and jars of wine were fetched, and the women servants brought out the bread which they had prepared during the day's travel.

Other boats were designed for the dead rather than the living. The funeral bark proper, which carried the dead pilgrim to the holy city of Abydos, was of a characteristic shape; the curved bows, ending in stylized papyrus flowers, recall very ancient boats made of papyrus or reeds. Other boats placed in the tomb were solar barks, like the ones used by the sun-god, or regular craft which the dead man might need in the hereafter—which was bound to be, the Egyptians argued, as full of water as this present world.

The height of Egyptian boatbuilding was reached during the New Kingdom. Models were dying out, but we have some lovely drawings of boats from tombs and from places such as Hatshepsut's mortuary temple. The great queen dispatched a fleet to the mysterious southern land of Punt in order to bring back exotic trees for the temple she was having built for herself and her father, the god Amon. Since there was no canal between the Nile and the Red Sea in ancient times, boats sailing south to Africa had to be built on the seacoast. There was an ancient port on the Red Sea, not far from the end of the Wadi Hammamat, which led east from the Nile in the vicinity of Coptos. Hatshepsut's great vessels may have been built there: they were true seagoing ships.

Ships sailing north to Asia had no such problem; they simply went down the Nile and out into the sea. There have been a number of wild claims as to the Egyptians' seafaring exploits, but so far there is no evidence from reliable sources that they circumnavigated Africa, or passed the Pillars of Hercules to carry civilization to the wild lands of the Western Hemisphere. Very little is known about their methods of navigation; but we suppose that, like most ancient sailors, they preferred to keep land in sight. This would have been possible during the voyages to Punt, or north to Syria-Palestine, but the Egyptians had commercial and diplomatic contacts with the Aegean islands and/or Crete, and later with Mycenaean cities on the mainland of Greece. They must have lost a lot of ships out there in the Great Green, but they were probably as skilled as any of their contemporaries. Indeed, it is now generally believed that instead of borrowing from their neighbors, the islanders of Crete or the famed seafarers of Phoenicia, the Egyptians actually originated certain types of ships used by the latter. The "Byblos" and "Cretan" vessels were built by the Egyptians for voyages to those places.

But back to the boats themselves. One authority has compared the lines of Eighteenth Dynasty boats to those of modern racing craft. The hull was deeper than that of older boats; the deck beams now passed through the hull and were fastened outside, for added strength. The sails had two yards, the lower of which was stationary. The deck was boarded across. The oars went through loops of rope which served as oarlocks and, perhaps, as a means of holding the oars when the boat was moored. Ships of this type are extremely attractive in appearance, and the size of the sail suggests that they were capable of considerable speed.

In addition to sailing ships, there were barges and freighters. Barges towed by regular boats were used for massive pieces of stone such as obelisks. Hatshepsut depicts two of her obelisks lying end to end on such a barge, which was pulled by thirty boats with almost a thousand rowers. The towing boats had to be rowed, since they were traveling downstream from Assuan to Thebes, against the wind.

Boats were also used in war. Most of them would probably be considered troop transports rather than warships, but some of the texts do mention battles on sea as well as on land. In the Twentieth Dynasty, Ramses III had to fight off a threatened invasion of the Sea Peoples, who came at him from every direction except the air. His warships had long low hulls with raised bulwarks to protect the rowers. They must have been fairly efficient; Ramses won the battle.

### Medicine

The next time a scorpion bites you, you might try this. Recite:

I am the King's son, the eldest and first, Anubis; my mother Sekhmet-Isis came after me forth to the land of Syria, to the hill of the land of Heh, to the nome of those cannibals, saying, "Haste, haste, my child, king's son, eldest and first, Anubis. . . ." And you lick [the bite] with your tongue, while it is bleeding, immediately; then you recite to some oil, you recite to it seven times, you put it on the bite daily; you soak a strip of linen, you put it on it.

There is no field of ancient Egyptian knowledge in which the mixture of magic, science and religion is seen so clearly as in medicine. Most of Egyptian medical lore is, in spirit as well as in form, like the prescription quoted. The only part we would consider efficacious is the licking of the wound, which may imply sucking out the venom. But perhaps the incantation, which invoked the divine names of Isis and Anubis, had some value if it strengthened the patient's will to live.

Egyptian physicians had an excellent reputation in Greek times; to some extent that reputation has survived today. Herodotus mentions that there was specialization, some doctors tending to the feet, some to the teeth, some to the eyes. We have evidence of this specialization even in the Pyramid Age, with Doctors of the Belly, the Head and the Teeth, among others. Physicians were men of some social standing. They owned handsome tombs, and equipped them well.

The diseases treated by these men were, in general, the same ones that afflict the fellahin of Egypt today. Eye trouble, especially ophthalmia, was prevalent. The ancients were also plagued by running ears, rheumatism, and worms. Among the diseases identified in mummies are Pott's disease, which results in spinal deformation; kidney stones and gallstones; arterial disease; and osteocarcoma. Young King Siptah had a club foot, and several of the women had died in childbed. The skin of one royal mummy showed irruptions which might have been caused by smallpox. Diseases which affected only the soft organs of the body are, as a rule, undiagnosable by modern mummy investigators. One poor old lady had been an invalid for so long that she developed a bad case of bedsores, but we do not know what her trouble was.

Since dentists keep telling us that cavities are a result of soft food and too many sweets, we expect people who do not enjoy these dangerous luxuries to have excellent teeth. To some extent this is true; dental caries, or cavities, are not usually found in the teeth of primitive men. But the poor folk of Egypt had other troubles. Their grain was coarsely ground to begin with, and sometimes it got mixed with sand and bits of gravel from the grinding stones. The result was attrition of the hard parts of the teeth, with resultant exposure of the pulp, and alveolar abscesses. After the Pyramid Age the well-to-do classes began to suffer from caries, sometimes in addition to their abscesses.

Now we come to the pertinent question: what did the Egyptian physician do to alleviate all these woes, and others which have left no traces on the physical remains of the long-dead sufferers? For this information we must rely, for the most part, on the medical texts.

In this field the Egyptians were—for them—surprisingly communicative. Considering the vast areas of knowledge and activity for which we have no written documentation, we are pleasantly surprised to find no less than seven papyri dealing with medical problems, from the pharaonic period alone. Several are specialized; the Kahun papyrus deals with gynecology and the Edwin Smith with the surgical treatment of wounds and fractures. Others are collections of miscellaneous material.

The information we derive from the medical texts is certainly useful, but not consistently so. The texts tell us something about medicine and drugs; yet we are still a long way from complete knowledge on this subject. Medicine was given internally in various liquids; water, milk, honey, wine and beer are mentioned. Other medicaments were applied externally, and these were usually mixed with fat to form a salve. The burning question for us is, what ingredients were mixed with the liquid or the fat? What, in other words, was the effective pharmacopia of the ancient Egyptian doctor?

Some ingredients came from animals, and these are fairly easy for us to identify. Blood, fat, bones and organs of various mammals, reptiles and insects were used, as well as entire bodies if they were small enough to be macerated or taken intact. One remedy used for children's diseases was a skinned mouse, swallowed whole; evidently this nasty object was a last resort, for the remains of the mouse have been found in the alimentary canals of several little bodies. Warren Dawson points out that the use of mice as a children's medicine has continued up to modern times, in Europe as well as in the Near East. However, an ordinary M.D. would not be apt to write you a prescription for it.

The plant and mineral ingredients in prescriptions are still giving archaeologists trouble. Perhaps an example will show why. Suppose that you find, in your medical papyrus, a word "abet." You know it is a vegetable substance because it has the determinative that signifies the category of "plants." But you have never met it in any but a medical context, and it is not related to any word you do know. You look at the prescriptions in which it occurs, and you find that it is used to prevent baldness and to cure excessive menstruation, eye infections, and warts. What is it?

Thanks to the really brilliant analyses of some specialized scholars, we can now identify a certain number of these vegetable substances. None suggests that the Egyptians had made any significant discoveries. Often plants seem to have been selected for magical values, as was also true in medieval leechcraft. Thus a red fruit might restore a patient's healthy color, or a plant leaf shaped like the organ affected might be selected to cure an injury to or deficiency in that organ.

Given the early development of medical specialization, as indicated by the titles of doctors, we might anticipate a high degree of anatomical and physiological knowledge. And, considering the dreadful condition of ancient teeth, we would expect the Doctors of the Teeth to be especially active.

One of the surprising facts brought out by the study of human remains from Egypt is the conspicuous absence of surgical treatment. Some operations certainly were performed. A very ancient scene shows the act of circumcision, which was commonly practiced in Egypt. In this picture the "doctor" squats on the ground in front of the patient, who is standing. Sometimes an attendant holds the victim's wrists, but one valiant lad is unconfined; he places one hand lightly on the operator's head and has the other resting nonchalantly on his hip. This surgery was performed with a stone knife, probably for ritual reasons, since the doctors, like other craftsmen, had copper tools available to them.

Although other ancient cultures certainly did practice trepanning there is no sign that the Egyptians tried it. Splints were used, and so were bandages and pads of various sorts, and in these cases the art of the embalmer and that of the physician may have overlapped. Splints were employed to hold damaged mummies together, and of course mummy bandaging was an old skill; but we cannot tell whether splints for the living preceded splints for the dead, or vice versa. One medical text describes how to treat a dislocated jaw; the procedure sounds effective, if painful.

Particularly noteworthy is the apparent absence of any sort of dentistry. I cannot imagine what the Doctors of the Teeth were doing! Great claims have been made for Egyptian dentistry on the basis of one hole in one jawbone from the Fourth Dynasty which, according to enthusiasts, was drilled in order to drain an abscess under a tooth. But if that was the purpose of the hole, it is very strange indeed to find no other evidence of the activity of the Doctors of the Tooth. If any man merited their attentions, it would have been the king; and yet one mummy—tentatively identified as that of Amenhotep III—had teeth so badly abscessed that they must have reduced the poor man to a state of screaming misery, and semi-invalidism. Yet nothing was done, so far as we can see, to relieve this condition.

Up to this point we have done nothing but criticize the ancient Egyptian physicians; now we must look at their accomplishments. In some areas these accomplishments were quite impressive. So once again let us abandon our mummies in favor of the medical papyri, and investigate these texts in greater detail. We are going to concentrate on one papyrus—the so-called "Edwin Smith." It is named after its first (modern) owner, an American who worked in Egypt in the 1860's.

Edwin Smith was a member of a class which has been—politely —called "adventurers." Many of the pioneers of Egyptology, such as the flamboyant ex-circus performer Belzoni, belong to the same category. Smith's avowed professions were those of moneylender and antiquities dealer. Both professions give, on occasion, ample scope for skulduggery. Few of the antiquities dealers of that era were overly scrupulous about the sources of the objects they bought, and Smith has been accused, among other things, of forging some of his stock.

In January of 1862 a group of turbaned Egyptians appeared in Smith's office with a papyrus roll for sale. It was incomplete, and looked rather as if someone had trimmed its edges to make them neater, but Smith recognized it as a valuable acquisition. He bought it. To this day, no one knows where the thieves found it—but that they were thieves no one can deny, since the previous owner had never officially bequeathed it to them. It may have come from the tomb of that owner—a physician of ancient Egypt.

Two months after the first sale, the Egyptians turned up with another medical roll. Smith looked it over and realized that it was a fake, made up of odds and ends, and covered, to lend it verisimilitude, with scraps which had been cut off the first papyrus! Nevertheless he bought this roll too; and among the fragments so rescued was one containing a particularly important section of the original scroll—a passage on the action of the heart.

Smith never disposed of this papyrus. He left it to his daughter, who gave it and his papers to the New York Historical Society. The Society called in James Henry Breasted to translate and publish the text, which he did in 1930. To his surprise, Breasted found that Smith had left extensive notes on the text, which he had tried to translate. Like many of his fellow "adventurers," he was no simpleminded crook. His notes display a surprising knowledge of the Egyptian language, considering that during his lifetime the modern knowledge of the hieroglyphs was less than fifty years old. The text is written in the cursive hieratic script, which was at that time even less well understood than hieroglyphic writing.

By a strange coincidence, Edwin Smith was also at one time in possession of another extremely important medical text—the papyrus later bought by the German Egyptologist Ebers, and named after him. The Ebers and the Edwin Smith papyri are the most useful and interesting of all the texts; the others are either fragmentary, or so hopelessly mixed with magic as to give little information on medical knowledge.

Ebers (Egyptologists often refer to papyri solely by name) is the longer of the two—the longest, in fact, of all the medical texts. It is twenty meters long—rather an unwieldy size, we might think, but the Egyptians were accustomed to handle such rolls. This text is really a mixture, much less homogeneous than Edwin Smith. It contains: recitals of incantations before treatment; internal diseases; diseases of the eye, skin, extremities, head and sense organs; diseases of women and housekeeping matters; general medical notes; surgical cases.

Much of this, particularly the earlier sections, belongs to the category which Warren Dawson has called "magico-medical," as opposed to true medicine. We cannot avoid the suspicion that what we have in Ebers is a one-volume reference library for a practicing physician, who copied down, perhaps from other volumes, all the remedies and reminders and prescriptions that he found useful in his daily profession. Yet there are sections in the Ebers papyrus which indicate an approach quite alien to the magico-medical parts. This approach can best be seen and described, however, in the shorter Edwin Smith papyrus.

The Edwin Smith text was probably written during the New Kingdom, but it contains material copied from a much older source—a source that may go back as far as the thirtieth century B.C., before the Pyramids were raised at Giza. The text, in its original form, is so old that four or five hundred years after it was first composed, a copyist decided that it would be a good idea to explain some of the then archaic terminology. He added a section of explanations—archaeologists call them "glosses"—after each case, a sort of commentary on confusing phrases and words.

Considering that we are living four thousand years after this first commentator felt it necessary to emend his "archaic" text, Professor Breasted's accomplishment in translating the papyrus becomes quite impressive. It is really an excellent translation; succeeding scholars have criticized various details of it, but very few of them have succeeded in offering anything better.

Edwin Smith deals with the surgical treatment of wounds and fractures. As it now stands, it contains forty-eight cases, starting with the top of the head and moving down; but unfortunately, our copy stops just below the shoulders. Was the scribe interrupted, or is the remainder lost? The order is interesting; it is a logical way of organizing cases dealing with the human body, and it was, in fact, the standard order through the Middle Ages.

I think we can do no better than to quote one of the cases from Edwin Smith. Here is case number seven:

> *Instructions:* a gaping wound in his head, penetrating to the bone, perforating the suture [?] of his skull.
>
> You should palpate his wound, [though] he shudders greatly. You should cause him to lift his face. [If] it is difficult for him to open his mouth, and his heart is weary to speak; if you observe his spit upon his lips, not falling to the ground, while he gives blood from his nostrils and ears, and he suffers a stiffness in his neck and is not able to look at his shoulders and breast; then you say concerning him:
>
> "One having a gaping wound in his head, reaching to the bone, perforating the sutures [?] of his skull; the cord of his mandible is contracted; he gives blood from his nostrils and ears; he suffers a stiffness in his neck;
>
> "An ailment with which I will contend."
>
> Now if you find the cord of that man's mandible—his jaw— is contracted, you should have made for him something hot, until he is comfortable, so that his mouth opens. You should bind it with fat, honey and lint, until you know that he has reached a decisive point.
>
> If then you find that man has developed fever from that wound which is in the sutures [?] of his skull, while that man has developed *ti3* from that wound: you should lay your hand upon him. Should you find his face is wet with sweat, the ligaments of his neck are tense, his face is ruddy, his teeth [and] his back . . . , the odor of the box of his head is like the urine of goats, his mouth is bound, his eyebrows are drawn, while his face is as if he wept, you should say concerning him:
>
> "One having a gaping wound in his head, reaching to the bone, perforating the sutures [?] of his skull; he has developed *ti3*, his mouth is bound, he suffers a stiffness in his neck;
>
> "An ailment not to be treated."
>
> If, however, you find that that man has become pale and has already shown exhaustion, you should have made for him a wooden brace, padded with linen, and put it in his mouth. You should have made for him a draught of *w'h* fruit. His treatment is sitting,

placed between two supports of brick, until you know he has reached a decisive point.

(Commentary)

As for "perforating the sutures [?] of his skull," it means: what is between shell and shell of his skull, and that the sutures [?] are of leather.

As for "the cord of his mandible is contracted," it means: a stiffening on the part of his ligaments at the end of his ramus, which are fastened to his cheekbone, that is, at the end of his jaw, without moving to and fro, so that it is not easy for him to open his mouth because of his pain.

As for "the cord of his mandible," it means: the ligaments which bind the end of his jaw, as one says "the cord" of a thing, as a splint.

As for "his countenance wet with sweat," it means that his head is a little sweaty, like "a thing is wet."

As for "the ligaments of his neck are tense," it means: that the ligaments of his neck are stiff because of his injury.

As for "his face is ruddy," it means: that the color of his face is red, like the color of the *tmst*-fruit.

As for "the box of his head is like the urine of goats," it means: that the odor of his crown is like the urine of goats.

As for "the box of his head," it means: the middle of his crown next to his brain; the likening of it is to a box.

As for "his mouth is bound, both his eyebrows are drawn, while his face is as if he wept," it means: that he does not open his mouth that he may speak, both his eyebrows are distorted, one drawing upward, the other drooping downward, like one who winks while his face weeps.

As for "he has become pale and has already shown exhaustion," it means: becoming pale, because he is a [case of] "Undertake him, do not abandon him, in view of the exhaustion."

At first glance this excerpt may seem long and confusing, but the more closely one considers it, the more fascinating it becomes. The first thing one notices is the striking difference in approach between Edwin Smith and texts like the one quoted at the beginning of this section. In the description of the skull fracture, and in the other cases discussed in Edwin Smith, the approach is rigorously matter-of-fact. There are no appeals to divinities, no dubious prescriptions, no incantations, and no mention of demons. In fact, another case explicitly states that the illness is not caused by something entering from without, like a malicious ghost; it is "a thing which [the patient's] own flesh has made."

All the cases in Edwin Smith are organized in the same manner as the one we have quoted, and the organization is admirable. First comes the title: "Instructions concerning" whatever it is. Then follows a description of the symptoms. The third element is the physician's diagnosis, beginning with "you should say concerning him," and ending with a prognosis, which may take one of three forms: 1) an ailment which I will treat; 2) an ailment with which I will contend; 3) an ailment not to be treated. Following the prognosis comes the suggested treatment. Then, at the end of the case we find the glosses, or comments which explain difficult phrases.

The Edwin Smith Papyrus is also noteworthy for the detail and accuracy of the physician's observations, which are meticulously recorded. The doctor recognizes the significance of various symptoms, and changes his treatment accordingly. His anatomical knowledge is very detailed. The texts give words for skull, for brain-pan or brain-case, and for the brain itself. Jawbone and cheekbone are distinguished; it is observed that the end of the jawbone joins to the cheekbone. The ramus of the mandible—or, in nonmedical terminology, the end of the jawbone—is described, in Egyptian, as a "claw"-shaped object. In the commentary to another case it is further explained as resembling the claw of a certain bird, which has two opposing members. Thus the bone, whose location is precisely named, ends in a double-headed connecting part; so the translation "ramus" is obvious.

The "cord" of the mandible is, equally obviously, the ligament or tendon of that bone. If it is "bound," or locked, the man cannot open and close his mouth. Here again the physician's knowledge is extremely accurate.

Tendons, muscles and ligaments were known, and their operations were understood. Yet here we come up against one of the gaps in ancient knowledge which is only to be expected, and yet which surprises us because the other information is so exact. The word used for muscles, tendons, and ligaments was the same word, and it could also mean "vessel"—a hollow tube which carried the bodily fluids. It is strange to find one word covering such disparate entities, particularly when, as seems probable, the Egyptians knew quite well the difference between the functions of a ligament and those of a blood vessel.

The section of the medical papyrus Edwin Smith which deals with the heart and the vessels—a section also found in Ebers—is one of the most interesting and significant aspects of Egyptian medical lore. These vessels run to various parts of the body—to the eye, to the anus, the arms, and so on. Yet it seems that vessels can carry not only blood, but other bodily fluids. It was well known that blood sometimes flowed from the nose, not only in an ordinary nosebleed, but as the result of a hard blow on the head. Therefore, some of the vessels leading to the nose must carry blood. But the nose also secretes mucus. Then, argued the Egyptians, two of the vessels must carry this mucus to the nose from somewhere inside the body. Vessels also carried urine, semen, and water.

Where did the vessels originate? They were connected with the heart; yet we cannot say that the Egyptians recognized the heart's function as a pump for passing blood around the body. The heart was a vital organ, perhaps the most vital of all. Other, nonmedical texts make it clear that the heart was thought to hold not only the emotions but also the functions we know to be connected with the brain.

One of the great achievements of Egyptian medicine was the discovery of the pulse. It was called the "voice of the heart," and in one section, found in both Ebers and Edwin Smith, the physician is told where in the body this voice "speaks." Remarkable as this is, it is not enough to let us claim that the Egyptians anticipated Harvey in the discovery of the circulatory system. Yet they knew not only that the pulse was connected in some way with the heart, but that it was a factor the physician had to note. They did not count the pulse; they could not have done so, since they could not measure small units of time accurately. But its usefulness as a general symptom was certainly known.

The functions of the brain were never really recognized. In mummification the brain was not even preserved, as were many of the organs removed from the body. It was often pulled out, in pieces, and discarded. Yet the surgical papyrus shows that the medical writer of the text recognized that injury to the brain could affect motor activities. One case gives a beautiful description of a case of partial paralysis of one side of the body resulting from a blow on the head.

The physician took full advantage of skull injuries to observe the brain. One case refers to something inside the skull which resembles copper slag; although Breasted's interpretation of this has been questioned, I fail to see how it could be anything except the gray brain matter itself, with its convolutions. There is mention of a membrane enveloping the brain, and of a liquid which can only be the cerebrospinal fluid.

The word we have translated as "sutures" is particularly difficult. Perhaps the ancient commentator found it difficult too; but it cannot be said that his explanation helps us a great deal. He says it is between two "shells" of the skull. These "shells" must be bones of the head, and the only things which can be said to be "between" them are the sutures, the lines of union. Yet the commentator adds that these "sutures," or whatever they are, resemble leather. This does not sound like a good description of the texture of the suture. However, no one has suggested a better translation, so I have retained that of Breasted—with a question mark.

The mention of leather in connection with this doubtful word does remind us of something else found inside the skull—the dura mater, or tough membrane, the outermost of the three membranes surrounding the brain. We would be tempted to translate our questionable word as "dura mater," except for two difficulties. First, the dura mater is not exactly between the bones of the skull; and, second, there is another word which almost certainly refers to the membrane enclosing the brain.

The Egyptian physician's extensive knowledge of the anatomy of the brain and skull must have been derived from his observation of head injuries; he could not have learned it from his friend the embalmer. The contributions of mummification to anatomy have probably been greatly overrated; the embalmer was not interested in how the parts went together, and the only area of the body in which he did any extensive excavating was the abdominal cavity.

I began this chapter on science by remarking that there was almost no such thing in Egypt. "Almost" is not "altogether"; and if any production of ancient man can be called scientific, the Edwin Smith surgical papyrus deserves that description. It is indeed one of the high points, not only of Egyptian empirical knowledge, but of thought and reasoning. In its sober, rational approach, its careful organization and meticulous documentation, and, above all, in its attempt to reason from observed data, without demons, Edwin Smith is a work of science, in the strictest sense of that word. Yet how are we to interpret it? As a separate, distinct current of speculative thought which existed side by side with the leech-magician's lore? As the work of a single great man or school, whose results were copied for countless generations not because the copyists recognized the greatness of its implicit content, but because they found it useful? Or as one aspect of the Egyptian "multiplicity of approaches," which excluded no idea simply because it was inconsistent with another, so long as it had limited value?

Being a romantic, I have been fired by the suggestion that Edwin Smith, and Ebers, and a few of the other texts, derive their surgical lore from a single, very old source. And my imagination inevitably reacts to the fact that this postulated source book may come from a period roughly contemporaneous with Imhotep, the Old Kingdom sage. Imhotep's reputation as a physician outshone even his fame as an architect; it was as a medical man that he was deified. We would be going far beyond the evidence if we suggested seriously that the surgical papyrus owes its existence to Imhotep. Still, if I were a physician today, I would join the movement—already begun, I believe, by some historically minded doctors—to give to Imhotep the honored position, now accorded Hippocrates, as the father of medicine. As George Sarton has pointed out, "Hippocrates comes about halfway between Imhotep and us." He also comes about halfway between us and the lost original of the Edwin Smith surgical papyrus, which is thus the oldest scientific document in the world; and its author, whether it was Imhotep or another, unknown genius, ought to rate, at the very least, a placque in some medical institution.

# XII
# "The God Is Satisfied with His Offerings"

## The Official Religion

There will come a time when it will be seen that in vain have the Egyptians honored the deity with heartfelt piety and assiduous service, and all our holy worship will be found bootless and ineffectual. . . . Oh Egypt, Egypt, of thy religion nothing will remain but an empty tale, which thine own children in time to come will not believe; nothing will be left but graven words, and only the stones will tell of thy piety. And so the gods will depart from mankind.

YES, the gods are gone—Amon and Isis, jackal-headed Anubis, even Osiris, lordly judge of the dead. In a way, it seems a pity. For if man does make gods in his own image, the Egyptian gods testify to the tolerance of their creators. They lacked the nasty habits of some other deities, who thrived on incinerated babies and dripping human hearts, or required the complete annihilation of people who held other opinions on religious matters. Except for one brief period, Egyptian religion was the most broad-minded of

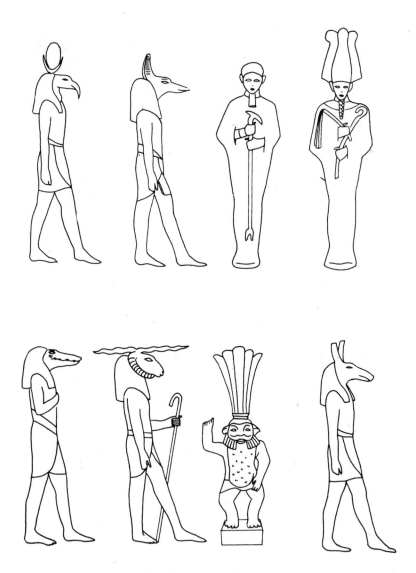

*Some of the principal gods*

Above left to right: Thoth, Anubis, Ptah, Osiris. Below,
left to right: Sobek, Khnum, Bes, Set

*Some of the principal goddesses*

Above, left to right: Bastet, Hathor, Maat, Nephthys. Below,
Taweret and Isis nursing Horus

faiths. If a foreigner could not find some Egyptian god or other to worship, he was very hard to please; but even in that case the amiable Egyptians allowed him to worship his own god, or even adopted it themselves.

The Egyptians were just about the most polytheistic people who ever lived. No one knows exactly how many gods they had; one list gives over eighty, and I suspect it is incomplete. Before we get into the mainstream of the symposium, we had better start with the Cast of Characters—a list, not of all eighty, but of the principal gods and their attributes, to whom we will be referring. The list itself is an oversimplification. There is still debate on who the gods were, how they got to be that way, and what they stood for:

Gods:

   *Amon*—One of the eight gods of chaos; god of wind or air. City: Thebes. Sacred animals: ram, goose; but always shown in human form. Wife: Mut. Son: Khonsu.

   *Anubis*—God of cemeteries, embalming. Animal: jackal. Son of Osiris and Nephthys.

   *Atum*—Creator god, identified with Re.

   *Bes*—Dwarfish bandy-legged god of bedchamber, toilet table; wears leopard skin and ostrich headdress.

   *Geb*—Earth god. Sacred animal: goose. Son of Shu and Tefnut. Wife: Nut. Children: Osiris, Isis, Nephthys, Set.

   *Hapi*—The Nile. Shown as a plump man with pendulous female breasts.

   *Horus*—Originally sky god, hawk-headed, whose eyes were sun and moon; identified with king. In his form of Horus of the Horizon, Harakhate, merged with Re to become Re-Harakhte. Became confused with Horus the son of Isis and Osiris, the great antagonist of Set.

   *Khephra*—Sun, creator god. Animal: beetle. Identified with Re.

   *Khonsu*—Moon god. Shown as handsome boy with sidelock. City: Thebes. Son of Amon and Mut.

   *Khnum*—The "Molder," creator god, who made mankind out of clay. City: Elephantine. Animal: ram.

   *Min*—Ithyphallic, fertility god, patron of desert and travelers. City: Coptos.

*Montu*—God of war. City: Hermonthis (Thebes). Animals: bull, falcon.

*Osiris*—God of the dead, judge of spirits. Shown in mummiform human shape. City: first Busiris, then Abydos. Wife: Isis. Son: Horus.

*Nefertum*—Son of Ptah and Sekhmet. Human form. Insignia: lotus.

*Ptah*—God of artisans, craftsmen; always in human form. Sacred animal: Apis bull. City: Memphis.

*Re*—Great sun-god. City: Heliopolis. Animals: falcon, Mnevis bull.

*Set*—Brother and murderer of Osiris. God of highlands, foreigners. Animal: doglike, unidentified beast. City: Ombos, later Tanis Avaris.

*Shu*—God of atmosphere, who separates Geb, earth, from Nut, sky. Son of Atum, husband of Tefnut.

*Sobek*—Crocodile god. Centers of worship: Fayum, Kom Ombo.

*Thoth*—Divine scribe, inventor of numbers. Associated with moon. Animals: ibis, baboon. City: Hermonthis.

*Wepwawet*—Mortuary god. City: Assiut. Animal: wolf.

GODDESSES:

*Bastet*—Goddess of warmth, pleasure, dancing, music. Animal: cat. City: Bubastis.

*Hathor*—Goddess of love, beauty, joy. Animal: cow. City: Denderah.

*Heket*—Frog goddess. Midwife who assisted birth of sun.

*Isis*—Symbol of devoted wife (of Osiris), mother (of Horus). Animal: cow.

*Maat*—Goddess of truth, law, order. Daughter of Re. Symbol: feather. Always in human form.

*Meskhenet*—Goddess of childbirth. Shown as woman with two long curved shoots on head.

*Mut*—(Pronounced mo͞ot.) Mother goddess. Wife of Amon. City: Thebes. Son: Khonsu.

*Neith*—(Pronounced like "night.") Goddess of hunting and war. Symbol: crossed arrows. City: Sais.

*Nekhbet*—One of the Two Ladies who protected the king, tutulary goddess of Upper Egypt. Animal: vulture. City: Nekheb.

*Nephthys*—Sister of Isis and Osiris, wife of Set, but sympathetic to Osiris; hence one of goddesses who guarded the dead.

*Nut*—(Pronounced nōōt.) Sky goddess. Animal: cow. Wife of Geb.

*Sekhmet*—Goddess of battle. Animal: lion. City: Memphis. Wife of Ptah. Associated with medical profession.

*Selket*—Daughter of Re, presides over embalmed entrails, protectress of the dead. Animal: scorpion.

*Seshat*—Goddess of learning. Symbol: star on a pole with inverted horns.

*Taweret*—Hippopotamus goddess of childbirth.

*Tefnut*—Goddess of moisture, mother of Geb and Nut, wife of Shu.

*Wadjet*—Second of the Two Ladies; goddess of Lower Egypt. Animal: cobra. City: Buto.

One of the things that makes a discussion of Egyptian religion so confusing is not so much the number of gods, but the fact that they refuse to stay in the neat little slots we construct for them. Through the process called syncretism, one god might assume the name and attributes of two or three others, as Amon of Thebes became Amon-Re Harakhte. Instead of sharing names, he might usurp some other god's titles, or insignia, or job. So Osiris took first the insignia of an ancient Delta god named Andjti and then the title and position of a mortuary god of Abydos. The animal-headed gods overlap frightfully—a falcon may represent Re, Horus, Montu, or any one of a number of others. All these factors are relatively unimportant, however, compared with a really serious problem of overlap which has annoyed most students of Egyptian religion. We will see it best through an example. So let us go back to the beginning of all things and see how, according to Egyptian dogma, the world was created.

In the beginning there was the primeval abyss—chaos—formlessness. Out of the waters of chaos there gradually emerged a small hillock of wet ground, just as, after the annual inundation begins to subside, little mounds of earth come into view above the falling waters. On this primeval mound appeared Atum, the Creator.

Atum was a male god. Despite this handicap, he produced the first couple, the god Shu and the goddess Tefnut, air and mois-

*Geb, Nut, and Shu*

ture. In a relatively refined version of the story he accomplished this by spitting. A more pragmatic version makes the hand and phallus of the god the agents of creation. Whatever his method, once the first pair of male and female deities appeared, reproduction proceeded normally thereafter. Shu and Tefnut bore Geb (earth—male) and Nut (sky—female), who bore Isis and Osiris, Set and Nephthys. This group of nine deities constituted the Ennead of Heliopolis; Atum had adopted the sun-god Re of that city, and was called Re-Atum.

Even this one creation story gives alternative explanations of the method of creation—a third version provides Atum with a female consort. But Atum was not the only creator. Khnum, the potter, who made mankind out of clay, was another. The most provocative of the creation stories is the one called the Memphite Theology. According to this text, the real creator was Ptah, chief god of Memphis:

> The sight of the eyes, the hearing of the ears, the smelling of air of the nose, they report to the heart. This it is which causes every completed conception to come forth, and it is the tongue which proclaims that which the heart thinks. . . . Indeed, every command of the god came into being through that which the heart thought and the tongue commanded.

Here we have creation viewed, not as a physical act, but as the result of divine *will* and divine *utterance*. For "heart" read "brain" or "mind"; the Egyptians thought of the heart as the seat of the intelligence.

The Memphite Theology is one of the Egyptians' finest achievements in philosophic thought. It is more abstract and more profound than the other creation stories; its resemblance to the doctrine of the Logos has been pointed out by many scholars. Yet—and this is the point of our example—neither the Memphite version nor any other creation story ever superseded all the others. For each cosmological phenomenon there was, not one explanation, but many; and all were equally valid.

For a more concrete example, let us look at the sun. Re was a sun-god, and so was Harakhte—Horus of the Horizon. Horus being originally a sky god, the sun was regarded as one of his eyes. But it was also a boat, in which Re sailed across the sky, and a hawk which flew on outspread wings. The most fetching of all the sun myths is the one which identifies the solar orb with Khephri, the beetle-headed god—that same beetle whose form is commemorated in scarabs. How did an earthbound insect get to be a sun-god? Well, you see, the dung beetle of Egypt may often be seen pushing a little round ball of clay along ahead of him as he plods through the sand. From this ball, the ancients believed, the beetle's young emerged, just as the new sun was reborn each morning. Modern science, always disillusioning, says that the clay ball does not, in fact, contain the grub of the beetle; but the Egyptians didn't know that.

A similar "multiplicity of approaches" can be found in almost every object or phenomenon the Egyptians thought seriously about—death, immortality, the rise of the Nile, the stars, and so on, *ad infinitum*. Some scholars find this lack of logical consistency infuriating, and there have been many attempts to pummel the

*The beetle pushing the divine sun disc*

big, floppy system into some sort of solid shape. It will not work. Egyptian religion was not consistent, in our terms. It may have had a consistency of its own, but it is so different from ours that we refuse to call it by the same name. We might reasonably ask how many theological systems are logical, to nonbelievers; the subject matter is not particularly suitable to principles of reason. Furthermore, what we see in Egyptian religion is not an artificially constructed theology, formalized by arbitrary pronouncements from a single source of authority, but a hodgepodge of superstition, magic, sophisticated theorizing, and myth, from dozens of different temples, covering a period of more than three millennia! Certainly we can construct a system to explain everything if we are determined to do so, but we may find ourselves in the awkward position immortalized by an old song:

> Last night I saw upon the stair
> A little man who wasn't there.

My tolerance of Egyptian inconsistency is perhaps, in part, personal; like the Egyptians I have no trouble believing several contradictory things all at once, and I find the universe too complex to be comprehended through a single system of thought. For this reason, or for others which are more defensible, I like Professor Frankfort's term, "multiplicity of approaches." It is a description of what the Egyptians did, rather than a pseudo-psychological explanation of why they did it; and it neatly, and correctly, describes the underlying assumption of Egyptian religion:

"There are a dozen different ways of explaining anything that really matters; and *all of them are right.*"

Our modern approaches to Egyptian religion are not necessarily inconsistent, but they are certainly numerous. No longer can a book on this subject restrict itself to a catalogue of deities. Some studies attempt to synthesize the theology and explain the symbolism—neither of which the Egyptians ever bothered to do; others investigate details of dogma or ritual. One school stresses the historical aspect. A fairly factual history of Egyptian religion can be written, on the basis of the texts and reliefs of dynastic Egypt, but some scholars have tried to penetrate far back into the misty, unknown years of prehistory to describe the very beginnings of religion in Egypt.

In the beginning, then, instead of Atum squatting on his primeval hill, we see Egypt as made of dozens of little villages, each with its own local chieftain and village god. Many of the local gods took animal forms, and they may have been the totems of the primitive communities. As time went on, two things happened. One was an amalgamation—under duress, usually—of the little villages into larger units. The other was a series of invasions of people from outside the valley. As the villages joined together, so did the gods join forces to form a pantheon; and they were accompanied by foreign gods imported by the invader, or invaders, or traders, or whatever they were. Among the invading gods, according to some scholars, was the well-known mortuary god Osiris, whose murder and resurrection form the Egyptian Passion. Settling first in the northern Delta, Osiris became god of the north, and eventually, when the two kingdoms of north and south came to blows, the conflict was viewed as a struggle between Osiris and the indigenous southern god, the red-headed warrior Set. The Great Antagonists, however, are not Osiris and Set, but Set and his nephew, Osiris' son Horus, who was also a northern god. The eventual defeat of Set by Horus commemorates, in mythological form, an ancient conquest of the south by the north.

Another powerful god whose fame goes back to prehistoric times was Re, the sun-god. His city was Heliopolis, but some scholars see him as another foreign god, from a northern region where the sun's life-giving warmth would be more valued than in Egypt. Unlike Osiris, who owed his popularity to the appeal of his resurrection, Re rose to power through the machinations of a clever, well-organized priesthood.

The reader can find one or more of these interpretations cited, as a fact, in most books about Egypt. Naturally the evidence for any one of them is pretty vague; one does not expect much in the way of historic proof from such a remote period. Yet the fragments of fact which we do have often contradict these theories. First and foremost, polytheism is not an additive process. It is unlikely that each little village worshiped only one god, distinct from all the other gods of all the other villages, and it is still more unlikely that the swarming pantheon of historic times was obtained by adding up all the monotheistic gods of all the villages. Totemism is another of those seemingly happy thoughts which cannot be supported. The distinctive traits of the totemic system, such as exogamy, and the identification of the members of the tribe with the animal of the totem, are not found in Egypt.

As for Egypt's famous animal gods, they cannot be described so simply. Some gods were never shown in animal form. Ptah was associated with a sacred bull, the Apis, but he never has a bull's head, nor are bulls, as such, sacred to Ptah. Amon, always depicted as a man, did not borrow even the head of his sacred animal, the goose. Other divinities sometimes have animal forms and sometimes human forms; Hathor may be shown as a shapely woman, or as a woman with a cow's head, or as a shapely cow. The gods were not conceived of as animals, nor were animals worshiped as gods. The gods were beings who could be, at times, interpreted as, or symbolized by, an animal or part animal form.

Egypt may have derived some of her gods from abroad; but as yet we cannot prove that Osiris or Re were immigrants. As for the conquest of the "Followers of Set" by the "Followers of Horus," the only conquest we know of was the historic event which marks the beginning of dynastic history, and that was vice versa—south conquered north. The only evidence for the predynastic conquest, which is often mentioned, is this very myth. Myth may be a poetic description of political or historical events, but this approach can be overworked. Some interpreters see every new, powerful god as the patron of a new, powerful invading army or political party. In these terms the spread of Christianity must have been owing to the ferocity of that conquering sect from Palestine, which first overran the Roman Empire and then defeated the rest of the western nations.

Even after the beginning of historic times—that is, the First Dynasty—we are exceedingly short on evidence with which to construct a legitimate history of Egyptian religion. The uncertainty and the debate over questions relating to prehistoric religion extend into the so-called archaic period. We know that many of the gods prominent during later periods were being worshiped then, and that Horus was already identified with the king. Strangely enough, the name of Set, Horus's implacable foe, also crops up in royal titles during the early dynasties. The quarrelsome red-headed god's significance, from the political and religious aspects, is still the subject of considerable academic discussion. Some authorities believe that Re of Heliopolis was already a powerful god; others argue that Osiris had established himself as Lord of Abydos by this time. The actual evidence for both these last statements is, at best, vague.

By the Old Kingdom we are in slightly better case; for one thing, the inscriptional material has increased. The belief in immortality goes back to the earliest periods in Egypt; prehistoric graves include such pathetic but significant vanities as cosmetic palettes, beads, and pots which once contained food and drink. But it is not until the Fifth and Sixth Dynasties that we know much more about mortuary religion. The Pyramid Texts of this age tell us that Re and Osiris had both acquired status as gods of the dead. During the same era we see an increased importance for Re, the sun-god, in court dogma as well as in the mortuary cult. However, despite the convincing, carefully documented arguments of several distinguished scholars, it is as yet impossible to explain why Re became so important.

During the Middle Kingdom, Re continued to hold his own as divine father of the king, who was at the same time Horus, son of Osiris. The cult of Osiris also spread during this period; the blessing of the resurrected god was now available to commoners, if it had not been so earlier. The rulers of the Middle Kingdom came originally from Thebes, and in the Twelfth Dynasty a hitherto minor god of that city, named Amon, becomes a major divinity. Amon's real nature is somewhat obscure. His name means something like "the Hidden One," and he may have represented the wind or the air. Early in the proceedings Amon associated himself with Re and other sun gods, and took the name of Amon-Re-Harakhte. Whether this was a sound political move, or merely sound theology, we do not know.

Amon's real rise to power did not begin until the Eighteenth Dynasty, when, after a second period of political breakdown, Egypt was reunited under a king of Thebes. Unlike the unifiers of the Twelfth Dynasty, the new Theban kings did not leave home

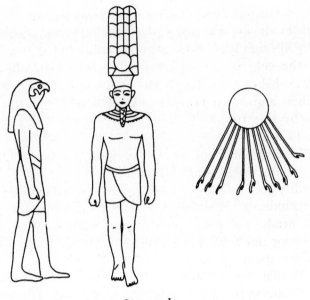

*Sun gods*

Left to right: Re-Harakhte, Amon-Re, Aton

after their conquest. When they set up the national capital in their native town, a temple to Amon was already there; and, as the little villages on the Theban plain grew into "Thebes of the Hundred Gates," so the humble temple of Amon mushroomed into the spectacular structure of Karnak, still, even in its ruins, one of the greatest sights coming down to us from the ancient world. Amon-Re was the divine father of the king and the patron of the warrior pharaohs of the early Eighteenth Dynasty. As Egypt spread out across the Near East, the spoils of empire poured into Thebes, and a goodly share of the booty fell to the temple of Amon-Re.

By the middle of the Eighteenth Dynasty the once-obscure local god of Thebes had become King of the Gods, and "the sole one, who made everything which is." Here, Amon is not only a creator, but he is the only creator—the only god, if we are to take the text literally. This cannot be done, however. The worship of the other gods continued, and some of them also claimed the epithet "sole god." It is only another example of that pleasant inconsistency which is so characteristic of Egyptian religion.

During the period of Amon's aggrandizement, we begin to find occasional references to a god called Aton. Like Amon-Re, he was a sun god, but he was a very small fish. Then, somewhere around the year 1390 B.C., a son and heir was born to the King Amenhotep III and his chief wife Ti, a woman of common birth. The young prince was named Amenhotep, in honor of Amon; he was raised in the royal palace in Thebes, where he surely was trained to pay homage to the gods, chief among them the patron of his house and his city. When the youthful Amenhotep III came to the throne, he was crowned at Thebes. He worshiped Amon. He also built a temple to the obscure godling Aton, who was shown in the form of a hawk-headed human figure, like Re-Harakhte.

Then—almost overnight, or so it seems to us across the gulf of the centuries—came the revolution. Amenhotep IV cast off his official name and chose a new one which incorporated the name of the god Aton—Akhenaton. He moved his court from Thebes to a brand-new city, also named after the Aton, and ordered his tomb to be built within its precincts. In the temples raised to his honor in the new city, Aton was shown, not as a man or an animal-headed man, but as a featureless disc whose only anthropomorphic feature was the row of rays ending in human hands, which extended the sign of life to the king. Some time after the move the king sent emissaries throughout the country, ordering them to chisel out the names of the ancient gods from the walls of tombs and temples. Amon was especially persecuted; not even the name of Akhenaton's father Amenhotep was spared, because it incorporated the hated element. In some cases the plural word "gods" was excised from the inscriptions.

So much is—we are fairly sure—fact. From this point on we enter into a realm of speculation and theory which is so permeated with unscholarly prejudices that it is almost impossible to separate people from their passions. I am certainly not free of prejudice myself; perhaps I still am affected by the glamour of my first meeting with Akhenaton in the pages of James Henry Breasted, who viewed the heretic king as "the first monotheist"

and "the first individual in history." Breasted admired Akhenaton; his masterful prose and his scholarly prestige created an unforgettable picture of a pale dreamer, frail in body but great of
soul, who stood out unflinchingly against the forces of reaction to
create a god who was—almost—God.

Who could resist an image like that one? It still clouds the
surface of my intellect when I try to talk rationally about Akhenaton; and I suspect that the violent antagonism of some scholars is
in direct ratio to the effort they must make to obliterate that same
glamorous picture. The reaction has been violent indeed. Some
modern interpreters see the whole Amarna experiment as the
degenerate product of a sick brain, and Akhenaton as deformed in
body and perverted in soul. He has been accused of marrying his
own eleven-year-old daughter and getting her with child; of di-
vorcing his beautiful wife Nefertiti; of displaying an abnormal
affection for his young son-in-law. The early grotesque statues of
the king are viewed as literal portraits of a pathological condition
which affected his virility; the fact—as certain as a fact can be, in
this uncertain world—that Akhenaton had six daughters is blandly
ignored by the scholars who propound this theory, and it is a good
example of how illogical and unscholarly the "Akhenaton debate"
has come to be. Even the *haute couture* of the period has been
interpreted as decadent—men wearing women's clothing and
copying female hair styles! All this is, of course, as exaggerated as
Breasted's romantic picture.

It is impossible to talk about the "Amarna period," as it is
called, without talking about Akhenaton himself; here, surely, is
one time when the individual, as a force in history, cannot be
denied. The difficulty is that we know almost nothing about
Akhenaton except what we can infer from his activities; and while
the activities are sometimes fairly clear, the interpretations which
can be made from them are manifold—and they are almost always
colored in some way by the personality of the interpreter. I would
like to cite a few examples, just to show the reader that the statements he finds in books about Akhenaton are often based on very
scrappy scraps of proof.

In our day and age it is taboo for a father to marry his daughter. We cannot be sure that the Egyptians would have felt the

same way; in fact, there are several other possible cases of father-daughter marriage in the royal families, one of them almost incontrovertible. However, Akhenaton's affair with his third daughter, that Ankhesenpaaton who later became Tutankhamon's wife, is based on one badly broken inscription which accompanies a picture of a young woman carrying a child. The inscription reads: "The king's daughter, of his body, whom he loves, Ankhesenpa——" then a break of indeterminate length, and then the words, "born of the king's daughter, of his body, whom he loves, Ankhesenpa——" Apparently the young princess was the mother of a child; but its father is not named, nor is there any reason to suppose that the first set of titles and name refers to the baby rather than to the mother. And yet some scholarly books state, without comment or qualification, that Akhenaton married his daughter and fathered her child, solely on the basis of this mutilated inscription.

Akhenaton's break with the lovely Nefertiti is another example of an assumption based on insufficient evidence. The romance between this royal couple is the great love affair of ancient Egypt—if we recall that neither Antony nor Cleopatra was an Egyptian. Yet at the end of his reign, it is supposed, Akhenaton abandoned Nefertiti, or she left him, and the romantic idyll came to a sad end. The evidence? In some of the Amarna inscriptions Nefertiti's name has been erased and replaced by that of her daughter—not Ankhesenpaaton, but Meritaton, the eldest. Furthermore, Akhenaton bestowed one of his wife's epithets on his son-in-law and first successor, Smenkhkare. From this evidence—if it can be called that—comes the theory of the estrangement of the once-devoted couple, which is even more often cited as fact than is the father-daughter marriage.

Just as we must view statements about Akhenaton the man with extreme caution, so we must be equally suspicious of interpretations of Akhenaton's new religion. The Amarna revolution—if we can apply that term to an upheaval in thought which was probably not accompanied by political revolution—involved several new ways of doing things. We have already mentioned the art forms in use at the time. It is possible to emphasize the new developments and stress the iconoclastic nature of the period; it is

equally possible to point out antecedents, and insist that Akhenaton really did not change so much. Although there are precedents
for some of the elements in the Aton faith, such as the claim "sole
god," which was also applied to Amon, I think it would be quibbling to deny that something strange, something radically different, was happening to Egyptian religion. What it was we will try
to ascertain.

The first, vital question is: What did Akhenaton actually
worship? The Aton was depicted as the rounded ball of the sun; it
is sometimes carved in very high relief, so that the three-dimen-
sional quality is unmistakable. Thus, to some scholars, it is the
most physical, the least abstract, of all the gods of Egypt. The
curious half-animal, half-human forms of other gods may have
been—they had to be!—symbolic; but the sun disc is *there,* up in
the sky. Other scholars say that the sun disc was a symbol, too; and
as such it was the most abstract of all the forms of the godhead.

I have my own prejudices about what Akhenaton worshiped;
but I think it is almost impossible to know what *he* thought he
was worshiping. The great Aton hymn, which has been compared
with the 104th Psalm, is not much help. It is full of beautiful but
vague compliments to the god, and it gives a charming picture of
the dependence of all creation, animal as well as human, on the
light and heat of the sun—or on the joy and love of the creator,
depending on how you want to interpret the words.

Another important question is whether the Aton faith was
monotheism or something else. Breasted thought it was monotheism. Most modern scholars are more cautious. The Aton had a set
of titles, a regular royal titulary, in which he was equated with
Shu and Atum and other gods. This, say the skeptics, is not
monotheism. The cautious scholars also point out that Aton was
not worshiped directly by anyone except the king; he was approached through Akhenaton, who was his son, the "only one who
knew him."

Since nothing can be written on the subject of the Aton
monotheism that is fact—it is only one man's theory against
another's—I might as well tell the reader what I think. Pure
monotheism, of the type implied by the reservations mentioned
above, is just about nonexistent. The idea of a divine son as an

intermediary between god and man can be found in modern times, in a faith which would certainly take affront if it were called polytheistic; it also admits a multiple godhead, and worships the deity under many names and epithets. To me the conclusive evidence of Akhenaton's faith being, so far as he was concerned, monotheistic can be found in the persecution of the other gods. Such bigotry is a sure sign of monotheism. It is true that Amon is particularly often defaced, but the other gods were not spared, and there are the rare, but extremely significant examples of the obliteration of the plural word "gods." At the city of Amarna itself no temples to other gods have ever been found. In the workman's village the old gods may have lived on, for official proscription does not destroy a divinity in the hearts of his worshipers. The question is not whether the Aton faith "caught on," but what its true nature was. And the answer, it seems to me, is a fairly good version of monotheism.

Perhaps one of the reasons for the reservations about this conclusion is the fact that Atonism, as we know it, seems to be lacking any ethical system. The "higher religions" have codes of conduct regulating the relations between god and man, and between man and other men. There is very little sign of moral values in the Aton hymn, which is the only statement of the faith surviving to us.

The Aton hymn is about the length of one of the longer Psalms; it is, like the Psalms, a hymn of praise. To assume, because we cannot find in it the Ten Commandments or the Sermon on the Mount, that equivalent statements did not exist is unfair argument. We have so little material, really, and we are accustomed to working over each little scrap so thoroughly, that we tend to forget that what we have is only a small percentage of the total picture. There are very few documents which could be called ethical or moralistic in all Egyptian literature. Akhenaton reigned for seventeen years (claims for a longer reign are based on misinterpretations of the inscriptions), and the religion he created died with him. It is not surprising that we lack documentary statements of belief from a period so short, when we have so few from the whole three-thousand-year span of pharaonic history. I cannot make any exalted claims for Akhenaton as a moralist; but neither can his adversaries dogmatically state that the Aton faith lacked this element.

We do not know the motives that impelled the *soi-disant* Amenhotep IV to take a step so alien to his heritage. Various theories have been suggested—naturally. There is the idea that the religious reformer was not Akhenaton, but his wife or mother and that this philosophically inclined female, whoever she was, came from one of the northern kingdoms—Mitanni is a favorite candidate—where a sun-god was worshiped. Others suggest that the court party (a strictly modern concept) had become alarmed at the growing temporal power of Amon's priesthood and sought to restrain it by setting up a new god. Neither theory makes any sense. The "evidence" of Ti's foreign ancestry is extremely tenuous, as we pointed out in the first chapter; Nefertiti's claim to Mitannian blood is now discounted by thoughtful scholars. As for the idea that someone other than Akhenaton was responsible for the Aton faith, there is nothing to support, or even suggest it. The political interpretation gives Akhenaton credit for political acumen so great as to amount to clairvoyance. We can see now, from where we stand, the development of a process which was to end, four hundred years after Akhenaton, with the High Priests of Amon as rulers of Thebes; but there is no reason to suppose that the king, or anyone else at court, could see it.

Both of these theories, like all the others, break down on the really essential point: that the Aton faith, if not true monotheism, was so different from true polytheism as to be quite alien to the thought of the time, in Egypt or Mitanni or anyplace else. The most obvious way of explaining the phenomenon of Amarna is to resort to the unpopular, but almost inescapable theory that Akhenaton himself was one of those rare, spiritually inspired individuals who occasionally emerge from the placid masses of mankind and, for better or worse, work their will on the course of history. No matter what we think of Breasted's fondness for Akhenaton, we must admit that there is a grain of truth in that sweeping characterization, "the first individual in history." Deformed, depraved, diseased, or what you will, Akhenaton is the only one of the pharaohs who has come down to us as more than a handsome hard-stone statue. The very magnitude of the controversy that rages around his vanished figure testifies to his uniqueness.

Whatever its character, it is probable that the religious revolution was the work of one man. When he died—how, we do not know—the new faith also died. Akhenaton's successors were boys; one of them, Smenkhkare, probably did not survive his father-in-law, and young Tutankhamon was only nine years old when he ascended the throne. A few years later he had abandoned the city of Aton and restored the worship of Amon, repaying the god fourfold for all that he had lost under the persecution. Tutankhamon was the last of the house of Amarna; he was succeeded by a man of unknown antecedents who reigned for only a few years. The next king, Harmhab, who had been—we think—a follower of Akhenaton's, completed the return to orthodoxy with a vengeance. Harmhab denied the existence of all the rulers between Amenhotep III and himself, claiming their years of kingship under his reign. Eventually Akhenaton's very name was wiped off the pages of history. The heretic king was referred to only as "that criminal." The victory of Amon was complete.

The new family of kings who made up the Nineteenth Dynasty were thoroughly orthodox except for one slightly peculiar factor—the prominence they gave to Set, the old enemy of Osiris. Osiris was not neglected. One of the most beautiful temples in Egypt was built in his honor, at Abydos, by two of the kings of this dynasty. Since one of them, Seti I, had a name which was singularly inappropriate at Abydos, incorporating as it did the name of Osiris's murderer, the little figure of Set in the king's cartouche was replaced, throughout the temple, by the Osiris figure. Even I find this inconsistency mildly startling; if the king's name was so offensive, he should never have selected it in the first place. The solution, of course, lies in the familiar "multiplicity of approaches." At Abydos, Set was his brother's murderer, and anathema; some place else he was something else, and perfectly all right. Set's position is an unusual one, and it is still imperfectly understood. Whether or not it is understandable in our terms is another matter.

The Nineteenth Dynasty kings tried, with some success, to reestablish the old Egyptian Asiatic empire, which had been lost under Akhenaton and his father. One result of foreign contacts was the introduction of alien gods into the Egyptian pantheon; Astarte, Baal, and others were worshiped in Egypt, though none of them ever became outstandingly popular.

Above all the others, supreme in the pantheon, Amon-Re continued his triumphant progress. By the end of the Twentieth Dynasty his priests were in control of a vast amount of property; one estimate makes it as high as 15 percent of the people and 30 percent of the land. The end of the dynasty saw what some scholars have viewed as the inevitable conclusion. The High Priest of Amon took over the functions, if not the titles, of the king. It does not matter whether he seized power by virtue of his priestly power or his control of the army; he ruled as spokesman of the god. At this time Egypt was again divided, the north being ruled by men who claimed the title of king, the south by the high priests. A reunification made no difference to Amon. A benevolent monarch, allowing many lesser suns to shine in his heavens, he continued to rule the pantheon until Greek times, and after; for Alexander the Great found it expedient to make the hard journey out to the Oasis of Siwa in order to be acknowledged King of Egypt by Amon of that place. Amon and his cohorts were not supplanted until Jehovah pushed Amon from his throne, and His Son replaced Osiris as a pledge of eternal life. Then, and not until then, could it be said that the gods of ancient Egypt were dead.

## Temples and Rituals

Anyone who has visited Egypt on one of those whirlwind, five-day tours probably comes back with jumbled memories of Egyptian temples—heavy towering gateways, forests of columns, headless statues, and walls of austere pale stone covered with unintelligible pictures. Many of the "tourist" temples are Ptolemaic in date. Edfu, Denderah, Kom Ombo, Philae—all were built during the Greek or Roman occupation of Egypt, after 300 B. C. Their plans are much the same as those of the dynastic temples, but the decoration and the overall impression are different.

Of the dynastic temples still surviving, the most famous are in Upper Egypt—Karnak, Luxor, Abu Simbel (in Nubia) and Abydos are the main ones. Some of the other conspicuous temples of the Theban area, such as the Ramesseum, Deir el Bahri, and Medinet Habu, were not primarily houses of the gods; they were dedicated to the mortuary cult of the king.

The earliest temples in Egypt were little one-room affairs made of reeds, wood, or brick. Naturally, none of them have survived, but archaeologists can guess at their appearance from pictures, especially the hieroglyphic signs. Few of the pre-Eighteenth Dynasty temples have survived. Perhaps the most interesting is the little temple of Senusert I, which dates from the beginning of the Twelfth Dynasty, but it was not found intact. Its stones were disinterred from the inside of one of the pylons at Karnak, and put together by archaeologists. The Egyptian kings were fond of claiming pious respect for the works of their ancestors, but, like so many virtues, it was more honored in the breach than in the observance. The royal builder of the third pylon, looking around for material, took the temple stones to prop up his pylon, and there they remained until they were found in modern times.

Senusert's temple is a very simple one—a plain rectangular building with a flat roof and big windows all around. It stands on a platform, reached by ramps on opposite sides; and it is, for all its simplicity, a handsome, dignified little structure. This type is called a peripteral temple, and others of the same type were built during the Eighteenth Dynasty.

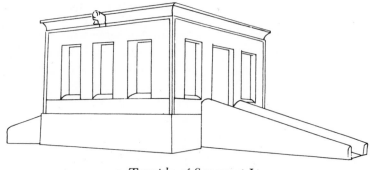

*Temple of Senusert I*

*Perspective of a New Kingdom temple*
Restoration of the temple of Amon-Re at Luxor

*Reconstruction of a pylon gateway*
With obelisks, statues, and standards. Temple of Amon-Re
at Luxor

The standard temple plan of the New Kingdom, which is
found in most surviving temples, is not so simple as that of the
peripteral temple, but it is not as complicated as it appears to be.
Basically it consisted of four elements: a pylon or gateway; a court
with rows of columns along one or more sides; a wide columned
(hypostyle) hall; and the sanctuary room itself.

The pylon gateway was made of two towers with sloping sides
and flat tops. The gate was between the towers. Beyond was the
colonnaded court, usually unroofed except for the part over the

colonnades. Beyond this came the hypostyle hall. The biggest and most impressive of these halls is the one at Karnak; it is a jungle of columns, so crowded together that it is hard to realize how big the place is. If you stand at one end and look down to the other end, and see a miniscule Arab squatting at the base of one of the mammoth pillars, you begin to grasp the size. Some of the columns in this hall are 42 and a half feet high, and 27 and a half feet around. The hall was lit by a clerestory raised on the two central rows of columns; the giants in these rows are 69 feet high, and it has been calculated that one hundred men could stand on each of the enormous capitals—although I would not care to be one of the ones who stood along the edges.

Behind the hypostyle hall the favored worshiper might enter the shrine itself—the dwelling place of the god. This was a simple rectangular room, without windows; at the far end stood a statue of the god. Some temples were dedicated to more than one god, or to a god and his family. Triads were popular, so often a temple will have three shrines. Surrounding the shrine were storerooms, offices, and the like.

The rock-cut temples, such as Abu Simbel, were essentially a transfer of the standard style into solid stone. The façade of Abu Simbel represents the pylon, with gigantic statues like the ones often found in front of the regular temples; inside the cliff are the usual pillared halls and the shrine.

The casual visitor finds it hard to trace this plan in the Egyptian temples of today. This is because the basic elements could be multiplied, not only by the original builder but by succeeding rulers. When a king wanted to improve a temple, the usual procedure was to build another court and/or pylon in front of the ones already there. Karnak demonstrates this procedure very well. As it stands today it represents the pious royal efforts of over a millennium, and that figure does not include the Middle Kingdom temple which is now lost. Karnak has eight pylons, not counting the ones which belong to the other nearby temples.

Prominent among the minor decorative elements of a temple were obelisks, and these also might be added by later kings, willy-nilly, to honor the god. Hatshepsut tore down part of her own father's hall at Karnak in order to insert, quite inappropriately, two fine obelisks. These tall slim square pillars, tapering to a pyramid point on top, often stood in front of the pylon gateway; their surfaces were covered with inscriptions praising, in no modest terms, the ruler who had erected them. The obelisks, some of which are almost a hundred feet high, are not what one would call easily transportable; and yet there are probably more standing obelisks today in Rome than there are in Egypt, and others are scattered all over the world from New York to Istanbul.

Statues were an important architectural element too, and in keeping with the massiveness of the temple they were large. They stood in rows against the walls, or between the columns of the courtyard; massive figures of the king might adorn the gateway as well. Like sculpture, reliefs and paintings played an important part in the decorative effect. Most of the flat wall surfaces were covered with carvings; the subject matter concerned the king and the gods.

Columns played an important part in Egyptian architecture. They were used in houses and palaces, but naturally we see them to their best advantage in temples, since these have survived better than has domestic architecture.

There were several distinct types of columns, characterized by their capitals. Most, archaeologists think, were derived from plant

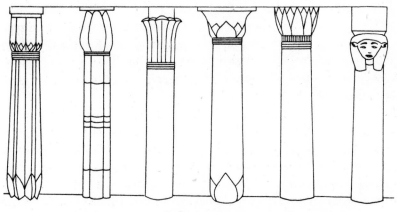

*Column types*

Left to right: papyrus cluster, lotus, palm, papyrus flower, multiple flower, Hathor

forms, even, in some cases, from bundles of reeds used to support the light roofs of early huts. The first column in our illustration was probably a bunch of papyrus stems, whose bound stiff tops form the capital. Another column derived from the ubiquitous and useful papyrus was Number Four, whose capital was a single papyrus top bent back, as would be natural, by the weight of the roof it supported. The second column looks, in actuality, so much like the papyrus cluster that it is hard to tell them apart. It is derived from the lotus. Its stems are rounded in section, while the papyrus stems are triangular, but the easiest way of distinguishing them is that the column base tapers in the papyrus type and is straight in the lotus.

The palm column, Number Three, is not so common, nor is the open-flower type. Our last example is a curious one; the squared capital has heads in bas-relief and full face of the goddess Hathor, with her cow ears. These columns were used in shrines dedicated to the goddess, and similar ones, with figures of the little pygmy god Bes, also appear now and then. In Ptolemaic times several complicated composite plant capitals appeared; dozens of them can be seen at Denderah, Edfu, and other late temples. We must not forget to mention the simplest and, in some ways, the most effective of all Egyptian columns, which require no illustration—the beautiful fluted cylinder which reminds us of Greek types. Archaeologists and art historians seem to agree that there is no connection between the Greek and Egyptian columns, although to an untrained eye they certainly look a lot alike. The Egyptian variety is probably seen to the best advantage at Hatshepsut's mortuary temple at Deir el Bahri, but the type goes back a long way in Egypt.

One other type of temple ought to be mentioned, although it survives today only in plans. The temples Akhenaton erected in honor of his sun-god Aton are quite different from the standard type. The glowing orb was not worshiped in a dark sanctuary but in an open court, approached by a series of colonnades and courtyards with great gateways. It was surrounded by offices and storerooms, and in the center, under the open sky, was the altar of the god, on a platform approached by steps. Akhenaton's temples may not be so heretical as they first appear; sun temples of the Fifth Dynasty also had an altar, surmounted by an obelisk court as the center of worship.

It is no wonder that the tourist (and I use this word in an honorable sense, referring to a group of which I am often one) comes away confused about temple plans. The real pity is that he gets a totally misleading impression of what these temples looked like. They seem austere and dignified, almost ponderously so, and they add to the impression many people have of Egyptian culture, as being equally ponderous and dignified. In their pristine state these temples were, of course, very big. But they blazed and glittered and shone as brilliantly as a sunlit baroque church.

As the visitor approached the pylon, his first impression was not so much one of size as of color, bright enough to hurt the eyes under the golden Egyptian sun. The flat surfaces of the towers which formed the pylon were painted with enormous figures of men and gods—orange and blue and green and red, they stood out against the clean white background as brilliantly as a billboard, and much more attractively. The obelisks before the gate might be tipped with gold or even completely covered with that gorgeous material. The tall flagstaffs in front of the portal also had golden tips, and floated scarlet pennants. Going in through the gate, the visitor found himself in a court whose pillars were painted in the same bright colors and were covered with the elegant little pictures of hieroglyphic inscriptions. The massive statues, in serried ranks, looked very handsome with their heads and arms and noses all in place, and with their surfaces polished to a gleaming sheen. The limestone statues were painted—dazzling white clothing, red-brown skin, inlays of semiprecious stones and gold on crowns and collars.

By the time the visitor passed from the sunlight of the court into the hypostyle hall, where shafts of clear light from the clerestory pierced the shadows, some of the brilliance of the first part of the temple was dimmed. But still the rich ornamentation continued. The doors might be of beautifully grained cedar or of copper plated with gold. . . . But the best picture comes from the words of the Egyptians themselves:

. . . a very great portal . . . wrought with gold throughout. The Divine Shadow, in the shape of a ram, is inlaid with real lapis lazuli wrought with gold and many precious stones. . . . Its floor is adorned with silver, towers are over against it. Stelae of lapis lazuli are set up, one on each side. Its pylons reach heaven like the four pillars of heaven, its flagstaffs shine more than the heavens, wrought with electrum.

Unlike churches, the temples were never filled with crowds of lay worshipers. Only the highest priests could enter the holy of holies and approach the god. By official dogma the king was the celebrant of the divine rites and high priest of all the gods; but, since he could not be in a dozen places at once, he had to delegate his duties.

In the morning, as the sun rose over the cliffs, the priest in charge of that day's ritual entered the sanctuary, breaking the seals on the shrine. Within was the god's statue, very possibly of solid gold. (Naturally, none of these have survived.) With the slow care of religious ritual the god was washed and anointed, clothed in a new shirt and kilt, and decked with jewels. The morning offerings of food and drink were made. Hymns of praise were chanted; the "Singers of the God" performed for his entertainment. At sundown the shrine was closed and sealed; the high priest, or priest in charge, backed out of the sanctuary, sweeping away the traces of his footprints in order to leave the sacred place ritually clean.

The priesthoods were organized into three groups, or *phyles*, each of which served for four months a year. The head of the establishment was the High Priest, usually called the First Prophet. The high priests of certain gods had special titles; the head of Re's temple at Heliopolis was the "Greatest of Seers." The word we translate "prophet" is somewhat misleading, for it does not imply prediction of future events but was simply the designation of certain high-ranking ecclesiastics, perhaps the ones who were allowed to meet the god face to face. Other orders were the "lector priests," the scholars in charge of the ritual and the sacred writings, and the *wab* or lustration priests. Women served the god as singers or concubines.

In all this elaborate activity the common people had little or no part. The only time they saw the god, or his gorgeous golden shrine, was when he went traveling on the occasion of some festival. Luckily for the Egyptian laboring man there were many festivals; at some periods almost one-third of the days were holy days. Evidently the gods became bored sitting all day in their shrines. Sometimes they visited one another, as when Hathor went from Denderah to call on Horus at Edfu.

One of the biggest festivals of the year was Amon's Feast of Opet, at Thebes, when he went down from Karnak to his Luxor temple to see what was going on there. The festival took place during the inundation, when the river was overflowing and many of the peasants were unable to work their land; they undoubtedly enjoyed the celebration very much. Amon was carried from his Karnak sanctuary to the divine boat at the river. This was a gorgeous affair built of cedar from Lebanon, gilded, and adorned with carvings, rich hangings, and flowers. On the deck was a dais for the shrine of the god. The barge was towed by a royal flagship manned by high-ranking officials who fought for the honor of transporting the god, and by gangs of workmen on towropes along the bank. The river must have been crowded with other boats—private vessels of well-to-do people dressed in their best, munching sweetmeats and singing songs; hired craft jammed with sightseers of the lower classes. Other spectators followed along the bank, dancing, buying trinkets and tidbits from the booths erected along the route, being robbed by pickpockets and solicited by prostitutes and whined at by legless beggars. When, amid shouts of rejoicing, the divine boat reached the Luxor temple, the god was carried in procession, led by the king, into his Luxor shrine. The crowd of followers stopped at the gates to the courtyard. There they could jostle and gape and point out important personages in the procession, like the crowds at the first-night performances of plays and films. Sooner or later free food would be distributed, with plenty of bread and beer, and perhaps even a cup of wine.

Perhaps the humble worshipers of the god actually did get to see a theatrical performance, of a sort. There is no evidence in ancient Egypt of secular drama, but several papyri mention dramatic performances in connection with the king's coronation, and other religious rites. The written dialogue is sometimes accompanied by specific stage directions. One Twelfth Dynasty official boasted of having been selected to play Horus—a starring role if ever there was one—in the mystery play of Osiris. This was probably the most famous of all Egyptian dramas, representing the god's death and triumphant resurrection. The devout Egyptian audience may have wept and cheered and hissed the villain at appropriate moments, just as medieval pilgrims did during the representation of the Christian Passion. One cannot help but speculate as to why Ikhernofret was chosen for the part of Horus. Dramatic talent? Good looks? I jest, of course. Ikhernofret was Chief Treasurer, among a lot of other important titles, and his selection was probably a mark of royal favor.

## The Contendings of Horus and Set

The temples, the state festivals, the solemn daily ritual—this is one aspect of Egyptian religion. Another attitude is illustrated by a story which was very popular in late times; it is worth summarizing in some detail since it shows, more vividly than my own words could do, how some Egyptians thought about the divine masters of their destiny.

The story opens in the supreme tribunal of the gods, who are here referred to as the Ennead; the word no longer means nine gods, just a lot of them. Chief of the court is Re Atum, and the case under consideration is that of Horus and Set, the contenders for the throne of Osiris.

In the beginning, everyone except the president of the court seems to agree that Horus ought to inherit his father's throne. Re Atum is in favor of Set—perhaps because that god helps him repel his snaky enemies during the trip through the underworld—and while his authority is not enough to overrule the rest of the council, it is strong enough to create a deadlock.

The gods then request Thoth, the scribe, to write asking the advice of Neith, the ancient goddess of Sais; perhaps, as an old lady, she is supposed to be wiser than the rest. Neith replies:

"Give the office of Osiris to his son Horus!" On hearing the letter, the council shouts with one voice: "This goddess is right!"

Re, the lofty god of the sun, then loses his temper. He sneers at Horus: "The office is too much for you—you boy, still smelling of sour milk!" A general slanging match ensues; the petty god Baba, drawing himself up, shrieks at Re: "Your shrine is empty!"

That is too much—telling Re that he is not a god. The scandalized Ennead scolds Baba for *lesè majesté*, and Re goes off to his tent to sulk. There he sits until Hathor, goddess of love, sidles in and exposes herself to him. This indelicate act restores the supreme god's good humor; he returns to the tribunal and tells the contestants to present their cases.

Set's plea is more notable for rhetoric than for reason. "As for me, I am Set, great of strength among the Ennead. Daily I slay the enemies of Re, I am in front of the Bark of Millions; no other god can do this. I should receive the office of Osiris!"

The fickle Ennead immediately bellows: "Set is right!" Thoth is almost the only consistent one. He speaks up for his candidate, Horus, but his reasoned arguments are submerged in an exchange of insults, which ends with Isis getting up and cursing the whole tribunal. Her threats terrify the immortals; they assure her that everything will be fine, everyone will get what is due him. Set promises to kill one god per day unless judgment is given in his favor, and he refuses to discuss the matter any further unless Isis is thrown out of court. In desperation Re suggests that they all move to an island where they can debate in peace. Strict orders are given to the ferrymen not to take any woman across the water.

Anti, the ferryman, is just as irresponsible as his betters. When Isis appears, disguised as an old woman, he lets himself be bribed into taking her to the island. Sneaking up, Isis sees the Ennead at dinner. She changes her form into that of a beautiful girl, and strolls back and forth outside the window until Set catches a glimpse of her. It is love at first sight; he rushes out. "Beautiful maiden, I am here with you!" he announces rapturously.

Isis slyly presents him with a fictitious case. She is the widow, she says, of a poor herdsman, and a foreigner has come and stolen all the cattle from her son, the heir. Set, inflamed by love or basically stupid, exclaims indignantly, "Shall the cattle be given to the foreigner while the son of the man is alive?" Isis turns herself into a bird and flies up into a tree, cawing triumphantly, "It is your own mouth which has said it; it is your own cleverness which has judged you!"

Set bursts into tears. Weeping copiously he returns to the tribunal and tells them the whole story. "Well," says Re, in effect, "now you've done it." Even the supreme god has no choice now but to decide in favor of Horus.

Stubborn Set refuses to accept the verdict; he demands a trial by combat. Changing themselves into hippopotami, the two gods plunge into the river to see who can stay down the longest. Isis, pacing up and down in an agony of concern for her son, finally can stand the suspense no longer. She heaves a harpoon into the water—like the heroines of modern thriller fiction who try to bat the villain on the head while he is wrestling with the hero. Naturally, her weapon misses Set and hits Horus; he has to come out of the water and tell her to take her magic weapon out of his hide. Next time, Isis manages to hit Set, but when he emerges, appealing to her as his sister, the inconsistent woman frees him too. This annoys Horus, who cuts off his mother's head to teach her a little lesson.

After a time, Isis' unpleasant condition dawns on Re. "Who is this woman who has no head?" he inquires. Thoth, who knows all, tells him, and Re decides that Horus shall be punished. In the meantime Set finds the boy asleep and gouges out his eyes. Horus is cured by Hathor's magic, and once again the Ennead goes into executive session to try to settle the case.

The story goes on and on. There is one bawdy episode in which Set tries to play an unsavory trick upon his nephew, but it is turned back on him by the wiles of Isis. There are battles, and more hippopotami, and endless ranting in the tribunal. The issue is finally decided by a threatening letter from no less a personage than Osiris; Set concedes to Horus, Horus is crowned, and everybody—except Set—is happy.

Obviously this story is not official dogma. It is rude, insulting, and frivolous, and I think there is no doubt but that the Egyptians regarded it as a humorous tale. It is a far cry from the solemn ritual which casual students think of as the only manifestation of the religious attitude in ancient Egypt. Yet frivolity was not the sole alternative to ritual, nor does the Horus and Set story represent the secret cynicism of the people as opposed to the official piety of the court. We know relatively little about popular religion in its day-by-day manifestations. But the few sources we do have give a third, and very significant, picture of religious attitudes.

## Religion of the People

Though they were not admitted to the precincts of the great temples, the people had their centers of worship. They made pilgrimages to certain shrines and they also worshiped at home. Poorer houses had a small shrine in one room of the house; nobles might possess a special pavilion set in the beauty of the garden. The gods worshiped in the household shrines could be the great gods of the pantheon, and perhaps a craftsman might prefer to offer to Ptah, and a scribe might choose Thoth, the inventor of numbers and patron of writing. Hathor was a favorite; her small shrine at Deir el Bahri yielded hundreds of pieces of broken faience objects which had been offered to her by pilgrims.

Two of the most popular household gods, whose worship was almost entirely restricted to small shrines, were very peculiar-looking. If we did not know that Taweret was a good-natured goddess, we would certainly take her for a monster. She was a hippopotamus goddess, and the protectress of women in childbirth. One would think that the sight of her would frighten a pregnant woman into fits, but evidently the Egyptians found her appealing. Another favored household god was Bes, whose grotesque figure often decorated the bedchamber. He is unusual in that he was the only Egyptian god to be painted, consistently, in direct front view. He does not look very Egyptian, really; his round homely face and dwarfish body suggest something from inner Africa, as does his costume. Perhaps he was imported. But although he was not handsome, Bes was a jolly monster, in charge of fun and games generally.

The most important documents relating to popular religion come from little memorial stones found at Deir el Medineh, the village of the necropolis workers of Thebes. One of these prayers is dedicated to a goddess named Mereseger, "She Who Loves Silence," who was also called "The Peak of the West" after a prominent mountain near Thebes. It was written by a necropolis worker named Neferabet, who calls himself "an ignorant and witless man." "I knew not good or evil," he says. "When I did the deed of transgression against the Peak, she punished me, and I was in her hand by night as well as day. . . . I called out to the wind, but it did not come to me. . . . But when I called to my mistress, I found her coming to me with sweet breezes. She showed mercy unto me, after she had let me see her hand. She turned about to me in mercy."

This is really an extraordinary text to have been written by one of the cheerful, bumptious Egyptians, who bought magic spells to keep their consciences from testifying against them on the day of judgment. It is not unique, however. Another prayer, in much the same tone, addresses itself to no less a divinity than Amon-Re, king of the gods. The petitioner, an artist named Nebre, appealed to the god when his son fell ill, "in a state of death." Amon, who is given the astonishing epithet "he who comes at the voice of the poor man," responded to the father's plea. He rescued the son from death. Nebre, filled with thanksgiving, praised the god in these words: "Though the servant is inclined to do wrong, yet the Lord is inclined to be merciful." In this prayer we see a consciousness of sin, a humility, and an awareness of divine mercy which, it has been claimed, does not occur in ancient times outside of the religious literature of the Hebrews. Yet it is surely a factor in Egyptian religion of the late period.

In a sense these prayers are the essence of ancient Egyptian religion. Long lists of bizarre deities, philosophic interpretations of what we think the Egyptians thought, are less significant than the actual words of a man to his god. The gods are dead, but once they lived—not as cold golden statues in a darkened shrine, but as forces which could command the awe and devotion of living men.

# PART TWO
# The World
# of the Dead

# XIII

# "An Excellent, Equipped Spirit"

## *Attitudes Toward the Dead*

THE subject of undertaking (and I wonder how that euphemism ever originated?) seems to have a macabre fascination for many people—witness the success of such books as Jessica Mitford's *The American Way of Death,* which provided me with a pleasant evening's entertainment not long ago. Miss Mitford was not the first commentator to criticize that earnest craftsman, the American undertaker, or to wonder at the position he has come to hold as arbiter of a mortuary etiquette which often contradicts traditional religious dogma. Mark Twain, who missed few of the follies of which men are capable, was roused to sardonic comment on the same subject almost a century ago. In *Life on the Mississippi,* he created a mortician—who, we devoutly hope, was purely fictitious—and had this personage make the following remarks:

"Why, just look at it. A rich man won't have anything but your very best; and you can just pile it on, too—pile it on and sock it to him—he won't ever holler. And you take a poor man, and if you work him right, he'll bust himself on a single lay-out. Or especially a woman." He goes on to explain how he got Mrs. O'Flaherty, widow of a poor workman, to "bust herself" on her husband's funeral.

The morality of this sort of thing is beyond the scope of our present discussion; it hardly requires comment in any case. What interests us as students of ancient Egypt is the ironic fact that we seem to see, today, the resurgence of a concept which was once believed to be limited to primitive heathens, back in the dawn of civilization—the idea that the dead body, the corpse, must be: a) preserved, and b) treated as if it retained the individuality of the deceased. The parallelism of our cult with those of primitive cultures is painfully close—the painting of the dead man's face, the burial of jewelry and trinkets in the coffin, the ornate and expensive coffin itself.

Modern embalmers would claim, no doubt, that the motivation underlying their activities destroys the apparent parallels. They are not assisting the dead by means of magic, they are comforting the survivors by "psychology." We may reasonably doubt whether the embalmer's psychology is any more valid than the sympathetic magic of the witch doctors. But most suggestive of all is the fact that, beneath all the psychological claptrap, we can discern an extremely ancient, dichotomous attitude toward death and the dead—an ambivalence which may be found also in the graves of the wandering hunters of paleolithic Europe.

Throughout the inhabited world, and far back beyond written history, there runs the unifying thread of agreement on one idea— survival after death. It is as old as man, older than Homo sapiens; it exists among Australian aborigines and African bushmen. We may find it hard to believe that the brutish Neanderthal hunters shared this same faith; and yet there is no other reasonable explanation for the skeletons carefully buried in the caves in which they had lived, laid to rest with their weapons beside them and their ornaments still resting on their crumbling bones. In these humble graves we see the beginning, not only of a belief in some sort of life after death, but of the careful tending of the physical remains.

Now any savage with two eyes in his unkempt head knows that the body is corruptible. After passing through changes which are perturbing to contemplate, the corpse is reduced, within the span of one observer's lifetime, to a state which bears little resemblance to the human form. We will not be crediting primitive man with too much insight if we assume that he knew the body itself did not survive. Whence, then, did he derive the immense concept of immortality?

Long before the processes of corruption attack the flesh, the great change of death manifests itself upon the body. The skin grows cold, the eyes dull; the lips do not speak nor the limbs move.

At first the visible signs of death resemble those of other phenomena, such as coma or sleep. "Sleep is a little death," and Thanatos and Hypnos, to many men, are brothers. But the sleeper awakes. And sometimes, in his waking state, he remembers adventures he had while his physical body lay unresponsive and inert, on his bed. In his unconscious travels the sleeper is not limited by physical time or space; he may even see friends who no longer exist in the waking world. From such experiences there might arise the concept of a Dweller within the House of the Flesh who can leave the sleeping body to venture abroad and who, at the time of death, abandons the empty dwelling forever.

This is not an answer to the question of how the notion of immortality began; it is only a suggestion of a possibility. But most people who have left us any statements of belief imagine a Dweller within the body—one or more. They call it by various names; we call it the soul.

The soul, outside its body, is of course invisible, and it is only seen by the living under special conditions. Unseen, it may linger near its old home or it may join other spirits in another place—a place which can be visited by the living in dreams. The views of the dreamland where the dead live vary considerably; sometimes they go down below, sometimes up above. The hereafter may be visualized as a Happy Hunting Ground, where the soul enjoys all the pleasures it cherished on earth, only more so, and experiences none of the pain. Sometimes the regions of the dead are sad and gloomy; sometimes they are etherealized and utterly removed from the gross activities of the body.

Happy Hunting Ground or melancholy Hades, in no culture do the living really look forward to the time when they will go there. The attitude of the living toward death is not ambivalent; they are most heartily against it. But there is an ambivalence to be observed in the attitude of the living toward the dead.

When Mark Twain's unpleasant undertaker described his exploitation of his customers, he ascribed his success to the application of an unworthy old principle—"keeping up with the Joneses." But this is only the superficial explanation of why people will beggar themselves to buy equipment which is not only superfluous, but slightly obscene. What the undertaker is really exploiting is the ancient ambivalence of the living toward the dead.

On the one hand there is grief and love which cries out for expression. But, mingled with grief and love is a complex of contradictory emotions which people do not so readily admit. Reactions to the corpse itself range from mild distaste to superstitious horror; and since the dead flesh was once the habitation of the beloved soul, the living relatives feel guilty about their repugnance. Another reaction of the living—though few of them will own it—is relief. "Whoever is dead, it is not I. Thank God!" Or, to paraphrase St. Augustine: "Lord, let me join my dear one in Paradise—but not just yet!" This sense of guilty relief has to be paid for—nowadays, apparently, with copper-sheathed, satin-lined coffins.

Frazer has said—very cogently, I think—that the fear of the dead arises out of the fear of death. If the living rejoice in the fact that they still breathe and eat and love and walk abroad under the sun, they can assume the corollary: that the dead hate not being alive. The malignancy of the dead is a logical next step—a blind malignancy, directed against all the living.

We do not have to leave our own, supposedly rational culture to find evidence of the fear of the dead. Few of us would care to spend the night with a dead body as sole company, and we still shun graveyards after dark. I don't believe in ghosts, but I prefer not to read Poe or Lovecraft when I am alone in the house at night. The ghost story itself specializes, not in kindly spirits, but in malignant specters; its wide appeal testifies to its probing of a deep-seated human emotion. And the principles of the modern ghost story, now relegated to folklore, were part of the tenets of the church not many centuries ago. Indeed, I believe there is still a formula for exorcism in some rituals.

We can jump back over ten thousand years and find the same belief. Among the oldest of all surviving burials, those of prehistoric man, there are a few unusual graves. The skeletons found in them had been laid in painfully cramped positions, knees drawn up against the chest and legs tightly flexed. Such a position could only have been maintained by binding the limbs of the corpse with cords, and it has been suggested that this was done in order to keep the dead man from wandering around and annoying the living.

There is a theory that burial itself did not originate from love or sanitary motives, but from fear. The very notion of inhumation, pinning the body down under earth and stones, may have arisen out of a desire to keep it confined. A more drastic method of restraint is dismemberment, and this too is found occasionally in prehistoric graves. Perhaps cremation was the most effective defense of all; there is no more thorough way of rendering a man powerless than by reducing him to ashes. If cremation, and dispersal of the ashes, was practiced by prehistoric man, we would naturally have no evidence of it; the partially burned bodies in some ancient graves were not cremated, and in these cases the fires may have been accidental. We cannot recognize cremation burials as such until the ashes are preserved in pots or urns; and by this time the fear of the dead has been superseded, consciously at least, by other motives.

Another method of defense against the dead is propitiation: If you keep them happy and well tended they will not harm, and may even help, you. They will be more favorably inclined, perhaps, if you keep your hands off their property. So, to be on the safe side, you bury it with them, including their women, horses, and slaves. This would explain the "grave goods" which, from earliest times, were buried with the dead. An alternate explanation is that such objects as jewelry, weapons, and wives were sent along with the dead man to be of use to him wherever he was going.

Propitiation has one advantage over violence and destruction as a method of rendering the dead harmless to the living: It does not offend the oft-simultaneous emotion of grief. The old argument as to whether burial of the dead was first motivated by fear or by affection is pointless; there is no reason why both should not have operated. They are contradictory emotions, perhaps, but they are not mutually exclusive.

One howling inconsistency still stands out. Whether we love them or whether we fear them, we all agree that the dead are dead—that the body is corruptible. Repugnance for the corpse and terror of the bodiless ghost are not the same, and attempts to control the ghost by binding the corpse seem senseless. So does the opposite technique, furnishing the unresponsive, insensible body with elegant tombs and dead slaves.

Yet there is a good deal of sense in the attentions paid to the dead body if we believe in sympathetic magic. Since the soul was once part of the body or intimately associated with it, then the soul can be affected by that which is done to the flesh. This principle is at the basis of many sorceries, those practiced for the benefit of the living as well as the dead. Many of the rituals in honor of the dead are explicable in these terms, including the effort to preserve the corpse and give it, at least temporarily, the appearance of life.

While the principle of sympathetic magic may account for dismemberment or mummification with equal facility, it does not have any bearing on the American way of death. We do not believe in magic. There must be some other reason for our desire to preserve the dead clay and to surround it with comforts which it cannot sense.

Some Christian sects include among the articles of their creeds the phrase: "I believe in the resurrection of the body." If these words are taken literally, they would account for embalming—indeed, they would justify far greater efforts than the ones we put forth. However, ministers and priests of all sects have been vehement in opposing the ostentation of American funeral customs, and the problems involved in the literal resurrection of the physical body are rationally insoluble. Some of these problems seem rather funny to us, but they were not at all amusing to the medieval theologians who propounded them so earnestly. Take the classic case of the cannibal who is converted to Christianity. He is assured of a resurrection in the flesh if he joins the right church; but whose flesh is it? What about the Christian missionaries whom he absorbed, in his unregenerate days, into that now-hallowed flesh of his? They are entitled to a resurrection in the body, too, but someone is going to be missing a part when the Day of Judgment comes around.

When I put the problem of the cannibal to a Jesuit friend, he gave me an answer suited to my simple mind: "But it is not the same body." Not really, no; but in one way it is the same. The God who made man out of the dust of the earth and woman out of one of his least important bones can, if He wills it, restore to the blessed any body He wants them to have—"the same body," if necessary—the cannibal's body and those of the missionaries, all complete and original. The somber words of Ecclesiastes, "Then shall the dust return to the earth as it was," are resolved by the magnificent paradox of Job: "And though worms destroy this body, yet in my flesh shall I see God."

In these terms the preservation of the body is irrelevant, and the American mortuary cult is inexplicable by the words of the very creed which is read over the coffins of the painted and embalmed dead.

I sometimes amuse myself by wondering whether archaeologists of a future day would be able to find our credo in the coffins of our dead. Suppose that by the year A.D. 5000 all written records of our culture are destroyed (not necessarily such a fantastic assumption) but that some of our frail bones do survive. Jones' guaranteed, lead-lined, moisture-proof coffins may, by pure accident, live up to their claims, and a few bodies may be found in all the bravery of tuxedos, toupees, and plastic surgery. How will the learned scholars of the intergalactic empire of A.D. 5000 interpret the mortuary beliefs of the primitive earthmen of our era? Sympathetic magic is the obvious answer; and perhaps, fantastically, the intergalactic experts may be right. How many of the people who submit to the witch doctors of the modern American mortuary cult do it because they still harbor, deep down in their livers and bowels, some seed of their primitive ancestors' faith in magic? Is it in the undying superstition of the human race that we must ultimately seek the reason for the American way of death, rather than in the overt appeals to pride, or misapplied piety, or love?

Let us turn now, with some relief, to a simpler cult—that of the ancient Egyptians. It, at least, makes sense in terms of its own expressed premises. Complex and bizarre as it seems, the Egyptian way of death is comprehensible on the basis of a few simple assumptions. The first assumption is that a man, or one aspect of him, can survive physical death. The second is that his postmortem existence is affected by what is done with, and to, his body. Neither of these assumptions is peculiar to Egypt; both form part of a very ancient and very widespread system of belief. In the light of this general background, we will begin with the first premise, and ask how, where and in what form the ancient Egyptian expected to live on after death.

## Heaven and the Soul

The road which led from Memphis and Thebes to Paradise was beset with perils, and the dead man could not even set foot upon it until he had fulfilled a number of ritual obligations. The fact of death did not make man immortal. A soul was made, not born.

Strictly speaking, there is no concept in ancient Egypt which corresponds to our idea of the soul: an invisible, nonmaterial dweller within the flesh which animates the body during life and leaves it after death to seek whatever fate its owner's deeds and beliefs have destined it for. The Egyptian texts refer to many nonmaterial aspects of a man as having some sort of existence apart from his body, including his shadow and his name. But there are only three entities which have a consistent application to life after death.

The *ba* is the easiest of these to describe; it took the form of a bird with a human head, sometimes preceded by a small lighted

Ba *bird*

lamp. Its normal environment was the tomb or its vicinity. We see it perching solicitously on the breast of the mummy, or flying down the tomb shaft to rejoin the mummy after a short trip outside. The word *ba* is often translated as "soul"; but as a rule it did not come into existence until after death, and even then only as a result of special ceremonies which were designed to "make a man into a *ba*."

Another candidate for the word "soul" is the *ka*. When the creator god Khnum shaped the body of a new child on his potter's wheel, he also made the child's *ka* in its exact image; in relief and in painting the *ka* is the double of the man to whom it belongs. But the *ka* is not quite the same as the soul, since it did not necessarily dwell within the body. When a man died, he joined his

*The god Khnum shaping the child and its* ka

*ka* in the hereafter. The *ka* needed to be nourished; offerings were made to it, and it seems to have been a helper in assuring post-mortem existence. It had roles to play in life, too, exerting a generally beneficent and protective influence. The concept of the *ka* is extremely difficult; the variety of ways in which it has been translated shows the lack of agreement as to its precise nature: "double," "guardian spirit," "personality," "vital essence," "will or power." However we translate it—and Egyptologists usually prefer not to translate it at all—it was, among other things, one aspect of a man after death.

The third of the trio, the *akh,* is the most abstract of all. It had no pictorial form. The word is written, in the texts, with the crested ibis, just as *ba* was written with another long-legged bird and *ka* was written with the two upraised arms. But unlike the *ba* and *ka,* the *akh* was never shown in relief or painting. The word can, like *ka,* mean a number of things, from "effective," and "beneficial," to "glorious." Sometimes it is rendered as "spirit," or "transfigured spirit." Often the word is used in the plural, as we use "the dead" or "the blessed" to refer to an impersonalized group. It is at once the vaguest and the most spiritualized of all the Egyptian words for the dead.

There is no point in trying to distinguish between these three forms of the spiritual man in logical terms. We cannot say that under condition A he might become a *ba,* while conditions B and C necessitated his appearance as *ka* and *akh* respectively. There is considerable overlap in the way the words are used.

We will not be surprised to discover that the Egyptians were no more consistent in their views of the hereafter than they were about the soul. We find almost the complete range, from a subterranean to a heavenly paradise; and the god of the dead may be celestial or chthonic.

Many of the gods and goddesses of Egypt had parts to play in the mortuary ritual, but some of them are specifically connected with the dead. Anubis the jackal-headed was the guide of the dead and the patron of cemeteries and embalming; he was a kindly deity despite his predatory head. Wepwawet of Assiut and Khentiamentiu of Abydos were also mortuary gods. Chief of them all, ruler of the regions of the dead, was Osiris. Plutarch has given us the oldest complete version of his story. The Egyptians never wrote it down, but they referred to it constantly and, despite minor descrepancies, the Greek and the Egyptians agree on the main points.

Osiris was an ancient king of Egypt who brought his people out of savagery, teaching them the arts of civilization and ruling them with benevolent kindness. Everyone loved him, including his sister-wife, Isis, with one exception—his brother Set grew jealous and decided Osiris must die. He and his adherents tricked the good king into lying down in a chest, which they promptly covered, nailed up, and threw into the water. The grieving wife, Isis, set out on a long and arduous search for her husband's body. Finally she found the chest at Byblos, where the sea had carried it, and brought it back to Egypt. In a lonely spot in the marshes she opened the chest and threw herself on her husband's body, weeping bitterly. The gods, pitying her grief, sent for Anubis to come and embalm the corpse. But first they revived Osiris sufficiently to impregnate his wife, so that she gave birth to a son called Horus. One day Set, out hunting, found the chest and its contents. This time he tore the body into fourteen pieces and scattered them up and down the length of Egypt. Patiently Isis set out again to collect them. She buried each piece of the body in the place where she found it; according to some versions of the story the head was buried in Abydos, hence this city became particularly sacred to Osiris. Other versions say that the god's entire body was buried there. Resurrected by the mercy of the gods, Osiris was set to rule over the dead in the Land of the Westerners, and his son, Horus, grown to manhood, fought his wicked uncle and regained his father's throne. The second sister of Osiris, Nephthys, often joined Isis in her search and in her mourning, despite the fact that she was the wife of Set.

Osiris belongs to a class which is well known, particularly in the Near East—the Dying Gods. His spiritual cousins are Tammuz and Adonis and Attis, fine young men whose premature death is a symbol of the annual death of vegetation, and whose resurrection is seen in the young green sprouts of the new crop. The appeal in the stories of Osiris and the other dying gods is obvious; here was a man who died, and who lived again. In his story there was hope for all men.

Osiris was not, however, the only king of the dead in Egypt. The withering of the grass suggests death; and so does the daily progress of the sun, which vanishes each night behind the western horizon. If the region of death is the west, then the east is, inescapably, the place of resurrection; for with the dawn comes the rebirth of the dying sun-god, Re.

Two supreme gods of the dead, and two afterworlds governed by them, are not so terribly inconsistent in themselves. Different elements of the population might have held different beliefs. But knowing the Egyptians as—I hope—we have come to know them, we will not expect to find the situation so clear. And it is not.

We can only guess about the prehistoric religion of Egypt; by the time we get a fairly coherent picture of the cult of the dead we find the Osiris faith and the solar faith existing side by side. Not only is there official acceptance of two gods of the dead, but any inner consistency is missing. The heavenly realm governed by Re is somewhere up in the sky, but he also passes through the underworld, which ought to be Osiris's sole responsibility. Re dies in the west each night, but he is not "Lord of the Westerners"; that title belongs to Osiris, who borrowed it from an even older mortuary god.

There are hints in the Pyramid Texts, the oldest body of mortuary texts known, that Re and Osiris were not always so compatible. A few puzzling passages in that great compilation of magico-religious spells speak of Osiris as an enemy; other passages reject the east, the region sacred to Re's resurrection. But these elusive hints are the only evidence we have of what may have been, at one time, a battle royal between two opposing cults, and it is impossible to attribute one cult to one part of the population and one to another. Some scholars believed that the solar faith was that of the king and the court, while the religion of Osiris belonged to the people. Neat as this theory is, it cannot be proved. Osiris and Re together were guardians of the king and of his people. Either or both could guarantee eternal life in the west—or the east—or the underworld.

All three regions are mentioned as locations for the realm of the dead. Another possible direction is north; for here lie the circumpolar stars, which never set, and one fate the dead may anticipate is to join these starry immortals. This concept is rather remote and etherealized; the Egyptians enjoyed the pleasures of life as much as, if not more than, we do, and they were just as susceptible to a super-earthly heaven, well supplied with tasty haunches of beef, foaming jugs of beer, sweet northern breezes, and a nice little house with a garden.

All these pleasant things could be found in the most comprehensible of the Egyptian versions of Paradise, a place called the Field, or Marsh, of Reeds. It seems to be a swampy region, rather like the scenery of the ancient Delta. Some texts contain little maps of the Field of Reeds, with rivers and islands and towns. In this happy land the grain grew ten cubits high, and other supplies were equally lavish.

Then there was a region known as the Dat, or Duat. Eventually this came to be located under the earth, but originally it was a typical Egyptian paradise in that it could have been almost anywhere. Water is a frequent feature of the afterworlds, in the form of rivers or lakes; the Lily Lake, in the eastern sky, had to be crossed by the dead before they could reach the court of Re, if that was their destination. Names for the next world were as numerous as they were poetic—the Land of the Westerners, the Beautiful Roads of the West, the Field of Offerings, the Land of Eternity.

Perhaps the Egyptian was not so much concerned with where he lived as with living itself. He would accept any place, any position, so long as he could win life thereby. The celestial circuit of the sun, which was sometimes viewed as a boat sailing the heavens, presented many possibilities for the dead man. He might become a rower in this boat of Re's, or carry a spear in order to fight the enemies of the god. If he was particularly fortunate, he would be invited to sit beside Re while other less well-equipped spirits toiled at the oars. If he journeyed to join the gods in their abodes, east or west, he would take any job that was open—he would be the god's secretary or servant.

The Egyptians were generally cheerful souls; their versions of the hereafter, divergent as they are in geography, generally agree on one thing. The Land of Eternity is "just and fair, without troubles." The dead are the "transfigured spirits," whom their mourning relatives expect to join in everlasting bliss.

Now and again, though, we detect a sour note in the hymns of praise. The regions of darkness under the earth, where the dead are sometimes thought to dwell, are illumined by the sun-god when he passes through them on his way to the eastern horizon to be reborn in glory; but his light gives no comfort to these dead, and they weep pitifully to see the waning of his splendor. In these dark realms the sun-god's boat encounters fearful dangers—hideous serpents attack it, demons must be fought off by force of arms. Here too, according to some references, there is a river of fire, where the souls of the enemies of Re burn in everlasting torment. And one text gives a discordant, and very poignant picture of the land of the "happy and just":

> Deep and dark is the dwelling place of the inhabitants of the West. It has no door and no window, no light to brighten it, no north wind to refresh the heart. The sun does not rise therein; each day they lie in darkness. . . . Those who are in the West, they are set apart and their existence is misery. One is loath to go and join them.

One is loath indeed. "As I love life and hate death" is a common adjuration in ancient Egyptian; it is a candid expression of the fear and doubt that must have lurked, skull-like, under the bright face of faith. Nowhere, I think, are these doubts expressed more eloquently than in one brief sentence from an Egyptian text: "None has returned from there, to tell us how they fare."

These simple words have always epitomized, for me, the doubts which are surely as universal as the belief, founded in desperate desire, in eternal life.

One interesting facet of the Egyptian language, which I suppose we could interpret as a psychological trait if we wanted to, is its reluctance to mention death. Ancient Egyptian had a word which meant "to die," but it was usually avoided in favor of any one of a dozen different euphemisms. When a king died he "went to join his father the sun," or "mingled with the gods," or "rested from life." In a land so dependent on water transportation, an image involving boats came readily to mind. Death was the time when "the mooring stake was driven in"—the final landing.

The ultimate proof of the Egyptians' fear of death is the mortuary cult itself—not only the time and money spent on tombs, coffins and other paraphernalia, but the fantastic imaginative attention to detail, which anticipated any possible—and some impossible—dangers that might prevent the resurrection so urgently desired. Death was an enemy, to be fought and conquered. And sometimes the dead, too, were hostile.

The prayer we quoted at the beginning of this book is a prayer against malevolent spirits. Sickness, as all Egyptian physicians knew, could be caused by the hatred of a dead man or dead woman, as well as by other hostile agencies. Most fascinating of all our sources are the texts called "letters to the dead." Scribbled on rough pots, they were "mailed" by being deposited in a tomb. Here are excerpts from one of them, written by a man to his deceased wife:

> To the excellent spirit, Ankhere. What evil thing have I done to you, that I should have come into this wretched state in which I am? What have I done to you? What you have done is that you have laid hands on me! . . . I made you a married woman, when I was a youth; I was with you, and I did not put you away. I did not cause your heart to grieve. . . . When you became ill, of the illness which you had, I [sent for] a master physician. . . . I wept exceedingly, with all my retinue, before all my neighbors. And I gave you linen cloths to wrap you, and I caused many cloths to be made, and I neglected no good thing that could be done for you. And now, look, I have spent three years living alone. . . . And, look, I did it because of you. But, look, you don't know good from bad. It will be decided between you and me! And, look, the sisters in the house, I have not entered into one of them!

The writer's extreme mental anguish even affected his spelling; the original is full of careless mistakes. The poor fellow reminds his wife of his many kindnesses to her, including the services of a good doctor during her last illness. As is common in Egyptian texts, the unpleasant fact of death is never explicitly stated; but the husband says he grieved publicly for his wife and gave her a good burial. Furthermore—and this obviously preys on his mind—not only has he remained unmarried for three long years, but he has not even had relations with any of the women in the house. Yet in spite of his kindness to his wife she has afflicted him with some unnamed but awful fate; and he threatens to call her up for judgment in the tribunal of the gods.

Obviously this man regards his dead wife as living on and as capable—in every sense of the word—of doing him an injury. They may have been as happy together as his letter implies; but catastrophic, undeserved bad luck could only be explained by the malice of some spirit.

It has been claimed that the Egyptians were not really afraid of the dead as a group. They feared only particular people who, having been unpleasant during life, might be equally nasty after they were dead. Yet the letters to the dead do not really bear out this theory. The afflicted husband, in the letter we have quoted, is outraged precisely because he had never given his wife cause to harm him and had no reason to expect her to do so. The argument that Egyptian tombs would not have been desecrated in such an efficient, wholehearted fashion if the robbers have been afraid of their occupants is not conclusive either; there are always people in any culture whose greed, or need, gives them enough intestinal fortitude to risk the sanctions the society sets up against antisocial behavior. We are supposed to have a healthy respect for the law and for policemen; but our jails are full of people who managed to rise above this inhibition. In many of the rifled tombs, the mummies have been brutally hacked apart in a manner as shocking as it was unnecessary; but this ferocity is understandable if we assume that the robbers were trying to protect themselves against the expected revenge of the violated dead by dismembering their bodies.

So, in the Egyptian faith we find, in addition to the inconsistency we have come to expect, a wide range of attitudes toward death and the dead. But we also find a unifying theme: the desire for survival in some, perhaps any, form. Let us go on to see how this survival was attained, and what a man had to do and possess in order to be "made into a living *ba*."

# XIV

## "My Body Shall Be Enduring"

### *Mummification—General*

THERE is no more typically Egyptian object than a mummy, unless it is a pyramid; and both represent essential elements in the equipment for eternity. Mummies have often been the villains in modern horror tales and films—another illustration of the fact that we still find a dead body an object of fear. Many years ago, when I first became interested in ancient Egypt, my indiscriminate reading led me to a particularly ghoulish mummy story. Efforts to trace it have failed, and one of the reasons why I would like to retell it, insofar as I can remember it, is because I hope some reader can identify it for me.

I have forgotten, among other vital statistics, the name of the archaeologist concerned. Let's call him Mr. Smith. Mr. Smith was excavating in Egypt, and one day he and his crew found a tomb wherein lay a mummy. By evening, when his crew had gone home, the gentleman we have named Mr. Smith was working with the mummy in the depths of the tomb, where he had descended by means of a rope. Absorbed in his task, he suddenly realized that the tomb had become very dark, and looking up, he was horrified to see a mass of black clouds obscuring the small square high above which led to the open air. One of the infrequent Egyptian storms had come up, as they do, with startling suddenness.

Mr. Smith knew that by morning, when his crew came back, the tomb would be flooded. He was in no danger, having his rope; but his now unwrapped mummy, for which he had apparently conceived an inordinate affection, would never survive a wetting. He had to get it up and out, or it would be lost.

Mr. Smith came to the conclusion that there was only one way out of the difficulty. He would have to sling the mummy on his back, and climb the rope. The problem was, how to get it attached to him? He seems not to have had any extra rope, which was careless, but by no means fatally so. He decided to put the mummy's arms around his neck and climb.

Painfully he inched his way up the rope, hand over hand and foot over foot. Above, the sky was ominously black; thunder rumbled distantly, like the remote roaring of an Egyptian lion goddess. All at once a bright streak of lightning cleft the threatening clouds; Mr. Smith, startled, slipped and slid down a few feet. And as he did so, the mummy moved. Its clasped hands slithered down over his breast and its head dropped; when he turned his own head he found himself staring directly into the withered eyes and fleshless grin of the old woman's face, which was now resting coquettishly on his shoulder.

The rest of the story is anticlimax; but even now, after an unmentionable number of years, I have not forgotten the impact of that grisly moment. Nor, I imagine, has Mr. Smith, if he is still alive—or if he ever lived, for I do not swear to the genuineness of the story. But I hope some reader can find Mr. Smith for me. I would hate to think that he is only the figment of some novelist's brain, or—worse still—of my own.*

---

* Much as I hate footnotes, I've got to put this one in to thank the kind readers of the first edition of this book who found "Mr. Smith" for me. He was Arthur Weigall, and he told the story, with characteristic gusto, in *Tutankhamen and Other Essays*, published in 1923 and, at this writing, unhappily still out of print. Mr. Robert Gibb of Aberdeen, Scotland, was the first reader to supply the information.

In one sense, it is irrelevant to ask why the ancient Egyptian needed a mummy in order to survive death. He obviously thought he did, or there would not be so many mummies. We have already mentioned the principle of sympathetic magic as one explanation for the attentions paid to the corpse, but it is not necessarily the complete answer. Once again, we will understand the Egyptian methods better if we' first look briefly at the techniques used by other people to dispose of their dead.

Although mummies have been found in many parts of the world beside Egypt, mummification as a method of disposal of the dead is comparatively rare. Leaving aside such exotic processes as exposure to birds of prey, and ritual cannibalism, the most common techniques, by a large margin, or two in number: inhumation and cremation.

Modern scholars who like logical systems have tried to find some relationship between the type of disposal used by a particular culture and the contemporary views of the hereafter. Is cremation in itself a denial of survival after death? No. We have already agreed that the body does not live again, no matter how carefully it is treated; therefore the destruction of the body need not affect the existence of the soul. But if the soul is freed by the conflagration which consumes the body, it ought to rise, on the lifting smoke, to a celestial paradise. Conversely, inhumation ought to imply a belief in a subterranean afterlife.

It doesn't work that way—possibly because ancient people were not as interested in consistency as the frustrated scholars who study them. Some cremation peoples believed in subterranean afterworlds and some inhumators thought of paradise as "heaven." There seems to be no essential difference in dogma between cremation and burial in the earth. Cremation burials include such features as elaborate tombs, sumptuous grave goods, and food offerings. In both methods of disposal something of the physical individual is preserved; and after a few hundred years or so there is very little difference to be seen in the final results of the two processes.

Mummification, then, cannot be regarded as the ultimate development of inhumation—the preservation of the body—as opposed to cremation—the utter destruction of the body. Mummification is a separate, and a special, technique.

We must distinguish first of all between embalming and mummification and between accidental and deliberate preservation of the body. Mummification, which is basically a process of desiccation, is only one form of embalming—the intentional preservation of the body from decay. Embalming by the injection of preservative materials is relatively new. Some attempts were made, in ancient and medieval times, to preserve tissue by the application of chemicals or vegetable substances, but most of the materials used by ancient embalmers were, in fact, quite useless for the purpose for which they were employed. In a few cases the embalmers hit on a substance which did preserve tissue; this was usually a desiccating agent, and the result was a mummy.

Mummies themselves may be deliberate or accidental. Perhaps the best preserved of all bodies—not really mummies—are products of a special environment: the peat bogs of Europe. These bodies are really remarkably well kept; they have none of the wrinkled, withered look of a genuine mummy, but preserve the texture of cloth and the very expression on the corpse's face. The chemicals in the soil transmuted cloth and flesh into a leatherlike substance. These bodies are the remains of careless pedestrians who missed their footing, or of criminals whose bodies were tossed into the bogs to get rid of them or of victims sacrificed to a god. They are accidentally preserved.

In classical and medieval times the bodies of royalty were often subjected to some sort of embalming. Some were successes, others were horrible failures. However, most of the successful examples must be viewed as accidental mummies, for they owe their survival to fortuitously favorable conditions of air or soil rather than to the materials which were meant to embalm them. Most of the bodies treated by the embalming techniques of olden times are in terrible condition today. Visitors to the catacombs of Rome are shown bodies of "embalmed" early Christians who, if they had known what they were going to look like 2,000 years later, would have begged to be excused. A skeleton is beautiful by comparison.

We must now consider cases of deliberate, successful mummification. Since the Egyptian mummies are the finest of the type, and the oldest, it was once suggested that all other intentional mummies were cases of cultural transmission from Egypt. Mummies are found in South America, Australia, and New Mexico, among other places, so this would mean that the Egyptians and their friends really got around.

The foremost exponent of the diffusion theory was no amateur, but a very distinguished scholar indeed—Grafton Elliot Smith, one of the first qualified medical men to study the physical anthropology of the ancient Egyptians. His book on Egyptian mummies, written in collaboration with Warren Dawson—another doctor, and a disciple of Smith's theories—is still the standard work on the subject. Smith's name is highly honored in Egyptology, but I doubt if any reputable scholar today would support his diffusion theory. None of the attempts to prove contact between the Old and New Worlds in ancient times has been successful, nor is there any real similarity between mummies of Egypt and those of the Western Hemisphere—except for the fact that all of them were mummified. As we shall see, Egyptian mummies were treated in a distinctive manner.

Peruvian mummies, perhaps the best known of all the New World types, were surely not accidental; they were meant to be preserved. Although there is some evidence of evisceration, they are primarily the product of climatic conditions as favorable as those of Egypt—dry cold instead of dry heat. The Egyptian cadavers were usually extended, but the Peruvian cases are bundled up; they look as if they were huddled against the cold. Cold has also preserved some bodies from the northern parts of north America—the Aleutians and Alaska. In the south of the same continent, another unique environment "pickled" the bodies of Indians of New Mexico and Kentucky in the saltpeter mines of those areas. These mummies, though deliberately placed in the mines, were not eviscerated.

The use of fire to dry bodies is also known; but in Nicaragua, for instance, this preliminary mummification was only temporary. After a year the body was cremated. A good many of these mummification techniques preserved the flesh for a limited time only. In various areas of the Pacific, evisceration and embalming of a rude sort was known, but infrequent. The Samoan mummies lasted for only thirty years or so, and the Tahitian variety were only good for a few months. A common procedure here was the pricking of the skin in order to allow the fluids of decomposition to escape, which, so far as we know, was never done in Egypt.

The same procedure was followed with the mummies from the Torres Straits area, between Australia and New Zealand. I have never seen one of these mummies—nor, to be honest, have I tried very hard to do so—but the photographs show them to have been fairly successful. They look vaguely like Egyptian mummies, except for the bamboo frames to which they are bound. It was on such frames that the embalming process was carried out; the body was raised, and suspended from the bamboo. I will spare the reader further details; they make rather repulsive reading. By comparison, the Egyptian process is quite antiseptic. Suffice it to say that the two techniques have nothing more in common than the aim of the process made inevitable. There are just too many difficulties in the diffusion theory, besides the fact that none of the other mummies show any important procedural resemblances to those of Egypt. Not only are the distances involved very great, but the time gap between ancient Egypt and the Pacific and American cultures is altogether too long.

In one case, however, the notion of mummification may have come to another society from Egypt. The Baganda tribe of Uganda mummify dead kings—or at least they used to; I don't know whether they have given it up now that Western culture has destroyed all the innocent old customs of the happy savages. Scholars who have studied the Baganda seem to think they exhibit other traits which resemble those of ancient Egypt, but whether the resemblance is more than coincidental, or, if it is, whether the connection lies in direct borrowing from Egypt by the Baganda ancestors or in a common "African" heritage—no man can say, nor I. At any rate, it is not impossible that the Egyptian and Bagandese embalmings are related.

Possible contacts between Egypt and the Canary Islands, where mummies were also manufactured, are hard to prove. The Guanches of the Canaries—who are, I understand, extinct—were of Berber stock, but it is unlikely that they left Africa, if that is where they came from, before the Egyptian mortuary cult faded out. According to reports, the Guanche mummies were preserved by the resin of a particular tree found in the islands. Resin was used in embalming by the Egyptians, but it was not the effective agent, and I have always had grave doubts about the Guanche method. These mummies were extremely desiccated, some weighing no more than seven pounds. It seems unlikely, offhand, that resin could so dehydrate the tissue.

Obviously, preservation of the body is not so much a result of theological notions relating to immortality as of more or less fortuitous physical conditions. Most of the people who believe in a life hereafter—which includes just about everyone—are satisfied with burial or with cremation. The preservation of the body is not a necessity for immortality. When the climate was right, or when the tribe had a handy natural embalming workshop such as the saltpeter mines, then we get mummies. Really effective embalming techniques could not be developed until a certain level of physiological and chemical knowledge had been attained. Sometimes a culture might stumble on an effective desiccating agent; but even then it was necessary to keep the body in a suitable environment or, sooner or later, decay took place.

We can't be sure how much Egyptian mummies depend for their endurance on the hot dry climate of Egypt. Mummies in damp tombs often decayed despite the best efforts of the embalmer; other mummies began to deteriorate after they were moved out of their tombs.

Of course the theological factor cannot be dismissed. Mummification in Egypt, as elsewhere, may have begun because of environmental conditions, but the complex profession we are about to study would not have developed if a need had not been felt. This need, as I have suggested, can probably be explained in terms of sympathetic magic. A man would live in Paradise as long as some part of him continued to exist in this world—but no longer. A statue, or even a name, could provide the necessary focal point for the spirit. But the best, and most direct, physical remnant of a man was his own body.

## Mummification—Egyptian

Everyone seems to agree that the Egyptians probably got the idea of embalming their dead from seeing the accidentally preserved bodies of their distant ancestors. In prehistoric times the dead were buried in the sand, without coffins or wrappings. The dry air and the hot, baking sand preserved the fragile flesh as they have also preserved cloth and wood and withered flowers. Laid in shallow graves, sometimes the dead reappeared. When Breasted was excavating in Nubia, he had to pass through a cemetery each day on his way to work, and, across his path, he saw the feet of a corpse which had been uncovered by the wind. They were as rough and callused as the feet of the living Nubians who worked at the excavation. As wind and time uncovered these remains for Breasted, so they must have exposed older specimens for the Egyptians of 3000 B.C., who lived at the time of the unification of the Two Lands.

The unification, and the beginning of the First Dynasty, marks the beginning of Egyptian civilization, as opposed to prehistory. Civilization means more complex ways of doing things. No longer were the dead shoveled directly into the sand. Graves were lined with wood, brick and stone; bodies were wrapped in cloth or enclosed in coffins. This care defeated one of the ends for which it was designed. Stone and wood shut out air and sand. Protected bodies decayed.

There is no evidence as yet from the First Dynasty to indicate that the Egyptians were trying to embalm their dead at this early period. They may have done; in the succeeding Dynasty, attempts were made. At Sakkara, Quibell found the remains of a woman who had been carefully prepared for the grave. The body lay on its side in a flexed position, knees bent. (The extended position, more convenient for mummy wrapping, did not come into general use until later.) Within the elaborate wrappings of this mummy there was a mass of corroded linen whose condition suggested that a material such as salt or natron had been applied to the surface of the body. The process did not work; only bones were left. But this example proves that a beginning had been made.

A few centuries later we are in the Pyramid Age, the time of the Fourth and Fifth Dynasties. It is a period of fantastic achievement in many areas, symbolized by the immense mass of the Great Pyramid. Mummification had not made the same strides as had tomb building, but the diligent embalmers had developed a new process which compensated, to some extent, for their inability to preserve the physical body. The corpse was treated with resin and wrapped in layer upon layer of linen bandages. While the outermost layer of bandage was still wet and sticky with resin, it was molded into the form of the body it covered, and the resin-soaked cloth set, forming a shell, or carapace, of stony hardness. The modeling was so exact that fine details of anatomy and expression are preserved. On one mummy, found at Medum by Petrie, the owner's neat mustache was reproduced in the linen, and the sexual organs were modeled with such care that we can tell that circumcision was practiced at that time. This mummy lay in the extended position, which was beginning to be the normal one. Its body cavity was packed with linen and the head rattled when it was shaken (to such extremes does a passion for truth lead archaeologists!), probably with bits of desiccated brain. At this period the brain was not removed, though the abdominal organs were.

Mummification gradually improved during the succeeding dynasties. By the Middle Kingdom the technique of modeling the surface of the body in plaster or linen had been abandoned. The body was eviscerated and treated with resin or gum; linen was used to fill the abdominal cavity. Sometimes sawdust was used for filling instead of linen. The brain was not removed.

The classic style of mummification did not appear until the New Kingdom. A new advance had been made—the removal of the brain by means of a hooked instrument which was inserted through the nostril and up, piercing the ethmoid bone, into the skull. The organs were removed from the abdominal cavity; the chest cavity was entered through an incision in the diaphragm, and all its contents were removed, with the exception of the heart.

*Mummy*

The heart was the seat not of romantic yearnings but of thought and memory, so we can see why it might be left in place. The other organs, with the exception of the kidneys, which were sometimes left in the body, were treated separately and then placed in four canopic jars.

This method is described by Herodotus, whom I do not intend to quote. For an Egyptologist the value of Herodotus rests almost entirely in the joy of his delightful prose. He was sometimes right but more often wrong, and his statements cannot be accepted without confirmation. He does, however, describe mummification fairly accurately, mentioning three different types. His first, and most expensive, method is the one just described. Methods two and three involve injecting cedar oil to dissolve the abdominal organs, and cleaning out the intestines with a purge. I am informed by those who ought to know that the second method would actually work, if an oleo-resin resembling turpentine was used, so Herodotus was right about this. He also scores on the most important point of all. So far we have only mentioned the preliminaries of mummification; the all-important desiccating agent has yet to be discussed. Herodotus correctly identified the agent and described the method.

In the past there was some disagreement about this vital substance, but recent experiments have pretty well settled the argument. If we wanted to duplicate an Egyptian mummy—and it appears, grotesquely enough, that some of us do!—we could.

The experts did not argue about what substance was used, but about how it was used. The substance is natron, a kind of salt whose dehydrating properties are very high. It is found in quantity in Egypt, particularly in the Wadi Natrun, one of the oases. There is no doubt that it was used in mummification; it has been chemically identified on many mummies and in canopic jars from as early as the Fourth Dynasty.

Herodotus says that the cadavers were placed in natron for a period of seventy days. Until recent times it was assumed that the natron was used in solution; so we had the novelist's gruesome version of an Egyptian embalmer's shop, with corpses floating in their salty baths. A thoughtful reader, however, might have found himself wondering. Baths? The aim was dehydration, wasn't it? Why add more water?

Herodotus used to be quoted as the authority for the natron baths, but here the interpreters, not the Greek, may be off the track. The word he uses is the word used to describe the salting of fish, which may be soaked, certainly, but which are often, in Egypt at least, preserved with dry salt.

One way of solving the problem was to try both wet and dry natron on tissue and see what would happen. This was done by Edward Lucas, the chemist who worked on the Tutankhamon objects, and the author of the definitive book on Egyptian materials. Another recent experimenter was Mr. Sandsson of the Department of Pathology of the University of Glasgow. Neither man—to still any apprehensions the reader may have—actually tried their experiments on a human body. Lucas used chickens and pigeons, and Sandsson used human toes. Both experimenters agree on the essential points: that it took an extremely high concentration of natron in the liquid state to preserve tissue, and that the results did not resemble Egyptian mummies; but that dry natron did produce specimens resembling Egyptian mummies. Dry natron seems to be the answer. The process might be recommended to modern morticians, if preservation is what they want. Some of the Egyptian specimens have lasted quite nicely for over 3,000 years, with the help of the admirable Egyptian climate.

The "classic" method of embalming continued with minor changes for several hundred years. It was quite a successful method; some of the mummies of this period, particularly those of Yuya and Seti I, are excellently preserved. Although the morticians could in many cases stave off the dangers of physical dissolution, there was one danger that threatened the mummy which they could not avert. Tomb robbers not only stole the goods buried in the tomb, but they often dismembered, mutilated, or burned the mummies themselves. During the Twenty-First Dynasty the situation got so bad that the pious priestly rulers of Thebes felt it necessary to restore and rebury the battered bodies of the ancient kings. The royal embalmers who picked up the pieces—quite literally, in some cases—had ample opportunity to view the results of the techniques they and their predecessors had practiced, and they may have decided that those results were not entirely satisfactory. Tissue was certainly preserved, but the mummies did not look lifelike. The skin was wrinkled and shrunken, the cheeks hollow, the flesh sunken.

Physicians have adopted Aesculapius as their patron; perhaps morticians, who are always seeking to improve their methods, ought to adopt one of these Twenty-First Dynasty embalmers. They were not disheartened; they were stimulated to do bigger and better things. But the techniques they adopted were rather peculiar.

This period is considered, by those who know, to be the height of mummification techniques. We ought to pause to consider the methods in some detail. There is no use warning off the squeamish, as Miss Mitford considerately did before leading them into the embalmers' workshop. What follows will be no worse than what has come before.

The undertaker of the Twenty-First Dynasty received his patient in a workshop which was not a permanent building but a temporary booth erected for the purpose. The body was laid out on a wooden table or platform. An incision was made in the left flank and all the internal organs except the heart, and perhaps the kidneys, were removed. The brain was extracted through one nostril. Then the entire body was covered with dry natron and allowed to remain in it for a period which was no longer than seventy days. This is the length of time assigned to the entire process by various texts; probably a good portion of the total was taken up by the bandaging and other parts of the process.

The organs removed from the body were also preserved in pots containing natron. At the end of the designated period the body emerged dry and desiccated, with loosened skin. It was at this point that the Twenty-First Dynasty embalmer departed from the practices of his predecessors and rose to heights of creative power. (Or, as Winlock puts it, he resorted to an expedient of somewhat doubtful taste.) He stuffed the body.

The abdominal cavity had always been stuffed, but this was different. Through slits made in the skin, the mummy was padded out with sawdust, salt, ashes, and so on, rammed in between skin and muscle until the desiccated form took on a shape resembling that which it had had in life—or perhaps any form that appealed to the undertaker.

After the body was stuffed, it was painted. The face was adorned with cosmetics, the lips rouged, artificial eyebrows gummed into place. If the natural hair was thinning it was eked out by false hair elaborately waved and curled. As a final touch, false eyes were inserted; they were of black-and-white stone or of linen with painted pupils.

The body itself being now prepared, the organs, which had been carefully preserved, were wrapped into seven packages, which were replaced in the body cavity along with small wax figures of four guardian genii of the dead. The incision was closed with a plug of paste or linen, or covered by a plate inscribed with magical figures.

The mummy was ready for wrapping. It was laid on wooden blocks for easier manipulation (modern archaeologists, when unwrapping mummies, sometimes use sawhorses), and a pile of old sheets, shirts and shawls was placed close at hand to be torn into strips of varying width as they were needed—narrow ones for fingers, wide ones for the torso. Before the first bandages were applied the amulets and ornaments of major importance were placed around the throat or wrist, or on the forehead. The fingers and toes were wrapped separately, with very narrow bandages; gloves or finger coverings of silver or gold, if the mummy were that of a royal personage, might go on the fingers first. Sandals have been found on the feet.

Bandaging a mummy took hundreds of yards of linen. It must have been a drain on the family linen closet. Perhaps the living saved old sheets and shawls toward the day of death, and extra supplies might be bought from temple warehouses or from thrifty individuals who had some to spare. We know, from the state of wear of much of the linen, and from the worn, washed-out laundry marks, that most of the material was not made specifically for mummy wrappings. The marks weren't really laundry marks, of course, but they are reminiscent of ours, being little scribbles in one corner which give the name of the owner or the warehouse to which the linen belonged. One Eleventh Dynasty mummy used 375 square meters of linen in its bandaging; the coffin was filled with extra sheets and these, with the palls used in the funeral procession, brought the total linen required to the staggering sum of 845 square meters.

After the first layer of bandages was applied, other amulets might be placed on the body. Then came more bandages, in a prescribed order—first wound spirally around the body, then a sheet covering the whole form, then more spiral bandages. At one point the head was fixed in position by a strip of linen around the face and neck. The arms were fastened to the thighs, and the legs were bound together. Twice during the wrapping process the bandages were covered with warm, melted resin. This substance, which has been erroneously called "bitumen," or "pitch," must have served some ritual purpose, since it did nothing to preserve tissue. In fact, it sometimes had precisely the opposite effect. Tutankhamon's mummy had been stuck to the coffin by the resin poured over it, which had hardened into a stony mass. Even more destructive was the spontaneous combustion brought about by the decomposition of the unguents, which carbonized the linen wrappings and reduced the flesh to a cracked and brittle state.

Finally the mummy was formed by the layers of bandaging into a rigid columnar shape. The final sheet was then applied.

Unlike the other bandages, it was made especially for the trade, being a sheet of coarse linen with a figure of Osiris drawn on its surface. This was covered by a piece of linen stitched up the back, and then a set of tapes was applied over the whole form. The mummy was now ready to be delivered to the family. The embalmers were through with him—almost.

Sometimes, in the course of excavation, archaeologists have found little deposits which seemed, at first glance, to be refuse—pots, some empty and some filled with rags; stained bits of linen; miscellaneous implements. We sometimes bury garbage, but the Egyptians were not so fastidious. It did not take much imagination to identify this particular trash as the residue from the undertaker's workshop. It could not be discarded; having touched the dead man, it partook to some extent of his essence, so it had to be given some sort of burial. Or, as Winlock cynically suggests, if a man wanted to be sure that *all* of him got into sacred ground, he would have to insist that even the sweepings of the embalmer's floor be gathered up.

There was good reason for such care. Some of the embalmers, certainly, were men of integrity. But in a number of cases, posterity has caught them out although their contemporaries were deceived. Even in carefully prepared mummies they sometimes slipped, letting bits and pieces of their equipment, or assorted small animals, be wrapped into a second or third layer of bandages. What difference did it make? The relatives of the dead man weren't going to unwrap him, and nothing essential had been left out.

More serious were cases like that of the woman whose inner workings had been lost or misplaced while the body was being mummified. The embalmer finally made up a set of organs out of a coil of rope and a bit of cowskin and some rags, bundled them up with the four sacred figures, and put them inside the lady. One would like to think that she encountered him later, in the hereafter; their conversation would have been interesting to hear.

The nastiest of all accusations, worse than carelessness or laziness, can also be levied against some ancient embalmers. The word is ghouls—robbers of the dead. Winlock describes one case which is an excellent example of archaeological detection; a process of reasoning which puts the blame for the robbery squarely and unmistakably on the shoulders of the men who had been paid to guard the mummy.

The mummies in question were those of two women. When Winlock first found them, they were lying just as they had been placed in the grave: tapes, outer sheet and Osiris sheet were in place. But as the archaeologist unwrapped the bodies, more and more confusion among the chest bandages became apparent. At last the bandages were off, down to the first layer of resin which had been applied; and there, in the hardened gum, was the imprint of the metal hawks which had once covered the ladies' chests. The hawks were gone. Around the torn bandages on the chests were fingerprints made by hands sticky with resin. The left hand of one woman had been laid bare in a search for finger rings.

Winlock concludes somberly, "The mummies had been rifled before they were even completely wrapped; and that must have taken place in the undertaker's own establishment."

Despite such cases of corruption and carelessness, the mummies of this period probably represent the height of Egyptian skill in embalming. From this point on the technique degenerated, and the carelessness increased. Some Ptolemaic mummies are very dark and hard and shiny, presumably from the application of resinous material (not bitumen, as is often claimed) directly to the skin. Poorly preserved mummies were kept intact by a long stick thrust through the body. Others can hardly be called mummies; they are only loose bones flung higgled-piggledy into a framework of palm fibers bandaged into the shape of a body. As the embalmers' skill decreased, the wrappings became very elaborate; the bandaging sometimes looks like woven basketing. The elaboration of bandaging reached its peak during the Roman period, and the mummies were at their lowest point. They were so thickly coated with resin that the material formed a cast all around the body, and sometimes we cannot even tell whether evisceration was carried out. The process had made a complete circle, back to the technique used in the earliest mummies—a cast or carapace covering the entire body.

Mummies, it may be thought, are not only an unpleasant topic of conversation, but an even more unpleasant object of research. This attitude is not only the squeamishness of our effete culture, it is a reflection of attitudes toward the dead which are a lot older than modern man. The other objects of an Egyptologist's study need no justification, but perhaps we ought to explain his interest in what may strike some people as a nasty business.

One reason for the study of mummification ought to be immediately obvious to any reader with archaeological know-how. The changes in embalming technique form a chronological sequence which can be pinned down by absolute dates. This means that otherwise undated mummies, and the contexts in which they are found, can sometimes be dated by means of this sequence, which was worked out so skillfully by men like Smith and Dawson.

The human remains found in some of the Old Kingdom pyramids illustrate how the sequence can be applied. In 1837, Colonel Vyse, an English explorer, was the first man in modern times to penetrate the interior of the third Giza pyramid, built by Menkaure. Vyse was several thousand years too late to find an undisturbed burial, but he did discover the king's sarcophagus and, in an upper chamber, scraps from a wooden coffin and from a mummy. It was only reasonable to suppose that the mummy fragments were the remains of the pyramid builder.

Another supposed mummy of the Pyramid Age was found in the tomb of King Mernere, near Cairo. Mernere was a Sixth Dynasty king. His remains were found in 1881, over 4,000 years after he had been sealed inside his pyramid.

But according to Smith's analysis of embalming techniques, the Mernere mummy is an Eighteenth Dynasty effort, coming from a period about a thousand years later than the pyramid in which it was found. The Mycerinus mummy is also later in date. Both were what archaeologists call "intrusive" burials—burials which made use of an already prepared tomb. Thus the study of mummification can correct a date based on misleading circumstances of discovery. It can even correct a date based on what would seem to be unarguable evidence—an inscription naming the mummy.

When the royal embalmers of the Twenty-First Dynasty gathered up the remains of the ancient kings for reburial, they sometimes found themselves doing a sort of ghoulish jigsaw puzzle with the pieces. It is not unlikely that they made mistakes. That is why you will sometimes find the identification of a particular royal mummy questioned. Most of the mummies in the collection were relabeled by the restorers, but occasionally the historical evidence does not fit the mummy; it may be too old or too young, or there may be other discrepancies. One of the questionable mummies is the one labeled Amenhotep III; actually, there are several names on the label. This king dates from the Eighteenth Dynasty; he was the father of Akhenaton and—I think—the grandfather of Tutankhamon. This mummy had been stuffed; packing had been introduced under the skin. Now this process, as we have seen, was not begun until the Twenty-First Dynasty, some 400 years after the age of Amenhotep III. When Elliot Smith examined the mummy he was unhappy about the attribution of it to an Eighteenth Dynasty king; he suggested, very tentatively, that the unique technique might be one of the heresies of the Amarna period, which was generally iconoclastic. But we now have other mummies dating from about the same period, and they show no signs of stuffing. The mummies of Yuya and of Tutankhamon were prepared in the traditional Eighteenth Dynasty manner. We cannot firmly deny that this mummy is that of Amenhotep III on typological evidence; the trouble with a noninclusive series is that a new example may turn up at any time to upset the arrangement. But it is clear that this particular mummy should be labeled with a big question mark.

Tutankhamon's mummy furnishes other examples of the useful application of the study of embalming. Incidentally, Carter's report on the unwrapping of the mummy is a superb illustration of the spirit in which archaeologists approach this task. Carter and Dr. Douglas Derry, who performed and reported the actual postmortem, were intelligent, sensitive human beings; both were soberly aware of their responsibilities, and keenly alive to the solemnity of the moment.

Derry's investigation of the mummy turned up one interesting and curious fact which had to do with the skull measurements.

Tutankhamon's skull was unusually broad, as well as flat-topped (platycephalic), with a markedly projecting occipital area. The general shape of the head was strikingly like that of another skull —the one found in the peculiar little Tomb No. 55, which was originally named "The Tomb of Queen Tiy." Both Derry and Smith—who examined the latter skull—commented independently on the unusual breadth and flatness of the two specimens. A later investigator, R. G. Harrison, who was a professor of anatomy, confirmed the resemblance, and praised Derry for the accuracy of his observations.

There seems to be no doubt that the owners of the skulls were related by blood, and this is a point of great importance. The most likely candidate for the occupant of Tomb 55 is Smenkhkare, the son-in-law and coregent of Akhenaton. If he and Tutankhamon were that much like one another, they must have been brothers, for they are too close in age to have been father and son. This is another useful fact to be learned from the study of mummies—the approximate age of the deceased. For example, Tutankhamon's age at death was somewhere in the neighborhood of eighteen years. Egyptian records give the number of years he reigned, so from the physical data we can deduce how old he was when he came to the throne. Smenkhkare—if the questionable skeleton is indeed his—was probably around twenty when he died. This would make him seventeen years old when he became king. Tutankhamon succeeded him; so if the two were brothers, Tutankhamon was the younger brother.

If you think there are a lot of "if's" in that paragraph, just wait. *If* Tutankhamon was a king's son, as one inscription states, then Smenkhkare must have been a king's son too, for a commoner, whatever his age, would not have preceded a prince of the blood onto the throne. Only two kings qualify for the paternal role. *If* there was a long coregency between Akhenaton and his father, then the latter monarch would have lived long enough to father Smenkhkare and Tutankhamon. *If* there wasn't a coregency, the father must have been Akhenaton, because that king reigned for seventeen years and Tutankhamon was only nine when he ascended the throne after Akhenaton's death.

Well, we seem to be getting off the subject of mummies. We

don't have Akhenaton's, and even if we did, we couldn't eliminate all the "if's." A close resemblance between his remains and those of Smenkhkare and Tutankhamon would not prove he was their father; he might equally well be their half brother. But we would be able to find out how old Akhenaton was when he died, and skeletal remains would settle, once and for all, the old argument as to whether Akhenaton suffered from a pathological condition severe enough to produce the deformities seen in some of his statues.

Those of us who are interested in Egyptology engage in this sort of guesswork all the time; it is going to be a blow to us if Akhenaton's mummy ever does turn up, because we enjoy our fantasies immensely, particularly when we label them "theories" and get into exciting arguments with other archaeologists.

We could go on listing the benefits to be derived from the study of mummies—the manner of death, the types of diseases prevalent, the state of medical treatment, styles of hairdressing and makeup, not to mention the all-important question of mortuary beliefs. Before I conclude our study of Egyptian mummies—which may have seemed, to the squeamish reader, inordinately long—I want to touch on one last value. It is the value of simple human interest. These poor scraps of mortality were once people; and if we have an ounce of imagination we cannot help wondering, when we see them in the unaesthetic but actual flesh, what they were like. How did they live—and how did they die?

Most of the time the last question is impossible to answer. The vicera of almost all mummies were removed and many specimens were damaged, by time or tomb robbers. Still, certain of the mummies have a story to tell. The two little mummies of the premature babies found in Tutankhamon's tomb suggest not only a father's disappointed hopes, but the fall of a dynasty. (The recent suggestion that these fetuses represent an otherwise unattested religious ritual is extremely farfetched.)

Detective story addicts who study the mummies mentioned in a book like Smith and Dawson's may be struck, as I was, by the apparent rarity of violent death. The great exception is the terrible mummy of King Sekenenre, who met an extremely violent

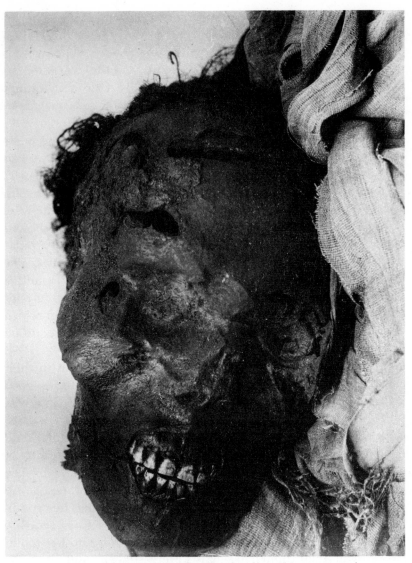

Mummy of Sekenenre. *The Metropolitan Museum of Art.*

end at the time of the Wars of Liberation, when the Theban rulers were beginning to object to the domination of the Hyksos invaders, who had controlled Egypt for many years. The wounds of ax and club can still be seen on the skull, and the expression on the face suggests that Sekenenre died painfully. Our fancy cannot lead us into overdramatizing Sekenenre's end; assassinated or struck down in battle, this man's death *was* dramatic.

Since I have a basically evil mind, I suspect that some other Egyptian kings did not die of old age. The histories of various nations, including those of the "enlightened" western world, indicate that the kingship was not the safest of all possible jobs. The royal mummies might not tell the complete story. Some were so badly battered that it is hard to tell whether they once showed signs of a violent attack; and poison, to name only one popular method of assassination, would not leave traces on the bones. The most recent investigation of Tutankhamon's mummy found a suspicious looking hole in the skull. This could have been a post-mortem injury, but the dramatic history of the period in which the boy lived and died certainly gives us grounds to speculate on *how* he died.

Smith and Dawson cite another case of violent death in their classic book, and, with the insight which distinguishes good archaeologists, they reconstructed another reasonable, and very pitiful, story to explain it. The mummy was that of a girl about sixteen years old. It had not been eviscerated, so the doctors could tell that the girl was six months pregnant. The probable cause of death was a fractured skull, and both forearms had been broken before death. Drawing on parallel cases from modern times, Smith suggested that the girl was unmarried and that when her condition was discovered by her family, her male relatives proceeded to wipe out the stain on their honor. When she flung up her hands to ward off their blows her wrists were broken, and then the murderers proceeded to beat her to death. It makes a plausible story, although we must state, in all fairness to the ancient Egyptians, that we have no reason to suppose that they were all as stupidly vicious about such matters as are some modern, civilized men.

The most mysteriously suggestive of all the mummies known to me was the body of a person who is still unidentified. It was found in 1872, when some lucky peasants stumbled upon a thieves' paradise. In a hidden cache in the cliffs near Thebes lay the bodies of the greatest kings and queens of Egypt, gathered from their desecrated tombs and secretly reburied, for safety, by the rulers of the Twenty-First Dynasty. For some time the happy tomb robbers, worthy descendants of forebears who had practiced the profession for generations, kept the secret of the discovery while marketing their find, but they were eventually caught by the shrewd detective work of the Department of Antiquities, then headed by Gaston Maspero. The cache was opened and the royal mummies taken to the Museum, where they were examined by experts.

Among the mummies of the blueboods was one which Maspero ignored at first. Enclosed in a plain white coffin, without name or inscriptions, it seemed hardly worthy of notice, except for the fact that it was sewed in a sheepskin of white wool—an unusual feature. With the change in temperature and humidity, however, the mummy was adversely affected, and eventually it forced itself upon Maspero's attention. He decided it had better be unwrapped at once. At first everything appeared to be normal; within the sheepskin the mummy was wrapped in typical Eighteenth Dynasty style. But as the unwrapping proceeded, the horrified archaeologists realized that this mummy, the body of a young man about five feet ten inches tall, was unlike any other they had seen. The body had never been eviscerated; it was preserved solely by dry natron which had been skillfully distributed on the surface of the body. Everyone who was present at the unwrapping seems to have been powerfully affected by the sight of the face; and, according to Maspero, all assumed immediately that death was the result of a convulsant poison. Maspero even suggested that the wrapping had been begun before life was completely extinct.

It comes as something of an anticlimax to realize, on sober reflection, that perhaps Maspero and his examining physician, Dr. Fouquet, let themselves be carried away just a bit. Of course there is no way of telling how this miserable wretch died; a number of diseases can cause considerable pain, and even if the young man had been poisoned, the venom might have come from a serpent's bite. However, even a photograph of the mummy shows us why the first beholders of the unwrapped face had to fight down a shudder of horror. (I am not reproducing this photograph.) It really is a terrible-looking thing; the impression it induces is not one of fear or terror, but of horrified pity. Occasionally mummies have been found which were not composed, as most were, into an attitude of repose. The most outstanding is Sekenenre, whom we have just described. Yet there is no mummy in the entire collection which arouses the painful emotions caused by this unknown young man. The surrounding circumstances—the plain unmarked coffin, the peculiar use of a sheepskin as wrapping, the failure of the embalmers to compose the body, and the fact, unique among all other mummies in the cache, that the body was not disemboweled—all this does justify a question as to how the man died. There is a mystery, even if it is not a murder mystery. We cannot even put up a reasonable guess as to who the man was. He must have been of royal birth or he would not have been included in the cache, and yet the cavalier treatment of the body suggests that he had been guilty of some crime.

Of course, there is one conspicuous omission in our royal male mummies of the Eighteenth Dynasty. We have most of them; but the great heretic, Akhenaton, is missing. I would love to think that this most unusual mummy is that of Egypt's most unusual king. But while such a fate would make a fine dramatic ending to the saga of Amarna, the scanty facts that we do have are all against such an identification. The age is too young—twenty-seven or eight, according to Elliot Smith—and, by the same expert's testimony, the wrappings seem to be early Eighteenth Dynasty rather than late. Nor does the mummy, which is straight and well formed except for the distorted face, conform to the bodily shape of Akhenaton as we know it from his statues. This is not, to me, a serious objection, but the other facts are. Most damning of all is the fact that the full reaction against Akhenaton did not begin until some years after his death. Even if some of his enemies, of whom he undoubtedly had a number, had managed to do away with him, his son-in-law, Tutankhaton as he was then, and his daughter, Tutankhaton's queen, would have seen to it that he was buried with fitting pomp. No—the Heretic King must remain, as he probably always will remain, lost to us; and the strange mummy of the royal cache should probably be considered that of a prince of the early Eighteenth Dynasty, whose fate not even Sherlock Holmes could unravel.

Of all the qualifications necessary for immortality, a physical simulacrum of the deceased was one of the most important. If we had no other evidence of this belief, the long centuries of scrupulous attention lavished on the corpse would be evidence enough. Admittedly, mummification is a curious custom; and it is a bit disconcerting to travel three thousand years into the past and find ourselves staring at a distorted, but recognizable, version of recent American funerary customs. Although embalming did not disappear entirely until Moslem times in Egypt, some of the early followers of Christ saw the impropriety which seems to elude American Christians. St. Anthony, son of a noble Egyptian family, addressed the faithful followers who surrounded him just before his death in these words:

> ". . . permit no man to take my body and carry it into Egypt, lest, according to the custom which they have, they embalm me and lay me up in their houses, for it was to avoid this that I came into the desert. . . . Dig a grave then . . . and hide my body under the earth . . . until the Resurrection of the dead, when I shall receive this body without corruption."

# XV

# "A Goodly Burial
in the Necropolis"

## *Tombs and Mortuary Temples*

ONCE the Egyptian had his mummy, he needed some place to put it. Simpleminded as this may sound, it is the basic reason for a tomb—a place in which the body can be protected. Like Egyptian mummies, Egyptian tombs are the quintessence of the type. Nothing bigger in the way of tombs exists than the Great Pyramid; no ruler's mortuary equipment ever outshone the treasures buried with the pharaohs.

Like those of primitive men everywhere, the earliest Egyptian graves were holes in the ground. The bodies, unembalmed except for the natural action of dry air and sand, lay on their sides with knees drawn up and hands folded before the face, in the attitude of sleep. As time went on, the holes were tidied up, squared at the corners and lined with mats and planks and bricks. Over the grave pit the earth was piled up in a low mound.

In the two elements, pit and mound, we see the constituents of the later tombs. Archaeologists call the pit the substructure; the superstructure is the part of the tomb which shows above ground. At the very beginning of the dynasties the Egyptians had devel-

oped these two elements into a surprisingly complex and handsome tomb, all the more amazing because of its nearness in time to
the prehistoric grave pits. Below the ground there was a substructure built of brick and consisting of several rooms, with the body
in the central, largest room. Surrounding rooms were used for the
storage of goods designed for the benefit of the dead. In the Second Dynasty the substructure developed into an imitation house,
complete with bathroom and toilet.

The superstructure was of a type common throughout Egyptian history. It is called a mastaba, and it is a flat-topped rectangular structure with sides that slope in a bit as they go up. The
earliest mastabas, some of which are as large as 180 by 90 feet,
were made of brick, with complex niches all around the outside.
Later the niching disappeared except for one recess, which developed into a mortuary chapel.

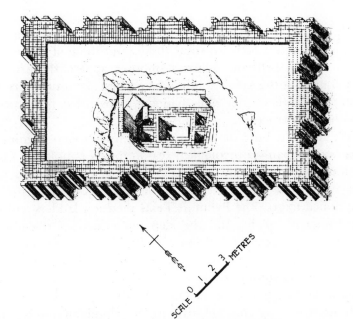

*Reconstruction of a niched mastaba*
*From* Archaic Egypt *by W. B. Emery.* © *1961. Reprinted by*
*permission of Penguin Books Ltd.*

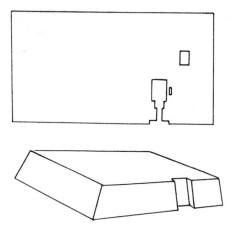

*Plan and reconstruction
of an Old Kingdom mastaba*

Up to the Third Dynasty there does not seem to have been any stylistic difference between royal tombs and those of the nobility. Djoser and his brilliant architect Imhotep apparently introduced the pyramid as the king's tomb. The earliest pyramids were built in steps or layers; later ones had the steps filled in to make a smooth-sided structure.

We may attribute the pyramid form to Imhotep's genius, but there was probably a theological reason for its popularity. One of the most plausible theories is that both step and true pyramid were symbols of the ascent to the regions of Re, where the dead king hoped to go. The Pyramid Texts mention ladders and stairs as methods of ascent, and the step pyramid does resemble the hieroglyphic sign for a staircase. As for the later pyramids, one ingenious explanation compares their smooth slopes to the slanting rays of the sun—another way of climbing to the celestial regions, according to the Texts. On a cloudy day at Giza, the rays of sunlight streaming through rifts in the clouds may take on the appearance of a shining, transparent pyramid of light, with the same angle of slope as those of the monuments of Giza.

The pyramids were only one part of the king's funerary complex, which also included two temples, one against the pyramid and one at the edge of the cultivated land, a causeway to connect the two, small subsidiary pyramids for the burial of the king's wives, and stone-lined pits containing huge boats. In 1954 an Egyptian archaeologist, Kamal el Mallakh, found one of these boats in almost perfect condition; it had been partly dismantled but the wood of which it was built was still sound. These boats have been called sun boats, but it is likely that they have some other significance. The spirits of the dead needed such transportation, for the Land of Eternity had many rivers and lakes. Boat pits have been found by Emery in connection with First Dynasty mastabas, so they were not restricted to pyramids.

The substructure of the pyramid in the Old Kingdom was fairly simple. Like that of the Great Pyramid, it consisted of a shaft going down under or into the heart of the superstructure and culminating in the burial chamber. The same type continued in the pyramids of the Fifth and Sixth Dynasties, which resemble their predecessors in general plan, but not in size or building technique. Later pyramids are shoddy affairs of mixed stone or rubble, held together by a limestone facing. When the outer layer of stone was removed by scavengers, chief among whom were kings of later times, the whole structure slid down into a limp heap. The late Fifth and Sixth Dynasty pyramids are notable for one thing, however—the famous inscriptions on the walls of the burial chambers known as the Pyramid Texts.

The mastaba continued to be the most popular type of non-royal tomb during the Old Kingdom. One Fourth Dynasty king built his tomb in this form. It has been suggested that this was a break with the solar religion, of which the pyramid was the symbol, but of course we do not have enough evidence to determine whether or not this theory is right. At Giza, mastabas were built by other Fourth Dynasty kings for their friends and relations; they were laid out like a genuine city of the dead, in neat rows, with streets between them. These private tombs are stone built and very simple, being smooth-sided except for the enclosed chapel, and having substructures which consisted of a shaft down into the ground, culminating in a tomb chamber.

The chapel, like the mortuary temple of the royal pyramid, represents the second reason for the building of tombs. The tomb itself sheltered the body; the chapel allowed for contact with the soul. At the far end of the small room was a "false door," shaped like a portal but made of solid stone. The figure of the dead man which was painted or carved on the door symbolized his coming forth into the regions of the living.

The dead were also represented physically by life-sized statues of stone or wood, painted in vivid colors. The statue was kept in a tiny room called the *serdab*, built into the superstructure and walled off from the outside world except for a small opening high in the wall, through which the statue could "see." The most famous of the Old Kingdom private statues came originally from the serdabs. In some Giza tombs the full-sized statue was replaced by a "reserve head."

At Giza we also find the first of a new type of tomb, which was to become as important as the mastaba—the "rock-cut" tomb. In one sense, of course, all tombs were rock-cut in part; the substructure went down into the ground. But the real rock-cut variety has no superstructure, only a room or series of rooms cut into a cliff face. As the Egyptians were to discover, rock-cut tombs had one great advantage over the type with a superstructure. They were not so conspicuous. As far back as the Fourth Dynasty, when King Khufu buried his mother in a deep, unmarked shaft near the causeway of his pyramid, he and his associates must have been aware of the need for secrecy; it is thought that the queen's original tomb had already been plundered, and that this was a re-burial. Of course Khufu could not know that his pious undertaking would survive forty centuries in safety, but it is surprising that he should have sought such secrecy for his mother, and then have himself buried in a monument that was visible for miles in every direction. It was almost a millennia later before the kings of Egypt learned the painful lesson, that secrecy was preferable to bombast in tomb-building. Even the earlier private rock-cut tombs sometimes defeated this advantage by adding porticos and courtyards and chapels—an "X marks the spot" for any interested tomb robber, of whom there were multitudes.

The Fifth and Sixth Dynasty private tombs are among the most beautiful found in Egypt, elaborate structures whose walls

The mastaba of Perneb, Fifth Dynasty. This model of the reconstructed tomb shows the *serdab* or statue chamber; the chapel, with the "false door"; the shaft leading to the burial chamber; and the facade of the tomb, with the entrance from a courtyard. The rock above the roof has been cut away to show the interior plan. *The Metropolitan Museum of Art.*

are carved and painted in exquisite low relief. Not only are the reliefs aesthetically pleasing, but they offer invaluable information on Egyptian life, since they depict the activities in which a wealthy man of that period engaged.

During the First Intermediate Period the country broke up into a number of separate states. With the collapse of royal power the kings' tombs diminished so thoroughly that they have practically disappeared; they were still pyramids, but that is about all we can say of them. Conversely, tombs of local chiefs, or nomarchs, became more elaborate; some of the handsomest are the rock-cut tombs of Beni Hassan, with their fine pillared porticos. The reliefs of these tombs, and others of the same period, have given us some of the most delightfully animated of all scenes of daily life—children playing, vigorous dancers, and wonderful, lively animals—but the technique of painting and carving is often crude compared with the delicate sophistication of the Old Kingdom reliefs.

When the reunification of the country was begun by the vigorous Theban rulers of the Eleventh Dynasty, the royal tombs adopted a new style. A great courtyard (called a *saff*) was dug out of the plain on the west bank of Thebes. It ended in a rock-cut façade surmounted by a small brick pyramid—no longer a tomb in itself, for the king was buried underground, beneath and behind the rock face. It was at one of these Eleventh Dynasty tombs that Maspero found the stela of Intef and his five dogs—the Cook Pot, Blackie, the Gazelle, and the others.

Nothing remains of these tombs today; but one can still make out the badly damaged foundations of the greatest Eleventh Dynasty tomb, which was built by the greatest of the kings of this dynasty. His name was Mentuhotep Nebhepetre, the man who completed the reunification and brought all of Egypt under a single king for the first time in many years. When his temple-tomb still stood, in all its glory, it must have been one of the handsomest buildings in Thebes. A huge courtyard, filled with the waving green branches of tamarisk and fig trees, ended in a ramp which led up to a monumental colonnaded portico. Atop this was another set of colonnades, and surmounting the whole a pyramid lifted up toward the sky. The king's tomb was under the temple, and behind the pyramid another court and a pillared hall served his mortuary cult.

Mentuhotep buried several of his wives in or near the temple, so that they could accompany him into the West. The tomb of Queen Neferu, later a tourist attraction, was one of them, and six other ladies found their last resting places within the temple precincts. One of them was a rather pitiful case; within the big, adult-sized coffin lay the body of a little girl only five years old, wearing the pretty necklaces with which she had dressed up during her brief lifetime. Her name was Mayet—"Kitten." But of the king, her husband—or, surely, husband-to-be—there was no trace.

Pyramids continued to be royal tombs during the Twelfth Dynasty. The "substructure," inside the pyramid now, became infinitely complicated, a real labyrinth of corridors and hidden chambers. The Labyrinth itself, mentioned by Strabo and other Greek tourists, was perhaps the mortuary temple of one of these Twelfth Dynasty pyramids. It covered an area greater than that of the temple of Karnak, but nothing remains of it today except acres of stone chips on the ground. The Middle Kingdom pyramids were built, in part, out of stones pilfered from earlier royal tombs—an unpious practice which was a direct violation of the Egyptian moral code. The Twelfth Dynasty kings got what was coming to them; later generations treated their pyramids in the same way, and today there is not much left of the tombs—and nothing of the men who built them.

For private tombs, mastaba and rock-cut types continued through the Middle Kingdom and Second Intermediate Period. In this period the country again fell into political anarchy, assisted, perhaps, by the mysterious invaders from Asia who are called the Hyksos. These people, whose origins are still unknown, adopted Egyptian customs, including their burial habits. We wish they had not been so accommodating; if we had a series of Hyksos graves we would know a lot more about these enigmatic people.

The Eighteenth Dynasty marks the beginning of the New Kingdom, with another unification of the country under Theban kings, and with a dramatic change in royal burials. The lesson that should have been obvious centuries before finally sank in, reinforced, perhaps, by an increase in tomb-robbing as a result of the breakdown of royal power. The kings of the Eighteenth Dynasty got the point their ancestors had been so obtuse about— the failure of massive monuments to fulfill their major function, the protection of the royal body. The most logical conclusion would have been the practicality of a humble burial, without the gold and rich oils that tempted the poor tomb robbers. But royal majesty and human pride could not face such a conclusion. Instead, the kings strove to attain safety through secrecy. From this time on the royal tombs were all rock cut. Dug into the cliffs of a remote valley on the west bank of Thebes, their entrances were hidden, unmarked by monument or temple. The temples of the pyramids could just as well stand next to the tombs they served, as convenience demanded, since the pyramids themselves were impossible to miss; but if the Eighteenth Dynasty temples had been built in front of the tombs, there would have been little point in trying to hide the tombs. So the temples were built on the edge of the cultivated land, miles away from the Valley which would be known as that of the Kings, and eventually there was a long row of them along the west bank of the Nile.

The tombs themselves are pretty much the same, although there are minor differences in internal arrangement: they consist of rooms and corridors and stairs dug into the cliffs. Many of them are open to visitors today, in the desolate valley across from modern Luxor. Perhaps the most impressive is that of Seti I, a king of the Nineteenth Dynasty. It is over 300 feet long, and is decorated with scenes of the king being welcomed and protected by various gods.

Some of the entrances to the tombs are easily accessible; others, like that of Thutmose III, are high up in the cliff and must have been reached by wooden stairs which were later demolished. The most famous of all the tombs in the Valley, that of Tutankhamon, is much smaller than the tombs of greater pharaohs and may have been hastily completed, or taken over from another owner, when the king died at the early age of eighteen.

Today, of course, the barren walls of the cliff are dotted with the black holes of tomb entrances. In ancient times the openings were concealed, and the Valley was heavily guarded. The rough

Royal rock-cut tomb at Thebes. The tomb of Seti I. *The Metropolitan Museum of Art, photo by Egyptian Expedition.*

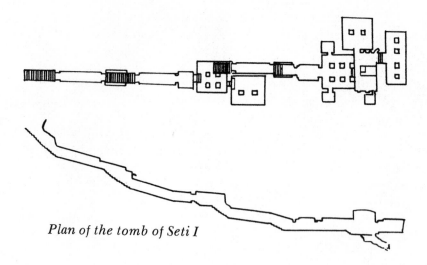

*Plan of the tomb of Seti I*

rock face of the cliffs gave no hint of the wonders that lay behind them; but men knew. It was impossible to build a tomb without employing hundreds of stonecutters, artists, and masons; and, contrary to what novelists have suggested, these workers were not slaughtered after the funeral. So even the hidden tombs were robbed, perhaps by the very workers who had built them. Only one survived the ages, and it did not go unrobbed; there is evidence, in Tutankhamon's tomb, of two successive attempts by tomb robbers who succeeded in making off with some of the contents. The only thing that saved it from being stripped was the fact that, in a later period, workmen's huts were built over it by a king who was constructing his own tomb nearby, and the location of Tutankhamon's last resting place was forgotten.

Every king who built a tomb in the Valley also built a mortuary temple along the river. Most of them have vanished today. That of Amenhotep III survives only in the gigantic and sadly battered Colossi of Memnon, which once guarded the pylon gates; others are completely gone. Like the humble chapels of the private tombs, the royal funerary temples served the cult of the dead, and were as necessary for the dead man's resurrection as was his tomb. Here the offerings were made which would give him nourishment in the next world. The royal mortuary temples also

Model of the Temple of Queen Hatshepsut at Deir el Bahri. Reconstructed as it was in 1480 B.C. (Scale: $\frac{1}{100}$) *The Metropolitan Museum of Art.*

served as homes for the gods. At Hatshepsut's temple there were also shrines to Amon, Anubis, and Hathor.

Hatshepsut's temple is a masterpiece and, according to many, the finest of all Egyptian temples. Like many masterpieces it was of an unusual type. It resembles the Eleventh Dynasty temple-tomb of Mentuhotep more than it does the standard temples, having a series of colonnaded terraces which rise up in several levels toward the cliffs behind it. A more typical temple is the one belonging to Ramses III, which is now called Medinet Habu. It has the elements we have already described as typical of the

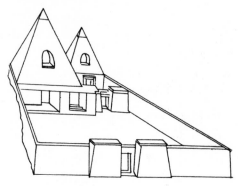

*Deir el Medineh tombs*

standard religious edifice: pylon, enclosing wall, pillared courts, and sanctuary.

After the Twentieth Dynasty the royal necropolis was moved from Thebes to Tanis, in the Delta. The royal tombs in this city were built within the temple precincts; they are sad degenerations of the great rock-cut tombs of Thebes.

Even before pyramids were abandoned by royalty they were, like other kingly elements of the mortuary cult, taken over by commoners. Some of the little mastabas of the Middle Kingdom at Abydos have diminutive pyramids of brick perched on top of them—how art the mighty fallen! Private tombs at Deir el Medineh, the workmen's town of the New Kingdom, also had little pyramids. Rock-cut and mastaba tombs of the New Kingdom became very elaborate, with courts and porches, all handsomely decorated. In the late period, Theban tombs of high officials be-

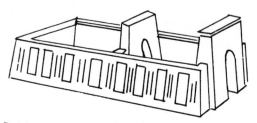

*Superstructure of the tomb of Pedamenopet*

come very pretentious; the tomb of a man named Pedamenopet, illustrated here, is a miniature brick temple up above. The substructure, below the temple, contained a court, many rooms, stairs, and long corridors. During the Saite or Twenty-Sixth Dynasty, there was a curious development in decoration. So great was the admiration of the men of this time for the wonders of their country's past that they copied not only scenes, but whole tombs of the Old and Middle Kingdoms, in their own burial places. Some are done so well that it is hard to tell which is a copy and which the original.

## Sarcophagi and Coffins

One thing leads to another. As tombs got more elaborate, coffins and other equipment went from bad to worse—if we look at the process from the point of view that coffins are pure vanity.

Next to the tomb, the coffin itself was the most important piece of equipment. The oldest coffins are plain boxes of wood, just big enough to hold a body in the contracted position then in vogue. As the body was extended, so was the coffin; by the Middle Kingdom it had become a sophisticated piece of wood painted inside and out with pictures and texts. The Herakleopolitan coffins, from a period just before the Middle Kingdom, show how elaborate the type could be. One important motif was the pair of eyes painted on one side of the coffin opposite the spot where the eyes of the corpse would be as it lay on its right side. The texts on these coffins—called, logically enough, the Coffin Texts—now fill six fat printed volumes. Not every coffin had all the texts; each bore a sort of anthology of the owner's favorites. Ultimately the texts derive from the Pyramid Texts of the Old Kingdom, although some spells have been discarded and new ones have been added.

A new fashion in coffins came in during the Second Intermediate Period with the adoption, by kings and commoners alike, of the type now thought of as typically Egyptian—the anthropoid, or man-shaped, coffin. For men and women, king and humble scribe, the form was the same, that of a wrapped mummy figure with a linen headdress. The earliest anthropoid coffins are of the

Herakleopolitan coffin. The type popular between the Ninth and Twelfth Dynasties. The elaborate paneling recalls the niched mastabas of the earliest dynasties; it may derive from ancient domestic architecture, and suggests that the coffin was conceived of as the house of the dead. *The Metropolitan Museum of Art, Rogers Fund, 1912.*

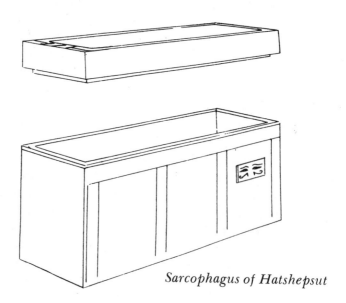

*Sarcophagus of Hatshepsut*

so-called *rishi* type; the word means "feathered," and it appropriately describes the decoration, which looks like wings spread protectively over the body. The *rishi* type soon died out, being replaced by the coffin with bands of inscriptions and rows of miniature scenes or divine figures. These continued until late times, but the *rishi* 'type survived in certain royal coffins, such as those of Tutankhamon, where the feathering takes on real beauty of technique and conception. The sweep of the wide wings, those of a protecting goddess, eloquently suggests the tender care of the dead.

We would know very little about royal burial equipment were it not for the fabulous discovery, by Lord Carnarvon and Howard Carter, of Tutankhamon's tomb. From it we learn that kings of this period had not one, but three coffins. Although they were made of wood, Tutankhamon's outer coffins became miracles of the jeweler's art, covered with sheet gold and marvelously inlaid. The innermost coffin had to be seen to be believed; it was 2,448 pounds of solid gold. That this incredible coffin was not unique we may deduce from late royal burials at Tanis. At this period royal power had declined tremendously, and yet Psousennes, an undistinguished pharaoh of the Twenty-First Dynasty, could still amass enough wealth to make his innermost coffin of solid silver. We must always remember, in assessing Tutankhamon's equipment, that it was that of a minor king—perhaps an unpopular king—who not only died young, but who lived at a time when the imperial revenues from Asia were low. Sometimes I dream of the impossible, and imagine finding the tomb of a king such as Amenhotep III still intact—the tomb of a king who had over thirty years to prepare his equipment, and the resources of Nubia and Asia with which to pay for it. This can never happen, except in dreams; the tomb of Amenhotep the Magnificent is rifled and empty, as are the other known tombs of the mightiest rulers of Egypt.

Tutankhamon's tomb not only demonstrates the incredible wealth with which pharaohs were buried, but it illustrated the Chinese-box character of these burials. The three coffins, nested one inside the other, were all contained inside a sarcophagus. The

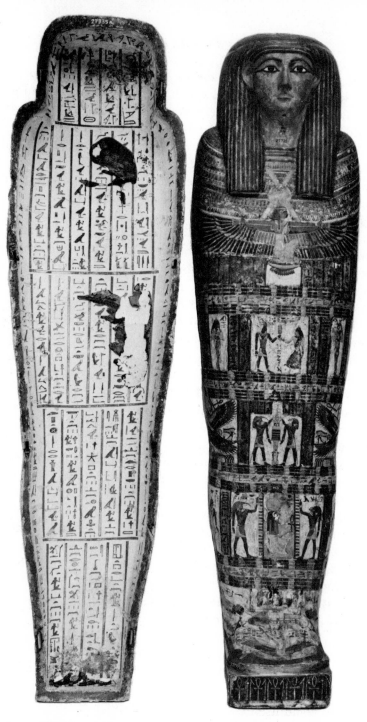

Anthropoid coffin. The standard type from the New Kingdom onward. Normally made of wood, sometimes covered with a thin coating of plaster. The decorations, painted or in relief, consist of mortuary gods and religious inscriptions. *The Trustees, British Museum.*

sarcophagus, as distinct from the coffin, was of stone—often wonderful stone such as quartzite, granite, or diorite. Sarcophagi had to be big to hold a body and three coffins; they are so heavy, weighing in tons, that even the masterful tomb robbers of Thebes, who ought to be made patron saints of the burglaring profession, could not steal them. I am sure they would have stolen them if they could have moved them; they stole everything else. The weight of the sarcophagi explains why we have a number of them with us today, while the coffins and the mummies which once lay within them have disappeared.

Few commoners could afford a sarcophagus; they usually had to settle for a coffin, and for one of those. Royal sarcophagi go back a long way, at least to the Third Dynasty. In the earliest time they were plain stone boxes, with separate lids of equally heavy stone. One exceptional Third Dynasty sarcophagus had, instead of a lid on top, a sliding panel at one end. By the New Kingdom, sarcophagi were covered with bands of inscription and with carved figures of the divinities who protected the dead.

So far, in Tutankhamon's burial, we have three coffins, and a sarcophagus enclosing the mummy. But that is not all. Enclosing the sarcophagus were three shrines, one inside the other; made of gilded wood, they carry the magical texts which were once written on the walls of the pyramid and which, later, would be inscribed on papyrus scrolls buried in the tomb. The outsides of the shrines were decorated with hieroglyphs which had religious meaning.

Three coffins, a sarcophagus, and three shrines—seven layers of physical protection, not counting the walls of the tomb itself. Yet the physical protection of the body was only a minor part of the mortuary cult, and most of the objects placed in the tomb served another purpose.

Even the physical equipment had a secondary significance. Originally a tomb may have been just a hole to hold the body, but its walls came to be used for texts and pictures designed to equip the dead with magical substitutes for the objects he would need in the Hereafter. A coffin could also kill two birds with one stone: enclosing the body and bearing still more magical texts. The anthropoid coffin itself was a simulacrum of the dying god Osiris, with whom the dead man was identified so that he could share in

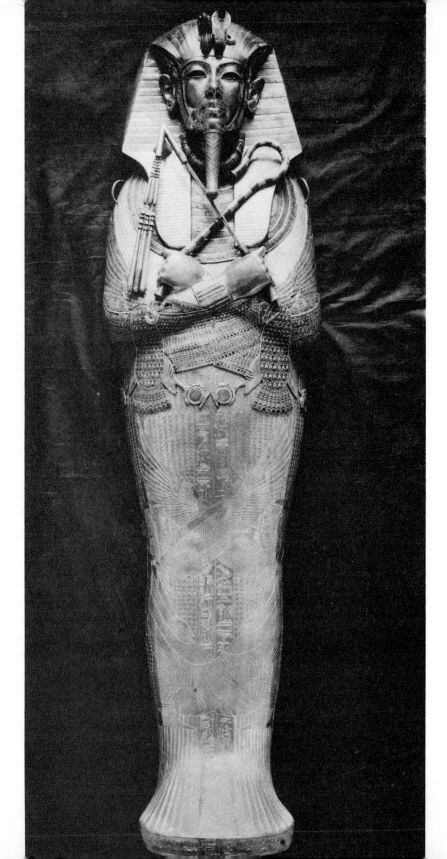

the death and glorious resurrection of the god. The figures of the winged goddesses on coffin and sarcophagus symbolized divine protection.

## Funerary Ritual

But coffin, tomb, and sarcophagus were only necessary prerequisites to immortality. They were not sufficient in themselves. A soul had to be fashioned out of the dead husk of the corpse.

Perhaps this process began with the embalming, but we have only a vague idea of the rites performed during the process of mummification. The vital ceremony was part of the funeral service; so let us see what happened after the mummy had been restored to the sorrowing family.

On the day of the funeral, a long procession set out for the tomb. Leading it was the mummy, on a sledge topped by an open shrine and pulled by oxen. Friends and relatives of the dead man lent a hand on the ropes, and the chief female mourners—wife and daughter, or wife and mother—walked at the head and foot of the bier. Priests accompanied the hearse. Other mourners walked behind, and all of them, male and female, expressed their grief in dramatic gestures. The women, as they were expected to do, exhibited less self-control than the men; with garments torn and streaming hair, they poured dust on their heads and cried aloud. When there were not enough women in the family to make a goodly show, or when the survivors wanted to be pretentious, professional female mourners were hired. Naturally they outshouted the ladies of the family, and the reliefs show them with rows of symmetrical tears flowing down their cheeks onto the ground. One painted scene depicts a little girl apprentice among the professionals; she seems to have considerable aptitude for the trade, and she always makes me think of poor little Oliver Twist, who made such a handsome mute—especially for children's funerals.

Following the mourners came servants carrying food, furniture, and chests containing clothing and other grave-goods.

*Rishi* coffin. The solid gold innermost coffin of Tutankhamon. *The Metropolitan Museum of Art, photo by Harry Burton.*

Another small sledge held the canopic box, with the four jars
containing the entrails.

In essence the funeral ritual was a recapitulation of the Osiris
legend, and an identification of the dead man with the god. The
coffin itself was made in the Osiris shape. The two mourning
women who accompanied the bier represented Isis and Nephthys,
weeping for their husband and brother. However, there are several elements of the ritual which do not obviously fit in with the
Osiris cult, and which are still mysteries.

One of them is the strange figure called the *tekenu*. In some
funeral scenes it is only a muffled ambiguous shape resting on a
sledge drawn by two men. Other scenes show it more clearly; it
seems to be a man wrapped in a cloth or skin, and lying in a
doubled-up position.

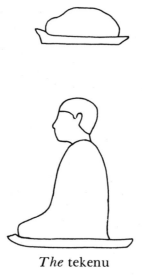

*The* tekenu

What function does this peculiar personage play in the funeral
ritual? No one knows exactly. To some scholars the pose suggests
the fetal position and the *tekenu* represents the rebirth of the
dead man into eternal life. Others see in it a symbolic survival of
ancient human sacrifice—a shedding of blood to give strength to
the strengthless dead—which may have been practiced in prehis-

Muu *dancer*

toric Egypt. Either idea may be correct, but we can't be sure. The *tekenu* had a short period of popularity; there is no sign of it—or him—in the Old Kingdom scenes, but then these are not normally of funerals. For the present the *tekenu* must remain one of those lost Egyptian mysteries that the occultists are so fond of.

When the funeral procession had toiled up to the desert plateau and reached the tomb, it was met by another unusual group—the *muu* dancers. These men were distinguished by strange crowns of reeds, whose shape and material strongly suggests the royal White Crown of Upper Egypt. There ought to be some clue in this, as to the origin and function of the dancers; but in fact none of the theories suggested by it really sounds convincing. The dancers perform a weird, jigging dance, something like a Highland fling with finger-snapping.

After the dance the mummy was lifted from the sledge and propped up in a standing position before the door of the tomb. The ceremony of the "Opening of the Mouth" was about to begin. It was conducted by the Sem or Setem priest, with his distinctive leopard-skin mantle and shaven head. First, the mummy was sprinkled with water and censed. Sacrifices of various animals were made. Then came the heart of the ceremony, the touching of various parts of the body with specially designed instruments which would restore the lost senses of the mummy. The mouth, as the organ of speech and of nourishment, was of particular importance. More censing and incense burning followed, and then the funerary meal was served; the dead man now had power to partake of it, and he was joined by his living relatives and close friends. It is significant that the "Opening of the Mouth" could be performed on a statue as well as on the mummy; as long as some physical representation of the dead man was operated on, his nonphysical aspect received the benefits of the operation.

Then the act of rebirth was completed; a new soul had been born. The members of the bereaved family, turning away to return to their homes, must have felt a lightening of their sorrow as they thought of the new-hatched soul, safely launched on the beautiful roads of the West, where they would one day join it—but not, they hoped, too very soon.

The act of rebirth was completed. But the newborn soul, like a newborn child, had to be kept alive. If we could visit the tomb once again, on the day after the funeral, we would find that the burial chamber had been sealed. But one part of the tomb was still accessible, and there certain activities were going on. Inside the painted chapel a priest deposited loaves of fresh bread and jars of water on the low altar. Every day of the year, from now to forever, the dead man was fed at this altar.

Food and drink were always buried with the dead. The poor man had a few jars filled with beer and some loaves of bread. The royal dead dined sumptuously—jars of vintage wines, haunches of beef, cakes, and the finest white bread were piled in heaps in the storage chambers of his tomb. But it was necessary to renew the food supply when it was used up, and so the funerary offering was instituted.

In theory the offering was made by the devoted son of the dead man, playing Horus to his Osiris, just as the son was responsible for all the other necessities of his father in the world to come. Some sons were as pious and dutiful about these responsibilities as they were supposed to be. In one inscription a man tells us that he caused himself to be buried in the same tomb as his father, not—and I love this touch of sinful human pride—not because he

*Offering table*

could not perfectly well afford a tomb of his own, but because he loved his father so much he wanted to be with him always. Still, human nature being what it is—and was—the wise Egyptian took steps to remove temptation from his offspring by providing for as many of his postmortem necessities as he could, while he could. Among these necessities was a daily food offering, and this was arranged by formal contract.

The contracts were made with *ka*-priests, like old Hekanakhte, whom we have already met; they agreed to substitute for the pious son, who naturally had no time to go traipsing over to his father's tomb every morning. Early in the game the methodical Egyptians formalized the problem of mortuary contracts, and some tomb owners had copies of them written on the walls of the tomb. The language of the texts is rather amusing, for its dry, legal tone seems far removed from the lofty business of immortality. Some contracts list not only the days on which offerings are to be made, but the precise number of loaves and jars which must be given. On festivals and holy days, extra food was provided.

A rich man might endow his tomb with five fields and their produce; a king could leave the riches of a dozen towns. The offerings themselves were not the only expenses involved, for the "wages" of the priest and his family also came out of the total. Such wages were paid in goods, since there was no money in pharaonic Egypt. Weights of copper or gold were sometimes used to calculate values; a sack of grain worth so many *deben* of copper could be traded for two linen sheets worth the same amount; but the parties to such transactions of barter, which made up most of the country's commerce, seldom actually saw the metal.

By now the economics majors among my readers are probably trying to calculate how long it would be before the entire national economy was sunk in tombs and tomb maintenance. It would not have taken long, if the contracts had actually been honored; they provided for food "in perpetuity." Luckily for society, if not for morality, there was a constant redistribution of wealth. Time passed, families died out, and the contracts quietly lapsed. Or else there was a change in dynasty, or confiscation, and contracts were reabsorbed into the treasury. Another class of people helped to keep the wealth in circulation, although the kings who gobbled up old mortuary contracts would have resented being compared with them—the tomb robbers. Something good can be said about them after all.

The Egyptians were well aware of this process. They knew that if their tombs were maintained for a century they were lucky. So what did they do? If the actual loaves of bread stopped coming, they could be replaced by magical substitutes. The tomb paintings which show rows of comely young women carrying food were magical insurance against the failing of forgetful *ka*-priests; so were the loaded offering tables which are depicted on tomb walls, stelae, and funerary slabs. A second line of defense in case of neglect was a written list. This became a formula; it is probably the best-known of all Egyptian texts to beginning students, who can rattle it off with their eyes closed, or read it glibly off the wall of any tomb. I have often done this to impress my non-Egyptological friends; I don't do it for Egyptologists, because they know quite well that all the formulae are alike.

The offering formula goes something like this: "A boon which the king gives, to Osiris, Lord of Abydos [or some other god], that he give invocation offerings of bread and beer, oxen and fowl, alabaster and clothing, and every good and pure thing for the *ka* of the venerated [So-and-so]."

The process seems unnecessarily complicated; the king pays Osiris or some other god who then makes the offerings to the *ka* of the dead man. Occasionally the king's "boon" may have been a real offering, made for a favorite courtier, but by the Middle Kingdom these formulae are inscribed for all sorts of people, including "nobodies" whom the Lord of the Two Lands did not know existed. The term translated "invocation offerings" is extremely significant; it means "a going-forth of the voice," and it suggests that the boon is a purely magical offering, a supply of spiritual food through the power of the spoken word. Although the lists of offerings vary, they include the staples of the Egyptian diet, beginning with the basic "bread and beer"; and they end with one of the typically Egyptian "et ceteras" to cover anything that might have been overlooked.

There was a last line of defense against spiritual starvation, in case all the others failed. It has always struck me with mingled pity and admiration—pity for the resigned acceptance of human frailty, which can visualize the necessity for such a desperate last resort, and admiration for the determination which refuses to give up the ghost. Some tombs carry an inscription which appeals to passersby—to any casual stranger who might be strolling in the vicinity of the tomb:

> Oh you who live and exist, who love life and hate death, who shall pass by this tomb: as you love life and hate death, so shall you offer to me that which is in your hands. If there is nothing in your hands, you shall speak thus: "A thousand of bread and beer, of oxen and geese, of alabaster and linen—a thousand of all good and pure things, for the venerated [So-and-so]."

Food, food, always food; it was the essential offering. But if food could be supplied, so could other things—things which would make the life hereafter a lot more comfortable.

Food, shelter, and clothing, the three basic necessities, were provided for. The tomb gave physical shelter and there was a formula which promised the spirit the means to build a house in Paradise. Tomb paintings of houses were another form of insurance. Middle Kingdom and First Intermediate tombs include house models, some of them delightful little miniatures of a rich nobleman's estate. As for clothing, we have seen the extent and richness of Tutankhamon's wardrobe.

Jars of fine oil, perfumes, and unguents were highly desired gifts for the living and hence for the dead; they were also irresistible to tomb robbers, who sometimes brought little bags along so that they could raid the contents of the heavy oil jars. All the amusements were provided for; a hunter had his bows and arrows, boomerangs and daggers. Women took into the tomb their elaborate toilet tables, complete with an extra wig or switch of false hair. More indolent men took their game boards along, and they

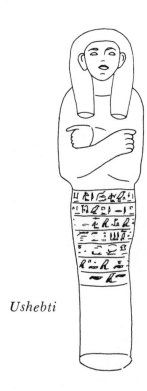

*Ushebti*

Magical concubine figure. The bed is a standard type, with footboard and headrest. *The Metropolitan Museum of Art, Rogers Fund, 1915.*

also had little naked female figurines, sometimes reclining on a model bed, whose magical purpose is obvious.

Human sacrifice died out in Egypt at the beginning of the dynasties. Since slaughtered servants were *de trop,* the Egyptians provided for their services as they provided for other necessities—by magical substitutes. In the Old Kingdom the wall paintings which showed scenes of daily life included multitudes of servants, making bread, reaping grain, carrying offerings, combing their mistresses' hair and dancing for the amusement of their masters. In the First Intermediate Period, when models came into style, we find charming little groups of miniature workers going about their chores. But the most enduring answer to the "servant problem" was one which has filled museum cases all over the world—the little human figurines called *ushebtis* or *shawabtis.* They are made of all sorts of materials from cheap faience to gilded wood, and represent all degrees of skill from crude figures just recognizable as human to beautiful little statuettes. All were designed to satisfy the same need—the need to avoid doing any work in heaven. Written somewhere on the figure was a text, another of the standardized mortuary formulae:

> O thou ushebti! If the deceased [So-and-so] is appointed to do any work which a man does in the necropolis—to cultivate the fields, to irrigate the banks, to transport sand of the East to the West—"Here am I!" thou shalt say.

This is really an admirable thought; I suppose the only reason it hasn't occurred to us is because we don't expect anyone to work in Paradise.

Most of the objects placed in the tomb can be interpreted as pleasures the dead man hoped to go on enjoying. Some attempts have been made to find a symbolic meaning for each object. The weapons represent the battle against the enemies of Re, the game board stands for the struggle between the powers of good and the powers of evil, and so on. Of course we can find a deeper significance in almost any object if we try hard enough; I don't recall that anyone has explained the symbolism of the cosmetic box, but I feel sure it could be done. Even the little female figurines with the decorations emphasizing the pubic region have been described as "fertility goddesses," or, more ponderously, "figures evocative of the female principle," which symbolized the rebirth of the dead man, procreated by himself!

Interpretations of this nature do more credit to the fertile imagination of the interpreter than to the speculative habits of the Egyptians. In particular, the habit of finding fertility symbols scattered all over the cultural landscape seems to be spreading from some schools of prehistorians into Egyptology. The other day, while reading a book on prehistoric religion, I ran across a statement which seems to me to represent the ultimate absurdity of this type of argument. The author denied, indignantly, that a certain object found in a paleolithic context could be a phallic symbol. Paleolithic man, said the author—probably correctly—knew nothing about the male role in procreation. How then, he demanded, could a phallus be an object of worship?

I am sorry to say that this naïve statement brought an unlady-like grin to my face. Certain Christian doctrines insist that the procreation of children is the only legitimate aim of the sexual act; my prehistorian wants to go the theologians one better, by maintaining that it is the *only* aim. Surely it is nonsense to suppose that this abstruse doctrine was held by paleolithic, or any other ancient, people. The best name for the little female figurines in Egyptian tombs is probably something like "magical concubines." To suggest that they had any other function is almost an insult to the Egyptians, who did not suffer from our neuroses in regard to sex.

Among the specifically funerary objects placed in the tomb, one of the most important was the structure which contained the viscera, removed from the body during the process of embalming. In the Late Period the embalmed entrails were replaced in the body, but before that, beginning in the Old Kingdom, they were put into four jars called "canopic jars," which in turn were enclosed in a canopic box or shrine. The canopic jars have a characteristic shape; at first they had plain stoppers, but later these were superseded by lids in the form of portrait heads of the deceased. One of the loveliest sets of these lids was found in the Tomb of Queen Ti. It was first thought to be a portrait of Akhenaton, then of Smenkhkare, and now scholars believe it is the head of a lady of the Amarna period, possible Akhenaton's eldest daughter, Princess Meritaton. Whoever it is, he or she was very handsome.

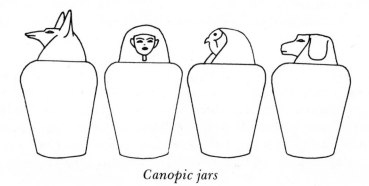

*Canopic jars*

The later canopic jars have, instead of "portrait" heads, the heads of the four mortuary genii, the sons of Horus—baboon, jackal, hawk, and human. The canopic shrine, in which the jars were placed, also had a standard shape and, as one might expect, the most elegant known is that of Tutankhamon. To me it is one of the loveliest objects ever found in Egypt, with its four protective goddesses standing with outspread arms on each side of the gilded box.

One other magical object found in many tombs was the Osiris bed, or "germinated Osiris figure," as it is called. A silhouette of the god was made out of wood and filled with rich earth; seeds were planted in the dirt and watered, so that when the figure was placed in the tomb, it was a green, living symbol of the resurrection of god and man. As Professor William C. Hayes has pointed out, the popular but erroneous notion of "mummy seeds" may have had its origin in these figures. Like the mummies of men and women, the seeds found in ancient tombs have never known a physical resurrection.

It is literally impossible to describe all the objects found in the tombs; the single burial of Tutankhamon included hundreds of separate items. We ought to mention, though, some of the things found on the mummy itself. One important object, in vogue from the late Old Kingdom down to Christian times, was the mask placed over the head of the dead man. Tutankhamon's mask was gold, and it is a gorgeous piece of work, like everything else he owned. Common masks were of the cartonnage type, made of layers of linen coated with glue or stucco, in a process resembling papier mâché.

The mummy was richly furnished with jewelry of various types—which led, inevitably, to the destruction of the precious body by hasty tomb robbers. The most popular piece of jewelry, in death as in life, was the broad collar made of beads or semiprecious stones. Not all the jewelry placed in the tomb had been worn; some was so fragile that it could only have been designed for the inactive dead. Bracelets, collars and rings might be purely ornamental in purpose, but some jewelry had a specific religious meaning. The broad vulture collars symbolized the care and love

Lid of a canopic jar, representing Princess Meritaton (?). Alabaster.
*The Metropolitan Museum of Art, The Theodore M. Davis Collection.*
*Bequest of Theodore M. Davis, 1915.*

of the goddess Mut, and various amulets stood for particular qualities the dead hoped to be endowed with.

The most important amulet was the heart scarab; after the Middle Kingdom, all mummies of any pretensions had them. The scarab amulets are well known; they are still being sold to tourists, and 99.99 percent of them are modern fakes. The heart scarabs were bigger than the usual variety, and, according to the magical texts, they ought to be made of a dark green stone. On the flat base there was a short inscription from the Book of the Dead.

*Horus eye amulet*

There are dozens of other amulets, some made of metal, some of faience, some of stone. They were hung around the neck or tied to the wrist or to another part of the body. Some took the shape of gods Bes and Taweret, the hideous but beloved household gods being quite popular, and others were made in the shape of hieroglyphic signs which signified life, stability, health, and other desirable attributes. A particularly vital amulet was the "Horus eye." It recalled the loss of the young god's eye during the battle against his father's murderer, and it was the symbol *par excellence* of offering to the dead.

# XVI

## "On That Day of Judging the Deficient"

### *Books of the Dead*

B ETWEEN the time when the newborn soul left the tomb and the moment when it settled down amid the comforts provided for it in the Land of Eternity, it had a long and dangerous journey to make. In order to reach the West the dead man had to cross water; for this he needed a boat. Perhaps there was a ferry; if so, the ferryman might prove hostile or indifferent. He would have to be bribed, or coerced, or wheedled into carrying the spirit across.

All along the way the dead man was beset by demons. If not properly handled, each and every one of these monsters—gigantic snakes, animal-headed monstrosities—could overpower and destroy the spirit. Supposing that he passed the demons unscathed and managed to cross the river, the dead man still had to face the gods. What if they didn't know him, or refused to accept him? All these possible emergencies had to be anticipated and prepared for. The whole process has always reminded me of a child's game: "Suppose this happens! But then suppose *that* happens!"

The defenses against dangers of this kind could only be of one sort. They consisted of magico-religious spells, and they make up

*Selected monsters*

Demigods and demons who might interfere with the dead
man during his journey to the hereafter. From a mortuary
papyrus. Left to right: the Devourer of Shades, a lion-
headed god, "Turn-Face" the ferryman, a great serpent

several sizable collections. The oldest collection is the Pyramid
Texts, which were inscribed in pretty blue hieroglyphs on the
walls of the Fifth and Sixth Dynasty pyramids. These texts are a
real hodgepodge; if we find Egyptian religion contradictory, the
Pyramid Texts are the epitome of contradiction. There are spells
invoking Osiris and spells asking for protection against Osiris;
spells hailing Re as god of the dead and other spells naming
Osiris. In one text the dead king humbly accepts the job of secretary to the god; in another he threatens to march in and *eat* Re
and the rest unless they submit to his demands.

The contradictions are to some extent resolved if we regard
the Pyramid Texts as an anthology, made up of spells from different places and times. And there is a unifying feature. Although a
few texts are in the form of hymns to the god, the great majority
deal, magically, with practical problems: how to reach the Hereafter, how to live once one gets there, how to control potential
antagonists.

The Pyramid Texts as such were used for the royal dead, although not all the privileges they claim for kings were their sole
prerogative. By the Middle Kingdom the magical collection had
been taken over by commoners. The Coffin Texts were not just
the Pyramid Texts in a new medium, but they include many of the
older spells and have the same purpose. In the New Kingdom and

thereafter the anthologies of magical incantations, greatly altered and revised, were written on papyrus scrolls, some of them handsomely decorated with miniature scenes, or vignettes, of the life to come. We call these scrolls the "Book of the Dead," but there were actually a number of different collections, for which the Egyptians had other names—the Book of Gates, the Book of That Which Is In the Afterworld, the Book of Coming Forth by Day.

"The Book of the Dead" is a title which would sell well; it is often mentioned in awed tones by the various schools of occultists. However, if a reader has the fortitude to wade through the entire collection, he is left with an impression not of mysterious, occult power, but of practical, thorough organization. The books of the dead, all of them, are guidebooks to the beautiful roads of the West, including useful phrases, explanations of local customs, and hints on how to deal with the natives. A sampling of chapter titles gives some idea of just how thorough the compilation was:

CHAPTER OF: not letting X be bitten by snakes
not dying a second time
not letting the head of a man be cut off from him
drinking water and not being burnt by fire
taking the form of a hawk of gold or whatever a man
    pleases
bringing along a boat
going into the boat of Re
giving funeral offerings
not allowing the body of a man to decay
not eating filth
making the *ushebti* figure do work

This is only the briefest sampling; there are hundreds of similar texts. It might be interesting to examine one in detail, to see how it works. If a man wants to avoid being bitten by snakes in the Afterworld, he says: "Oh Serpent! I am the flame which shines on the Opener of hundreds of thousands of years, the standard of the god Tenpu."

Offhand, this may not strike us as very effective. But we are not tuned to this variety of magic. Underlying all the seemingly meaningless verbiage was the basic power of all spells, the power of the word. Even the spoken word had effectiveness; the written was even more powerful, and the very fact that the handsome, and costly, papyrus said, in writing, that these words would eliminate the danger from serpents meant that that danger was thereby eliminated.

Above all, the books of the dead, from Pyramid Texts to papyrus scrolls, decree life for the lifeless. In their affirmation of life, the texts deny death. There is a majestic power even in our pedantic translations of the rolling, constantly repeated demand for existence: "King Teti has not died the death! He does not die! This king lives forever!"

Affirmation of a desire, or denial of a fear, have magical potency in themselves. Some words had more power than others, and one of the most significant magical words was a man's name. Like his image and his blood and his spittle and all the other elements that resembled him or were part of him, his name contained the essence of his being. To know a man's secret name is to have power over him. In many cultures the names of the gods were sacred, not to be spoken. This is not only respect, it is a reflection of the idea that the name was power. When Herodotus describes the rites of the Dying God in Egypt, he refers to the deity as "a god whose name a religious scruple prevents me from mentioning." Another example is the name of God which devout Jews still refuse to pronounce aloud.

In Egypt, to know the name of a god or of any man or object was to have power over it. The magical texts are full of the phrase, "I know you, I know your name!" The dead man, confronted by the watchful assembly of the gods, gives each of them his name and passes in, triumphant. There is even a spell to keep a man from forgetting his own name—tantamount to a loss of identity, and hence, of existence. The magical compilations were the final bulwark against "dying a second time." Not only did they protect the dead from danger but they provided substitutes for necessities which might fail or be missing. And all this could be done for the price of a painted coffin or a written scroll.

Thus the dead were guarded against neglect of their funerary cult and against purely spiritual dangers. Another peril had its magical defense as well. The Egyptians were painfully well aware

of the industry of the tomb robber. Ancient tombs gaped for-
lornly in various abandoned cemeteries, thieves were constantly
being punished by local or royal courts. Perhaps the best defense
against these ghouls (or redistributors of wealth) was to die and
be buried in the reign of a strong, ferocious pharaoh who would
put up with no nonsense in the necropoli. But this was at best a
temporary expedient; so, once again, the power of the written
word was called in to defend the tomb and its occupant.

> As for any man who shall enter into this tomb in his impurity,
> and who shall do a thing evilly against it, or who shall damage any
> stone or any brick in this tomb, or who shall erase the writing
> herein, I shall seize his neck like a bird. . . . I shall be judged with
> him in the august council of magistrates of the great god. But as
> for any man who shall enter into this tomb, being pure with regard
> to it, I shall be his partisan.

From texts like these (the quotation is a composite) come the
exciting but incorrect journalists' stories of "curses" in ancient
Egyptian tombs. As our quotation shows, these texts were not so
much curses as threats—not of ghostly ghastly terror, but of a
lawsuit in the court of the gods! And the threats were not against
visitors to the tomb as such, but against violators. In these terms,
archaeologists should stand high in the favor of the ancient Egyptian *kas* whose tombs they discover, for most of them would rather
cut off a hand than destroy a stone or a sign; indeed, the archaeologists of past generations not infrequently defended tombs,
sometimes physically, against the modern descendants of the tomb
robbers. If an Egyptologist ever reaches the Field of Reeds, he
should find "partisans" in plenty among the *akhu*.

Neither threats of divine retribution nor physical barriers
availed against the real desecraters. Egyptian doctrine could not
allow the only sure defense against despoilation—a burial so poor
in worldly goods that no robber would waste his time on it. In
Egypt, you *could* take it with you. At least you could take your
worldly goods as far as the tomb, and the chance that you might
succeed in carrying them all the way into the West was well worth
taking.

But what about the men and women who had nothing to take, who could not even afford the cheapest type of embalming? It has been suggested that the poor man in Egypt lacked even the hope of immortality; there was no "pie in the sky" to make up for the conspicuous lack of that commodity on earth. The theory that the lowest classes gave their dead to the animal scavengers of the river and the desert instead of burying them is contradicted by hundreds of proofs—the graves of ordinary men, women and children. We see, today, that people are willing to impoverish themselves to give their dead a "nice" funeral; the principle must have operated even more strongly in Egypt, where survival depended on the preservation of the body and where a cheap, accessible embalming material was available to everyone in the desert sand.

At all periods of Egyptian history the poor found the same grave—a hole in the ground—and they were laid to rest in the dignity of their own unembalmed flesh and bone. (No one can deny that there is something very undignified about embalming.) These people had no coffins; sometimes the survivors could not spare so much as a pot of food from the scanty household store. Yet the naked, hungry soul could have one hope of nourishment. As a beggar squats at a rich man's gate, the bodies of the poor were often buried near a nobleman's tomb, where they could catch the crumbs from his well-stocked offering table. This process reached its logical conclusion when the tombs themselves were invaded. Such intrusive burials, tucked cozily away in someone else's tomb, are not uncommon; even the Pyramids were not exempt, and some tombs have half a dozen burials ranging over as many generations. Ironically enough, the poorest of the poor sometimes attained that physical survival which was denied the divine pharaoh. The coffins and sarcophagi, the very unguents used in the ritual of resurrection, helped to destroy the flesh they were designed to protect; and if time and decay spared the royal bones, the tomb robbers did not. There is a moral in all of this, of course; but perhaps we are in no position to sneer at the Egyptians because they failed to see it.

## The Last Judgment

Tomb, mummy, magic, food offerings—in all this there is one conspicuous omission—any reference to an ethical or moral requirement for eternal life. Some scholars believe it was actually missing—that anybody could get to heaven from Egypt if he could pay the price. Contrarily, other scholars have claimed for the Egyptians the "Dawn of Conscience," and the first demonstration of righteousness as a prerequisite for immortality.

The truth probably lies somewhere between the two extremes, as it so often, boringly, does. The phrase "dawn of conscience" comes from James Henry Breasted. His argument, presented with enthusiasm and elegance of expression, was very persuasive; today, however, most Egyptologists would qualify it almost out of recognition. And yet we cannot dismiss all of the Egyptian mortuary cult as magic. There was, for one thing, the Judgment.

On the walls of the Sistine Chapel, Michelangelo's masterpiece gives an unforgettable picture of the Last Judgment in Christian terms. Christ, enthroned aloft, is not the merciful Redeemer, but the stern Judge. With upraised hand He sifts the risen dead, lifting the blessed into Paradise and sending the wailing shapes of the damned to Hell.

The Egyptian judgment had its majestic aspect too, but it was the formal majesty of the law court, complete with judge and jury, recording secretary, prosecutor, defendant, and witness. Two of our common symbols of law were present in the courtroom—the scales of justice and the goddess of truth.

In the Hall of the Two Truths sat the judge, the resurrected Osiris, with his wife Isis behind him. The jury consisted of forty-two personages instead of twelve, and all were gods. In the center of the hall, the focus of the scene, was a huge pair of scales. Thoth, the divine scribe, stood beside it, his pen poised and ready to record the judgment. Sometimes he was accompanied by the goddess Ma'at, Truth; sometimes she was represented by a small figure or

*Scales of the judgment, with heart and feather*

by the feather which was her symbol, occupying one pan of the scales. In the opposite pan was the heart of the man or woman to be judged. Near the scales hovered one other essential member of the court—a beast with the head of a crocodile, the midsection of a lion, and the hindquarters of a hippopotamus. Its name was "Devourer of Shades."

Into the court came Anubis Psychopompus, leading the defendant by the hand. The dead man was dressed in his best, just as he would be for such an occasion today. The dead ladies, in their finest filmy linen and curled wigs, irresistibly suggest the attractive females who try to explain to a sympathetic male jury why they felt it necessary to shoot their husbands.

The image of the feather in the pan of the scales is one I find very appealing. The feather was the symbol of truth, the goddess; but the idea that the heart of the dead man must be so light, so free of evil, as to balance the featherweight on the other pan of the scales is my interpretation rather than that of the Egyptians. But it is still a significant symbol—the weighing of the heart against truth.

The heart was the seat of the emotions and the organ of intelligence, memory, and will. With its accumulated memories of passions and deeds, the heart was the sole witness for or against a man in the case of his own salvation.

This was the Egyptian judgment in its developed form, known to us not only from descriptions in the book of the Dead but also from the pictures with which such texts were illustrated. The idea of a judging of the dead goes back a long way, however, to a period long before the papyrus scrolls came into use, and our knowledge of the earlier conception is not so clear.

The first judge may not have been Osiris. He is called, significantly, the "Great God"; and although there has been a lot of debate about his real name, we cannot be entirely sure who he was. His identity is less important than his function. Assisted by a tribunal of divine magistrates he, like Osiris, judged the fitness of the soul for immortality, on the basis of the defendant's plea:

> I gave bread to the hungry, water to the thirsty, clothes to the naked. Never have I done anything evilly against any man. I rescued the wretched man from one who was stronger than he. I judged two men so that they might be satisfied. I was respectful to my father, pleasant to my mother. Never did I take a thing belonging to any man. Never have I said anything evilly against any person. I spoke truth, I rendered justice.

There is quite a contrast between texts like this, which were written on tombstones of the late Old Kingdom and First Intermediate Period, and the Pyramid Texts, which were used at approximately the same time. The truth or falsehood of the claims to virtue are immaterial, as is the possibility that the mere statement of them had magical import. What is important is that they state a moral code, and that a man's behavior during his lifetime had a bearing on what happened to him after he died. "I spoke truth, I rendered justice."

However, there has been a lot of debate in Egyptological circles about the key words in that last sentence. They are the same word in Egyptian—the word *ma'at*. As we mentioned earlier, this word can be translated as "candor," as well as "truth" or "justice." It has also been read as "the divine order," that arrangement of the universe which was established by the god creator at the beginning of the world. This last rendering more or less negates the ethical content of *ma'at*; conformity with the divine order is not moral behavior, it is only good sense.

To render *ma'at* only in its pragmatic meaning is, I think, to lean over backwards in a reaction against Breasted's admittedly idealized notion of the dawn of conscience. Our word truth means many things in different contexts, and it is clear that *ma'at* has no one meaning. The men whose tombstones claim that they spoke *ma'at* and rendered *ma'at* give a number of specific examples of the acts they thought of as just and true, and these are moral qualities—charity toward the poor, help for the helpless.

Later in the First Intermediate Period a royal father, composing a series of precepts for the guidance of his son, had this to say about the day of judgment:

> Perform justice while you endure on earth. Quiet the one who weeps; do not oppress the widow; supplant no man in the property of his father; impair no officials at their posts. Be on guard against punishing unfairly. . . . The council which judges the deficient— you know they are not lenient on that day of judging. . . . Existence yonder is for eternity . . . but as for him who reaches it without wrongdoing, he shall exist yonder like a god, striding freely like the lords of eternity!

This is, I think, an impressive statement. My omissions, represented by dots, give the text more coherence than it actually has; but the development of the idea is really there.

About the same time that King Achtoy wrote his Instructions, the Coffin Texts were beginning to be inscribed. Once again there is a distinct difference between the mortuary magic of the Texts and the mortuary ethics of the Instructions.

After the Coffin Texts came the Book of the Dead; and by now we have reached the judgment as it has been described, with Osiris as supreme judge, and all the trappings of the formal court. What about the moral aspect of this version of the judgment?

I am afraid there is some excuse for the attitude of the skeptic, who claims that even this noble conception degenerated into another attempt to reduce all problems to those which could be solved by magic spells. The Book of the Dead is quite wordy on the judgment. Chapter 125 (the number is that of a modern classification) is the one dealing specifically with the Hall of the Two

Truths and what went on there. It gives, at some length, the speech of the defendant to the tribunal. The chapter in question used to be called the "Negative Confession"—a well-turned but essentially meaningless phrase, which has now been replaced by other titles such as "The Declaration of Innocence." In his peroration the dead man makes a statement to each of the forty-two gods, denying that he has committed a particular sin. We find all the Ten Commandments mentioned, except for the first two— Egyptian gods were not at all jealous, and they were very fond of graven images. In place of these there is a long list of ritual sins. The dead man tells the god "Dangerous of Face" that he has not committed murder, and informs the "Devourer of Shades" that he has not stolen. Lying, assault and battery, deceit, gossip, adultery, homosexuality, general violence, arrogant behavior, inordinate ambition—the list is much longer than the Judao-Christian cata-logue of prohibitions, which, we must recall, is also negative in character.

As an implicit ethical code, the "Declaration of Innocence" is fairly impressive. A certain number of rather picayune ritual sins are mentioned, but in general the list compares favorably with any other morality statement I can think of. However, the shining air of virtue is sullied by the fact that this chapter forms part of a book made up almost entirely of magical spells. The format makes it clear that this is only another formula, another incantation against danger. The denial of sin negates the sin, and the gods can be mastered by telling them their names.

But the judge, Osiris, surely reaches his verdict through the evidence given by that impartial witness, the heart. Can the deci-sion of the "Foremost of the Westerners" be subverted by a petty official armed with a papyrus scroll?

It could be; but there is an easier way out of the difficulty. The most disillusioning of all the spells in the Book of the Dead is Chapter 30, the text written on the base of the ubiquitous heart scarabs. Its intent, candidly stated, is to gag that one essential witness: "My heart of my mother! My heart of my mother! Do not stand up against me as witness! Do not create opposition against me as witness! Do not create opposition against me among the magistrates! Do not weigh heavy against me in the presence of the keeper of the scales!"

No, there is not much ethical content in this. It is said that there is more rejoicing in our heaven over a repentant sinner than over many of the faithful. The Egyptian did not even need to repent; all he needed was enough money to buy a scroll that *said* he had repented.

Yet it would not be entirely fair to see in the corruption of the judgment a shift from primitive ethics to sophisticated cynicism. The Pyramid Texts are just as "magical" as the Book of the Dead, and the later literature contains statements which show not only a striving for moral virtue, but a new humbleness before the god, and an awareness of man's sinful nature. The "Declaration of Innocence" is corrupt, but its content cannot be wholly ignored. To the literal sinner—a category not restricted to ancient Egypt— the magic of the written word might be assurance enough. To a more thoughtful believer, it might be a statement of a creed he had honestly tried to follow. In Egypt even the gods could err; and knowing human courts, the man preparing himself for the judgment from which there was no appeal might feel more secure in the knowledge that he had a written statement of the innocence he had tried to maintain. Perhaps the humble burials of the poor are themselves a testimonial to the enduring faith in the purity of the judgment. If these men could hope for survival, without the aid of heart scarabs or magical scrolls, they must have had some spiritual claim to be included among the followers of Osiris.

There was no appeal from the judgment; the sentence for the guilty was annihilation, that "dying a second time" which the Egyptians dreaded beyond all else. The little vignettes of the judgment hall always include a picture of the monster called the "Devourer of Shades"—his name makes his role fairly evident, and sometimes he is so impatient for his prey that he stands on his hind legs, fairly drooling. I find this monster rather charming, myself, and it is possible that the Egyptians did not take him too seriously. Even in the scenes where he sits poised, hungrily watching his potential dinner, the dead man smirks and bows, fully confident that the judgment will be in his favor.

We do not find the Egyptian monsters very frightening; the neat crisp drawing and the conventional types reduce them to abstractions. But perhaps the Egyptians were not always so blasé about them. It is not always easy to distinguish between gods and demons, for some of the gods were strange composites of men and beasts, and even they might be hostile toward an unprotected spirit. Serpents are among the commonest of the demons; the great enemy of Re, who attacked his boat each night in the Underworld, was a snake named Apophis. However, there is no real Devil in Egyptian theology. Set, the murderer of Osiris, was only evil in this specific context. In his other activities he could be personable and agreeable, holding the ladder for the dead king to mount to heaven, and helping Re repel the threatening serpent. In the Nineteenth Dynasty he was one of the patrons of the Royal House.

Whether they feared their demons or not, the Egyptians did fear death—the first physical death and that second death from which there was no resurrection. They spent a good part of their lives fighting annihilation, and in so doing they built up the most complicated structure of mortuary ritual any people has ever produced. We are the beneficiaries of it, in terms of museum collections and scholarly books; and perhaps we will not find the painted mummy cases and weird amulets so bizarre if we see, beneath their extravagance, a common human terror and a common hope.

# Historical Summary

<table>
<tr><td>? to 3110 B.C.</td><td>PREDYNASTIC OR PREHISTORIC PERIOD.</td></tr>
</table>

? to 3110 B.C.     PREDYNASTIC OR PREHISTORIC PERIOD.

3110–2686     ARCHAIC, PROTODYNASTIC, OR EARLY DYNASTIC. DYNASTIES I-III

Unification of two predynastic kingdoms under Menes. Djoser, Imhotep and the Step Pyramid.

2686–2181     OLD KINGDOM. DYNASTIES IV-VI

First flowering of high Egyptian culture in art, architecture, technology, speculative thought. Establishment of canons of art. Great Pyramid, Pyramid Texts. Centralized state of Fourth Dynasty breaks down at end of Sixth Dynasty.

2181–2040     FIRST INTERMEDIATE PERIOD. DYNASTIES VII-X

Political upheaval, dissolution of centralized state. Literature indicates search for ethical values. Ninth,

369

Tenth Dynasties, under Herakleopolitan rulers, control large territory but finally come into conflict with rising power of Thebes.

2134–1786  MIDDLE KINGDOM. DYNASTIES XI-XII

Eleventh Theban Dynasty reunites Egypt. Mentuhotep's temple at Deir el Bahri. Twelfth Dynasty Amenemhats and Senuserts move capital to Fayum. Conquest of Nubia, great irrigation work, contact with Asia.

1786–1570  SECOND INTERMEDIATE PERIOD. DYNASTIES XIII-XVII

Political collapse, fragmentation. Some of these dynasties contemporaneous. Accompanied by invasion and control of most of Egypt by Hyksos from Asia. Seventeenth Theban Dynasty under Kings Sekenenre and Kamose begins expulsion of Hyksos.

1570–1085  NEW KINGDOM, EMPIRE. DYNASTIES XVIII-XX

Ahmose completes conquest of Hyksos. Eighteenth Dynasty Thutmoses and Amenhoteps conquer Asian empire. Usurpation of Queen Hatshepsut and triumph of her nephew Thutmose III. Rise of Amon, religious revolution of Akhenaton. Tutankhamon. Fall of the dynasty with loss of Asian empire. Nineteenth Dynasty Setis and Ramses regain some of empire. Great building works at Abydos, Thebes, Abu Simbel, etc. First attack of Sea Peoples. End of dynasty with female king Tausert, ephemeral weak rulers. Twentieth Dynasty Ramses III repels invasion of Sea People, builds greatly. A series of weak Ramessids ends the dynasty.

1085–332  THE LATE PERIOD. DYNASTIES XXI-XXX

Two sets of rulers during Twenty-First Dynasty: high priests of Amon at Thebes, others at Tanis in Delta.

Libyan kings make up Twenty-Second Dynasty, Nubian kings the Twenty-Fifth. Sheshonk the Nubian fights in Asia but his successors lose Egypt to the Assyrians. In the Twenty-Sixth or Saite Dynasty native kings restore some of lost glory; temporary unification, renaissance of art. Persian conquest, 525 B.C. Followed by alternating periods of freedom under local kings and Persian domination.

332–30          PTOLEMAIC PERIOD.

Conquest by Alexander the Great, 332 B.C., ends Egyptian independence permanently. His successors, descendants of his general Ptolemy, are Greeks, but rule in Egyptian style. Cleopatra, Antony, Caesar, end this period.

30 B.C.–A.D. 364          ROMAN PERIOD.

Egypt becomes a Roman province under Augustus. About A.D. 200, Christianity widespread. A.D. 250–350, spread of Coptic language. About A.D. 270, life of St. Antony, the first famous hermit. Christianity becomes religion of Egypt until Arab conquest, in A.D. 640.

# READING LIST

For the reader who wishes to pursue certain topics in greater detail, or to investigate some interpretations which differ from those of the present author, here are a few suggested readings. I have tried to restrict the list to works in English which are more apt to be readily available than the professional journals and publications, and I have cited these latter only in the cases of references mentioned in the text, or when I have relied so heavily on a particular work that it would be an act of injustice not to acknowledge my debt.

For the fanatical reader (bless him) who has a good library at his disposal, I can do no better than to refer him to the bibliographies. The best is the one compiled by Ida A. Pratt and published by the New York Public Library. It is called *Ancient Egypt*; the first volume appeared in 1925 and the Supplement in 1942. There is an excellent bibliography in Hayes (see below), and a good one in Smith's *Art and Architecture*. I have ruthlessly omitted some wonderful books because they deal with history rather than with Egyptian culture and daily life, but Drioton and Vandier's *L'Égypte* is included because it has, at the end of each section, superb summaries, with references, of the major problems still being debated in Egyptology.

*Symbols and Abbreviations*
   *—available in paperback edition
   JEA—Journal of Egyptian Archaeology
   JNES—Journal of Near Eastern Studies
   JARCE—Journal of the American Research Center in Egypt
   PSBA—Proceedings of the Society of Biblical Archaeology

GENERAL

*Aldred, C., *Egypt to the End of the Old Kingdom*. London, Thames and Hudson, 1965.

Carter, H., *The Tomb of Tutankhamon*. 3 vols. New York, Cooper Square Publishers, Inc., 1963.

Drioton, É., and Vandier, J., *L'Égypte*. 3rd ed. Presses Universitaires de France, Paris, 1942.

*Emery, W. B., *Archaic Egypt*. Harmonsworth, Middlesex, Penguin Books.

*Erman, Adolf, *Life in Ancient Egypt*, tr. by H. M. Tirard. Dover Publications, 1971.

Hayes, W. C., *The Sceptre of Egypt*. 2 vols. Cambridge, Mass., Harvard University Press, 1953-1959.

———, "Daily Life in Ancient Egypt." *National Geographic* LXXX, no. 4 (Oct. 1941), 419.

*Herodotus, *The Persian Wars*, Book II. Transl. by George Rawlinson in *The Greek Historians*, Vol. I. New York, Random House, 1942.

Lucas, A., *Ancient Egyptian Materials and Industries*. 4th ed., rev. and enlarged by J. B. Harris. London, 1962.

Riefstahl, E., *Thebes in the Time of Amunhotep III*. Norman, Okla., University of Oklahoma Press, 1964.

Smith, J. C., *Tombs, Temples and Ancient Art*. Norman, Okla., University of Oklahoma Press, 1958.

*Wilson, J. A., *The Culture of Ancient Egypt*. Chicago, University of Chicago Press, 1956.

Winlock, H. E., *Excavations at Deir el Bahri, 1911-1931*. New York, 1942.


TRANSLATIONS

*Erman, A., *The Ancient Egyptians: A Sourcebook of Their Writings*, tr. by A. M. Blackman. New York, Harper Torchbooks, 1966.

Schott, S., *Altägyptische Liebeslieder*. Zürich, Artemis-Verlag, 1950.

*Simpson, William K., ed. *The Literature of Ancient Egypt*. New Haven, Yale University Press, 1973.

Wilson, J. A., "Egyptian Texts," in Pritchard, J. B., ed., *Ancient Near Eastern Texts Relating to the Old Testament*. 2nd ed. Princeton, Princeton University Press, 1955.

## JEWELRY

Aldred, Cyril, *Jewels of the Pharaohs*. New York and Washington, Praeger, 1971.

## LAND AND PEOPLE

Baedeker, K., *Egypt and the Sudan: Handbook for Travellers*. 8th ed. Leipsic, K. Baedeker, 1929.

Černý, J., "Consanguineous Marriages in Pharaonic Egypt," *JEA* 40 (1954), 23.

Derry, D. E., "The Dynastic Race in Egypt," *JEA* 42 (1956), 80.

James, T. G. H., *The Hekanakhte Papers and other Early Middle Kingdom Documents*. New York, 1962.

Kees, H., *Ancient Egypt. A Cultural Topography*. Chicago, University of Chicago Press, 1961.

## ARMY

Faulkner, R. O., "Egyptian Military Standards," *JEA* 27 (1941), 12.

———, "Egyptian Military Organization," *JEA* 29 (1943), 32.

Schulman, Alan R., "Egyptian Chariotry," *JARCE* 2 (1963), 92.

## ART: GENERAL

Aldred, C., "Art in Ancient Egypt": *Old Kingdom*, London, Alec Tiranti, Ltd., 1949; *Middle Kingdom*, 1950; *New Kingdom*, Alec Tiranti, Ltd., 1951.

Frankfort, H., "On Egyptian Art," *JEA* 18 (1932), 33.

Iverson, E., *Canon and Proportion in Egyptian Art*. London [1955].

Schäfer, H., *Von ägyptischer Kunst. Eine Grundlage*. 4th improved edition, ed. by E. Brunner Traut. Wiesbaden, 1963.

Smith, W. S., *The Art and Architecture of Ancient Egypt*. Pelican History of Art. Harmondsworth, Middlesex, Penguin Books, 1958.

Wilson, J. A., "The Artist of the Egyptian Old Kingdom," *JNES* 6 (1947), 231.


ARCHITECTURE
Badawy, A., *A History of Egyptian Architecture*. Vol. I. Lawrence, Kansas, Marvin Hall, 1954.
Clarke, S., and Engelbach, R., *Ancient Egyptian Masonry*. London, Oxford University Press, 1930.
Smith, E. B., *Egyptian Architecture as Cultural Expression*. New York, D. Appleton Century Co., 1938.


TOMBS
*Edwards, I. E. S., *The Pyramids of Egypt*. 2nd ed. Harmondsworth, Middlesex, Penguin Books, 1961.
Emery, W. B., *Great Tombs of the First Dynasty*. 3 vols. Cairo, 1949; London, 1954, 1958.
Grinsell, L., *Egyptian Pyramids*. Gloucester, John Bellows, Ltd., 1947.
Reisner, G. A., *The Development of the Egyptian Tomb Down to the Accession of Cheops*. Cambridge, Mass., Harvard University Press, 1936.


HOUSES
Bruyère, B., *Rapport sur les fouilles de Deir el Médineh 1922-1935*. Cairo, Institut français d'archéologie orientale, 1924-37.
Davies, N. de G., "The Town House in Ancient Egypt," *Metropolitan Museum Studies* I, 1928-29.
Peet, T. E., et al., *The City of Akhenaton*. (4 vols.) London, Egypt Exploration Society, 1923-41.


PICTURE BOOKS
Davies, Nina M., *Ancient Egyptian Paintings*. (3 vols.) Chicago, University of Chicago Press, 1936.
Davies, Norman de G., Publications of tombs, such as:
   *The Tomb of Nakht*. New York, Metropolitan Museum of Art, 1917.

   *The Tomb of Puyemre*. (2 vols.) New York, Metropolitan Museum of Art, 1922-23.

*The Tomb of Rekhmire.* (2 vols.) New York, Metropolitan Museum of Art, 1943.

Desroches Noblecourt, C., *Tutankhamon.* New York, New York Graphic Society, 1963.

Lange, K. and Heimer, M., *Egypt.* 2nd ed. rev. London, Phaidon, 1957.

Vandier, J., *Egyptian Sculpture.* London, A. Zwemmer [1951].


MAGIC, SCIENCE AND RELIGION: GENERAL

Frazer, J., *The Golden Bough.* Vols. I and II, The Magic Art. 3rd ed. London, Macmillan and Co., 1913, 1920.

James, E. O., *Prehistoric Religion.* London, 1957.

*Levy, G. R., *The Gate of Horn.* London, Faber and Faber, 1958.

Levy-Bruhl, L., *Primitive Mentality.* Trans. by Lilian A. Clare. London, 1923.

*Malinowski, B., *Magic, Science and Religion and Other Essays.* New York, Doubleday and Co., Inc., 1954.

*Otto, R., *The Idea of the Holy.* Harmondsworth, Middlesex, Penguin Books, 1959.

*Wilson, J. A., et al., *Before Philosophy.* Harmondsworth, Middlesex, Penguin Books, 1949.


MAGIC

Budge, E. A. W., *Egyptian Magic.* London, K. Paul, Trench, Trübner & Co., 1899.

Gardiner, A. H., "Professional Magicians in Ancient Egypt," *PSBA* 37 (1915), 253; 39 (1917), 31.

Lexa, G., *La Magie dans l'Egypte antique.* (3 vols.) Paris, P. Geuthner, 1925.


SCIENCE AND TECHNOLOGY

Neugebauer, O., *The Exact Sciences in Antiquity.* Princeton, Princeton University Press, 1952.

Neugebauer, O., and Parker, R., *Egyptian Astronomical Tests.* (2 vols.) Providence, R.I., Brown University Press, 1960, 1964.

Sarton, George, *A History of Science: Vol. I, Ancient Science Through the Golden Age of Greece.* Cambridge, Mass., Harvard University Press, 1952.

## BOATS
Faulkner, R. O., "Egyptian Sea-Going Ships," *JEA* 26 (1940), 3.

## MEDICINE
Breasted, J. H., *The Edwin Smith Surgical Papyrus*. (2 vols.) Chicago, University of Chicago Press, 1930.
Dawson, W. R., *Magician and Leech*. London, Methuen & Co., Ltd. [1929].
Grapow, H., *Grundriss der Medizin der Alten Agypten*. (3 vols.) Berlin, Akademie-Verlag, 1954-56.
Jonckheere, F., *La Médicine égyptienne*. (3 vols.) Brussels, Fondation Égyptologique Reine Elisabeth, 1958.
Leigh, R. Wood, *Notes on the Somatology and Pathology of Ancient Egypt*. Berkeley, Calif., University of California Press, 1934.

## RELIGION
*Breasted, J. H., *The Development of Religion and Thought in Ancient Egypt*. New York, Harper Torchbooks, 1959.
————, *The Dawn of Conscience*. New York, Chas. Scribner's Sons, 1933.
Černý, J., *Ancient Egyptian Religion*. London, 1952.
Clark, R. T. R., *Myth and Symbol in Ancient Egypt*. London, 1959.
*Frankfort, H., *Ancient Egyptian Religion*. New York, Harper Torchbooks, 1961.
————, *Kingship and the Gods*. Chicago, University of Chicago Press, 1948.
Gunn, B., "Religion of the Poor," *JEA* 5 (1917), 81.
Mercer, S. A. B., *The Religion of Ancient Egypt*. London, Luzac and Co., Ltd., 1949.
Wainright, G. A., *The Sky Religion in Egypt*. Cambridge, University Press, 1938.
Zabkhar, L. V., "The Theocracy of Amarna and the Doctrine of the Ba," *JNES* 13 (1954), 87.

## DEATH AND THE DEAD
Budge, E. A. W., *The Book of the Dead*. (3 vols.) London, Kegan Paul, Trench, Trübner and Co., 1901.

de Buck, A., *The Egyptian Coffin Texts.* (7 vols.) Chicago, University of Chicago Press, 1935-62.

Gardiner, A. H., *Attitude of the Ancient Egyptians toward Death and the Dead.* Cambridge, University Press, 1935.

Gardiner, A. H. and Sethe, K., *Egyptian Letters to the Dead.* London, Egypt Exploration Society, 1928.

Mercer, S. A. B., *Pyramid Texts.* (4 vols.) New York, Longmans, Green & Co., 1952.

## MUMMIFICATION

Harris, James E. and Weeks, Kent R., *X-Raying the Pharaohs.* New York: Charles Scribner's Sons, 1973.

Maspero, G., *Les momies royales de Deir el-Bahari.* Cairo, Mission archéologique française au Caire, 1889.

Murray, M. A., "Burial Customs and Beliefs in the Hereafter in Predynastic Egypt," *JEA* 42 (1956), 86.

Sandison, A. T., "The Use of Natron in Mummification in Ancient Egypt," *JNES* 22 (1963), 269.

Smith, G. E., *The Royal Mummies.* Cairo, Imprimerie de l'Institut français d'archéologie orientale, 1912.

Smith, G. E., and Dawson, W. R., *Egyptian Mummies.* London, George Allen and Unwin, Ltd., 1924.

# INDEX